VEHICLE BRAKING

VEHICLE BRAKING

A.K. Baker, *CEng, MIMechE*
Technical Services Manager, Ferodo Limited

PENTECH PRESS
London: Plymouth

Published by Pentech Press Limited
Graham Lodge, Graham Road
London NW4 3DG

British Library Cataloguing in Publication Data

Baker, A.K.
  Vehicle braking.
  1. Motor vehicles——Brakes
  I. Title
  629.2'46   TL269

  ISBN 0-7273-2202-8

Printed in Great Britain

CONTENTS

CONTENTS

Preface

The components used to form vehicle braking systems and the layouts into which they are combined have progressively increased in number and complexity. The aim of this book is to deal with virtually all of the braking equipment likely to be found in normal use at the present time, so its coverage begins in the mid 1950s, just as the disc brake was becoming a reality on production cars; although much of interest came before, space permits only brief references to earlier components. Cars are by far the most numerous class of vehicle on the roads, but equal attention is given to the braking of commercial vehicles of all categories; equipment for motor cycles, trailers, agricultural tractors and other kinds of vehicle is also covered, as are auxiliary braking systems, including retarders.

The book has been written particularly for those who require a practical approach to the subject but, nevertheless, some theoretical understanding is necessary of what is involved in stopping a moving mass; the first chapter therefore considers this in simple but adequate terms. The second chapter examines the fundamentals of actual braking, including the matter of friction; the following nine chapters then go into all necessary detail in describing drum and disc brakes and hydraulic and air braking systems, while Chapter twelve looks at what happens in service.

No book dealing with the construction and functioning of complex devices and systems can be complete without illustrations and an unusually large number have been brought together here to augment the descriptions given in the text; as these have largely been obtained from or prepared with the benefit of information from the many manufacturers named – to whom my thanks are due – their authenticity is well established.

The book is based principally on European practice, from which that of the Far East has been largely derived, but it also takes account of American practice in certain important respects and so it will be found of virtually universal relevance. In this connection, it should be noted that world harmonisation of braking standards and test methods is under active consideration so, whilst diversity of components will still be found, braking engineers are tending increasingly to have common aims.

The subject of vehicle braking is a fascinating one, with boundaries which are constantly being enlarged; concealed behind the factual descriptions of the hardware and its application, there is the largely unwritten story of the many engineers and others who have played some part in this ongoing development.

Alan K. Baker

1

Stopping

Before considering brakes themselves, it is necessary to appreciate what they have to do in order to decelerate or stop a vehicle.

1.1 Kinetic energy

In simple terms, a moving vehicle may be considered as a mass concentrated at a single point, which stores energy by reason of its motion. In order to reduce the velocity of this mass, a force must act on it in such a direction as to oppose the motion; braking equipment must first, therefore, be capable of generating such a force. Because the force applied to decelerate a mass acts through a distance during the time taken to slow down or stop, work is done and some or all of the stored energy is converted to a different form. The second requirement for braking equipment is, therefore, that it can effect this conversion of energy in a convenient manner.

The stored energy is known as kinetic energy; its magnitude at any instant of time is related to the magnitude of the mass and to its velocity, in a relationship which will be examined below. Calculations can determine how much of the energy has to be converted for any specified change of velocity; if the mass is brought to rest, the whole of this energy has to be converted to a different form.

The storage of this energy occurs during the acceleration of the mass m from rest, when the application of an external force p (assumed to be constant) causes an acceleration a which, ignoring effects such as friction and wind resistance, is proportional to m, i.e.

$$p = ma \tag{1.1}$$

In the period of time during which the force acts, the mass will be propelled along a straight path at an increasing velocity v which, at time t, will be equal to the product of the acceleration and the time; in what follows it is to be understood that both the force and the acceleration caused are constant.

$$v = at \tag{1.2}$$

1

At that instant of time, the distance s travelled since the moment of application of the force will be the product of the average velocity $\frac{1}{2}at$ during the period and the time t,

$$s = \tfrac{1}{2}at \times t = \tfrac{1}{2}at^2 \tag{1.3}$$

The work done during this period will be the product of the force p and the distance travelled s; hence from Equations 1.1 and 1.3

$$\text{Work done} = p \times s$$
$$= ma \times \tfrac{1}{2}at^2 = \tfrac{1}{2}ma^2t^2$$

But $at = v$ (Equation 1.2), so

$$\text{Work done} = \tfrac{1}{2}mv^2$$

As all losses have been ignored in these calculations, this amount of energy—which has been expended in accelerating the mass—is now stored by it; this is, in fact, the kinetic energy of the mass and, as can be seen from Equation 1.4, it depends only on the magnitude of the mass and its velocity. The form of Equation 1.4 shows that kinetic energy relates directly to mass but to the square of velocity; this is of particular significance when considering braking and may easily be considered by reference to Fig. 1.1.

Figure 1.1 relates kinetic energy to velocity on the basis of Equation

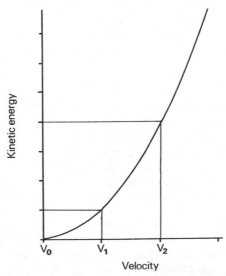

Fig. 1.1   The relationship between velocity and kinetic energy ($V_2 = 2V_1$)

1.4 and it can be seen that as velocity is doubled from a value v_1 to v_2, the magnitude of the kinetic energy is multiplied by a factor of four. This can be explained by consideration of the way in which energy was expended to accelerate the vehicle, when equal periods of time would have been taken to accelerate from rest (velocity v_0) to v_1 and from v_1 to v_2. Because the average velocity in the first period ($v_1/2$) is only one third of that in the second period $[(v_2+v_1)/2=(2v_1+v_1)/2=3v_1/2]$, the distance travelled during the second period is three times that covered during the first period, so that three times the work is done during that period by the constant force applied, the total at velocity v_2 being four times the value at v_1.

When braking, the amounts of energy to be dealt with in reducing the velocity from v_2 to v_1 and from v_1 to v_0 correspond to those stored during acceleration; three quarters of the kinetic energy of a moving mass therefore has to be dealt with in halving its velocity. It follows that, in a given amount of time, much more energy has to be dealt with if a mass is successively braked to a lower velocity and accelerated to the higher value than if it is successively braked to rest and accelerated to its initial velocity. Appreciation of this is important when comparing the severity of different sequences of brake applications.

It is because kinetic energy is proportional to the square of the velocity, but only directly proportional to mass, that excessive speed can impose much heavier duty on brakes than the same percentage of excess load. For example, a 10% increase in velocity raises the kinetic energy by 21%, which is equivalent to the effect of a 21% increase in mass. This is of particular significance when considering a vehicle, the performance of which has been uprated in some way, without any change having been made to the braking equipment.

1.2 Potential energy

So far, mention has been made of only one way in which energy is stored by a mass which is accelerated from rest, because it has been assumed that the motion considered is in a horizontal plane. If, however, the mass is accelerated up an incline, not only is energy expended in accelerating it, work also has to be done in lifting the mass and this is subsequently recoverable if the mass descends to its former level. If, conversely, the mass is initially accelerated down an incline, the energy immediately gained from the descent reduces the energy input needed to cause the acceleration.

This form of energy is called potential energy and it is calculated as the product of the mass and the vertical distance through which it moves. If, while descending an incline, the velocity of the mass is maintained at a constant value by use of brakes, it is potential energy only which has to be converted to another form; the kinetic energy remains constant. If the velocity of the mass is reduced while descending an incline then both potential energy and kinetic energy have to be converted at the same time.

When making successive decelerations on the level, the average rate of conversion of energy during a period of time is limited by the magnitude of the force (the engine power of the vehicle) available to accelerate the mass back to a higher velocity after a deceleration; moderately powered family cars are, therefore, seldom in braking trouble under these conditions unless the driver is misusing his car. A large amount of potential energy may, however, be stored by such a car over a long period when slowly climbing a long but slight gradient. This may subsequently be converted in a very short period of time during an incautious steep descent, during which the brakes of a heavily laden car can easily be subjected to excessive duty, causing overheating of the brake linings.

It can therefore be seen that the total amount of energy which has to be considered when a mass is decelerated is calculated on the basis of both kinetic and potential energy. It will, however, be shown later that in considering a brake installation as a whole, it is not only the condition of maximum energy dissipation which has to be taken into account, but the typical mixture of all conditions.

1.3 Braking efficiency

Further to the matter of energy which has to be converted when a mass is decelerated, it is convenient to include here some consideration of how deceleration may be measured. The need to make such an assessment arises, for example, when making comparisons during tests of components and vehicles under development, when carrying out a routine check that standards are being maintained or when seeking to satisfy legislation by demonstrating that a specified minimum value can be attained.

Although deceleration is the immediate effect of the application of a retarding force to a moving mass, the distance taken to stop is more significant in terms of the avoidance of a hazard, especially as the deceleration may vary during the stop, and the stopping time is a further measure which may be of some interest. In fact the four quantities—applied force, deceleration, stopping distance and stopping time—are, for a given mass, intimately related by the calculations set out above; any one of them might, therefore, be taken as a measure of what is now increasingly commonly called the braking efficiency.

It is, however, first necessary to clarify the use of the word efficiency in the present sense. It takes no account of the way in which an effort applied to a brake pedal is related to the braking force developed and applied to a moving vehicle to oppose its motion; no brake actuation system has a mechanical efficiency of 100% but braking efficiency is not concerned with the efforts always being made to improve this. Braking efficiency, in the sense in which the phrase is applied to stopping, is simply the ratio of the applied retarding force to the magnitude of the gravitational force on the mass concerned.

For satisfying the requirements of legislation, it has been found convenient to measure the forces developed by individual vehicle brakes by using stationary test machines, having rollers on which the wheels of each axle are positioned in turn; these measure the forces developed at the tyre surface for each wheel and, from a knowledge of the axle loadings, the overall braking efficiency can be calculated. Such a method is not, however, particularly useful for assessing the braking performance characteristics of a vehicle under the widely varying conditions encountered on the road, so other methods are in use for such purposes.

Stopping times are extremely short, unless decelerations are very low; they cannot easily be measured with sufficient accuracy to be useful. The accurate measurement of stopping distances, which is important for some purposes, requires the use at least of moderately specialised equipment and, if a measuring tape has to be used, is time consuming.

Deceleration itself has, for many years, been measured by using an instrument such as a simple pendulum type decelerometer (Fig. 1.2), a liquid filled U tube or a recording decelerometer; the latter type of

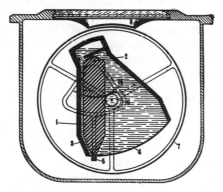

Fig. 1.2   A section through the Tapley meter, showing the magnetised pendulum 1 and armature 5 which moves the cylindrical scale to indicate deceleration (courtesy of Tapley Instrumentation Ltd.)

Fig. 1.3   A fifth wheel device used in conjunction with instrumentation on the vehicle to record velocity and deceleration

instrument yields a permanent record of deceleration versus time, enabling braking to be analysed at leisure. The particular value of the U tube is that for closed circuit testing it can be mounted so that the driver can observe it and vary his pedal effort so as to achieve a predetermined deceleration.

A test vehicle may also be equipped with a fifth wheel type of attachment (Fig. 1.3), which is used for determining speed as well as deceleration; electrical signals are generated as the wheel rotates and processed by instrumentation on the vehicle to yield the desired data. Such equipment is costly and is usually only used for making detailed assessments when particular accuracy is required.

1.4 Adhesion and static weight distribution

So far, consideration has been limited to the deceleration of a hypothetical concentrated mass, with no regard for the configuration of real vehicles, the actual roads on which they run or the way in which a retarding force may be developed and applied to them. Attention is, therefore, now given to a representative vehicle (Fig. 1.4) and the way in which some of the simple concepts dealt with can be related to it.

A four wheeled vehicle is shown in schematic form and the diagram

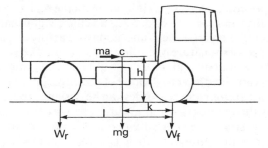

Fig. 1.4   Stopping a vehicle on a level road

includes the position of the centre of gravity, c; it will be realised that, although the mass m of the vehicle is not really concentrated at this point, there are a number of calculations which can be performed on the basis that this is, in fact, the case. The height above the road surface of the centre of gravity and its horizontal distance from either the front or rear wheel centre need to be known, as does the wheelbase; for the general stability of the vehicle, the centre of gravity should lie on the longitudinal centre line of the vehicle.

All convenient forms of braking system are applied to the wheels of the vehicle, either directly or by way of the transmission; they therefore take effect at the road surface, utilising the adhesion between the tyres and the road. The adhesion at each wheel is the product of the load on that wheel and the coefficient of adhesion (an alternative name for the coefficient of friction in this case) of the two materials—the tread rubber of the tyres and the surface coating of the road—which are in contact. With the centre of gravity on the longitudinal centre line and the vehicle on a road with no camber, the loads on each of the two wheels on each axle will be equal; it is therefore usual to consider axle loadings, rather than individual wheel loadings.

The mass of the vehicle is supported by the two (or more) axles but is seldom equally distributed; for basic design purposes, the distribution is determined for the static condition, with the vehicle stationary on a level surface. By taking moments of the forces concerned about the contact point of either the front (as in the example which follows) or the rear wheels, the static weight distribution may be found, W_f and W_r being the loads on the front and rear axles respectively and mg the total gravitational force on the vehicle

$$mgk - W_r l = 0$$

$$\therefore \quad W_r = mg \frac{k}{l} \tag{1.5}$$

The proportion of the total axle loading on the rear axle is therefore k/l and on the front axle $(1 - k/l)$; since a vehicle will usually have the same type of tyre on all wheels, and it may be assumed that the road surface is of constant nature over the area on which the vehicle stands, the adhesion at the individual axles will be in the same proportion.

Without knowing the actual value of the adhesion in any case, the braking effort at front and rear axles can be designed to be in the same ratio as for the loading at front and rear so that the total available adhesion can largely be utilised when it is necessary to achieve the maximum possible braking efficiency. Maximum deceleration is achieved when all wheels are braked almost to the point at which they lock.

It must be noted that the adhesion between the tyres and the road is not only used for braking but may also be used simultaneously for directional control (alternatively, for directional control at the same time as acceleration), each function making its demands on the total available. If a vehicle is being steered on a curved path when the brakes are applied, less adhesion is available for braking than would otherwise be the case.

The coefficient of adhesion between the tyres and road at any moment will be determined by the nature of the material of which each is constructed, the state of wear of each and their condition in terms of the presence of contaminants such as dust, water, ice, frost, mud, oil, etc. The most common contaminant of road surfaces in the UK is water and the design both of good tyres and of good road surfaces takes account of the need to deal with this; not only has the tyre/road combination to be capable of dispelling the thick layer of water which may be laying on the road, it must also penetrate the residual film which will be left between the two surfaces.

The bulk of the water present must be drained from the contact patch extremely rapidly by the tyre tread and the large scale roughness (known as macro-roughness) of the road surface (hence the relevance of the state of wear of each); the residual film trapped between the tread blocks and the road material should be penetrated by the surface roughness (micro-roughness) of the stone which, suitably bound together, is the usual major constituent of modern road surfaces. Only when the tread rubber of the tyres and the road surface material are in intimate contact is a coefficient of adhesion developed between them.

It is not so long since the combination of uncambered surfaces on roads such as motorways, with unsatisfactory macro-roughness, and insufficiently developed tyre tread designs led to the phenomenon of aquaplaning under wet conditions. A thick film of water, trapped between tyres and road kept the surfaces apart so that there was no contact and, therefore, no adhesion; usually affecting front wheels only (the rear wheels benefited from the partial clearance caused by the front ones), the condition caused the driver of any vehicle troubled in this way to be robbed of directional control and front wheel braking. Were it not for the necessity for the tyre to play a major part in dealing with water on the road, there would be little need for tread patterns for on-the-road vehicles.

1.5 Miscellaneous effects on braking

Before proceeding further, there are several miscellaneous effects on the braking of a vehicle which may conveniently be grouped together, their importance varying considerably from one to another. Most obvious is the direct effect of a gradient (a further effect is considered in the next section); quite simply, it is easier to stop a vehicle going uphill than if it is on a level road and harder to stop one going downhill.

Gradients may be described either in terms of their angle from the horizontal, in terms of the vertical distance travelled in relation to the horizontal distance travelled or by converting the latter figures to a percentage (for example, 1 in 20 is equivalent to 5%). If a vehicle is climbing a 1 in 20 gradient and the brakes are applied, the resulting brake efficiency is the sum of that due to the brakes alone and the 5% due to the rising gradient; similarly, on a falling gradient, the resultant braking efficiency is that due to the brakes less the gradient percentage.

Any vehicle in motion is subject to rolling resistance due to tyre losses, bearing friction and the natural wind resistance due to its road speed; this always acts to retard the vehicle and is commonly of the order of 2–3% at moderate speeds; rolling resistance will be augmented by engine braking if the vehicle is left in gear during braking and this also acts to increase the braking effect. The effect of a strong wind should not be overlooked, but this will naturally depend on its direction relative to the vehicle as well as on its speed.

When comparative tests of brakes and brake linings are being conducted, it is necessary to make allowance for these effects as far as is possible, otherwise the conclusions reached may be misleading.

1.6 Weight transfer

As stated above, the starting point of braking system design is the static weight distribution; under normal operating conditions, however, there are factors which modify this and which need to be taken into account.

The first of these is the secondary effect of a gradient, referred to above, the magnitude of which, like the direct effect, depends on the severity of the slope. When a vehicle is facing down a gradient, weight is transferred from the rear to the front axle, simply because the vertical line through the centre of gravity moves nearer to the contact point of the front wheels (Fig. 1.5); the converse is true if the vehicle is facing up the gradient.

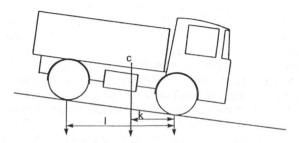

Fig. 1.5   A falling gradient causes a forward transfer of weight

The weight transfer caused in this way is seldom significant when considering the braking of a moving vehicle. Either, if the gradient is very slight, the effect is negligible anyway or, if the gradient is severe, it may be expected that the vehicle will be moving relatively slowly and able to achieve a sufficient braking effect within the limits of the adhesion as modified.

Problems can, however, arise with regard to the parking brake system which usually operates on the wheels of one axle only. In certain cases, it has been found necessary to incorporate the parking brake mechanism in the front brakes of a vehicle to meet the parking requirement on a steep falling gradient.

Another factor relates to the load carried; not so much with regard to the magnitude of the load, which forms part of the total mass of the vehicle and therefore affects braking directly, but with regard to its position or distribution. In the case of a car, the maximum payload of passengers and luggage is only a fraction of the mass of the empty vehicle; because of this, and because there is only a limited scope for varying the position of the load, variation in the load carried has only a limited effect on the calculated static weight distribution.

In the case of a truck, however, the magnitude of the maximum payload frequently is much larger than the mass of the empty vehicle so, from unladen to fully laden there is a very considerable change in the total mass; because the payload is largely carried by the rear axle or axles, this change in the total mass is accompanied by a considerable change in the proportion of the whole carried by each axle.

The vehicle designer will usually calculate the static weight distribution on the basis of the load being spread evenly over the body of the truck but this will often not be the case; when a concentrated load is carried which is less than the maximum, it may often be the case that it has to be carried in such a position that the normal pattern of distribution is disturbed, even though the maximum permitted axle loadings are in no case exceeded. Alternatively, the load may initially be evenly distributed but may be discharged in stages, with a corresponding progressive change in the proportions of the remainder carried by each axle.

Finally, there is weight transfer due to the way in which the braking force is applied to the vehicle. Referring to Fig. 1.4, the individual braking forces act at the road surface whereas the mass of the vehicle is considered as being concentrated at the centre of gravity c, a distance h above the road surface. A reaction to the braking force, of magnitude ma, where a is the deceleration (negative acceleration) of the vehicle, will therefore act at this distance h from it and a couple will be set up, tending to rotate the vehicle in such a way that the loading of the front axle will increase and that on the rear axle decrease.

In the case of the two axle vehicle shown schematically in Fig. 1.4 the weight transfer may be calculated as follows, by considering the tendency for the reaction force to rotate the vehicle about the contact point of the front wheels and the road. Since the couple referred to above is equal to mah, the reduction in load on the rear axle will be given by

$$\frac{mah}{l} \tag{1.6}$$

and the load on the front axle will be increased by the same amount.

It will be noted that the magnitude of the weight transfer during braking at any particular value of braking efficiency is dependent on the ratio of h, the height of the centre of gravity, to l, the wheelbase; this indicates that the effect is particularly marked in the case of short wheelbase vehicles, especially if the centre of gravity is high as is often the case with four wheeled tipping trucks. Weight transfer is an important factor, to which it is necessary to pay considerable attention; some of the ways in which allowance is made for this and for variation in loading will be examined in Chapter 11.

2

Braking

2.1 Introduction

As noted in Chapter 1, wheeled vehicles are usually braked by way of their wheels and, although there are various types of auxiliary braking system in use (considered in Chapter 10), in all but a few special cases friction brakes are used as the means of slowing down or stopping. In the past, tram cars have sometimes used an electromagnetic system of braking, in which brake shoes articulated to the care were drawn into contact with the running rails to develop a friction force, but no equivalent exists for road vehicles; instead friction is developed between rotating and non-rotating members of the vehicle itself.

Friction is, of course, a phenomenon which designers of engines and transmissions go to great lengths to minimise because, in such components, it is the cause of energy wastage and wear which are undesirable in the extreme. Ideally, the energy which has to be converted when braking takes place should be reclaimed for subsequent use and there are ways in which this can be done—at a price; regenerative braking in appropriate cases, either by electrical means or by storing energy in a flywheel, has been a practical possibility for some time and work on this continues in certain fields of operation.

The friction brake is, however, an extremely simple, compact, reliable and inexpensive device by comparison with the available alternatives; it is therefore unlikely to be displaced for general purposes within the foreseeable future. The systems of which friction brakes form a part are continually being refined in various ways and there is no reason to suppose that finality is yet near at hand.

2.2 Friction

Reference has been made above to friction as a phenomenon which occurs in mechanical devices and which, in general, is unwanted. It is, in fact an entirely natural phenomenon which forms part of the everyday experience of all human beings since, without it, such actions as walking and gripping objects between the fingers would be difficult to accomplish.

Friction is an elusive phenomenon when a precise definition is sought and it continues to be the subject of research. In simplified terms, however, friction can be said to result from the attraction which occurs between two surfaces which are brought into intimate contact with each other; it is not the same thing as the effects of surface roughness, referred to later. It is forces of molecular attraction which bind together all the substances which we know and use and these forces also come into being when two such substances are brought together but, because this attraction is only effective over extremely small distances, truly close contact is essential for its existence; because even polished surfaces are far from flat when considered under high magnification, such contact as this occurs only where opposing high points touch each other.

The forces of attraction referred to above come into existence whenever surfaces come into intimate contact but there is no friction until relative motion is initiated; for this to take place, the various individual contacts must first be broken and to do this a tangential force has to be exerted. As opposing pairs of high points are separated, other pairs come together so that the process of making and breaking of contacts is a continuous one and the force which is necessary to maintain steady motion is virtually constant.

The attractive force between the surfaces depends on their nature, as might be expected; friction is therefore dependent on the nature of the rubbing surfaces involved. The resistance to motion at any instant will depend on the true contact area, which will be only a small part of the apparent contact area; under load, deflection of the high points of the surfaces in contact will cause additional areas to come together so that the attractive force is increased and greater resistance to motion will be experienced. As, within limits, the deflection of the materials concerned will be more or less directly proportional to the load, so it is common experience that a frictional force also is virtually in direct proportion to the load.

One effect of any temperature rise to which the surfaces may be subject will be to soften the substances of which they consist so that, for a given load per unit of area, the true contact area will increase; at the same time, however, the shear strength of the substances will decrease so that, as will be considered below, there may be a change in the overall force required to sustain motion. A temperature rise may also affect the substances by altering them chemically so that their nature changes and the attractive forces are modified as well as their strength.

There is, however, at least one other feature of the contact between two surfaces which must be referred to and which relates to their roughness; in addition to the contact between opposing pairs of high points, there can be interlocking of these points so that there is a contribution to the resistance to motion from the forces of cohesion within the materials, as distinct from that due to the forces of attraction between them. Depending on the respective natures of the two substances, cold welds may be formed between them and subsequently sheared, the high points or asperities of the harder material may plough through the softer one or there may be shearing off of material from both surfaces; as noted above, the surface temperature will affect the shear strength, which is partly involved in determining the magnitude of these forces.

Large scale or macro-roughness is undesirable in surfaces which have to rub together; not only would the resistance to motion be high and erratic, considerable surface damage would be inevitable. Even the degree and nature of small scale or micro-roughness is important when surfaces are intended to be often in sliding contact—as in the case of friction brakes—if the wear rate of either or both is to be acceptable and if the frictional force is to be as expected.

The force necessary to cause relative motion between loaded surfaces in contact consists, then, of two principal components; part is required to overcome the attraction between the areas of true contact (the frictional resistance) and part to overcome the physical interference which occurs. As two well chosen surfaces are rubbed together they will 'bed in' to each other, removing most of those asperities which contribute to the physical interference so that the first component referred to above becomes the significant one, the resistance to motion assumes a steady value and the wear rate of both surfaces reduces to a minimum; however, as referred to later in this chapter, there is as yet no complete understanding of this process.

It is relevant to point out here that whilst it may be desirable at times to machine the surfaces of friction materials in service—perhaps to remove contamination or some other unwanted surface condition—they should be left with as smooth a finish as is practicable, in addition to maintaining their curvature or flatness; roughness plays no part in friction proper and the traditional use of a coarse file on brake linings will increase the rate of wear until full bedding has again been achieved.

Finally, and of great significance, the overcoming of the resistance to motion generates heat. In deforming and shearing the asperities of the surfaces, energy has to be expended and is converted into heat; the same is true of the breaking of the attractive ties between the materials. Friction brakes draw the energy which has to be expended in this way from the kinetic and potential energy stored by the vehicle, thus reducing its speed; a considerable quantity of heat is therefore generated during braking.

Depending on the thermal capacity of the brake parts and the rate of heat loss by conduction, convection and radiation, the generation of heat will lead to a temperature rise at the rubbing surfaces which causes the effects noted above. The provision of an adequate flow of air to promote satisfactory cooling by convection and the limitation of any harmful effects of the heat losses by conduction and radiation are problems which the brake and vehicle designers have to overcome.

2.3 Friction materials

When it is necessary for materials to slide one on the other, the basis on which they are chosen is closely related to the circumstances of the movement. If the components concerned are parts of a mechanism in which friction is an unwanted by-product, then the materials will be chosen for the relatively low attraction (low friction) between them and the small likelihood of them damaging each other. If the components are to form the working surfaces of a friction device, such as a brake or clutch, the second consideration will still apply but a high degree of inter-surface attraction (high friction), subject to other properties being acceptable, will be sought. The measure of this attraction is called the coefficient of friction and it is commonly denoted by the Greek letter μ (mu); this coefficient is the ratio of the force needed to initiate relative movement of the two surfaces to the normal force pressing them into contact.

A great variety of materials and substances can be used as friction materials but only a limited number can satisfy the ever increasing stringency of the demands made by the automotive industry. It has long been the established practice for one of the two materials in contact to be metallic (the mating surface), so that it can conduct away the heat generated at the working surfaces, withstand the applied forces and resist wear; the other material (the friction material) has been looked on as the one whose composition could be varied so as to yield the required performance characteristics and which—being subject to the greater amount of wear—could readily be replaced when the acceptable wear limit was reached.

Before the turn of the century, the materials used for frictional purposes were natural or processed substances which were readily available, although originally utilised for other purposes; examples of such materials are wood (Fig. 2.1), leather, cotton fabric and rubberised canvas. These materials had long been used on industrial friction devices and the brakes of horse drawn vehicles and, when the

Fig. 2.1   Wooden brake block on farm cart

early cars took to the road, were the only substances available for the rather more demanding duty involved.

These makeshift friction materials soon showed their limitations in terms of erratic friction level, poor temperature resistance and rapid wear, among other things; better alternatives, initially based on woven cotton but later utilising asbestos, were then developed. Herbert Frood of Combs in Derbyshire pioneered the friction materials industry in 1897 and soon adopted the brand name Ferodo. Cotton based materials continue in use for certain purposes, as do woven asbestos based ones (Fig. 2.2); greater scope for the formulators came, however, with the introduction of moulded asbestos based linings, as these permit the inclusion of an almost unlimited range of metallic and non metallic constituents, in addition to fibre and resin.

Whilst the brakes of older vehicles—and any others for which moulded linings are not available—are still serviced with woven roll material, moulded materials have been the subject of intensive development—especially those for disc brake pads—and currently offer high standards of consistency and wear resistance. Moulded roll materials are made with sufficient flexibility for them to be formed to shoes of various radius and are sometimes used in the replacement market.

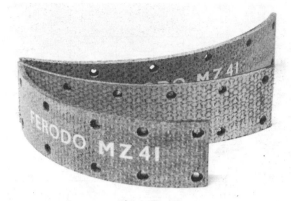

Fig. 2.2   Woven asbestos based brake linings (courtesy of Ferodo Ltd.)

The introduction of rigid moulded materials has eliminated the need for the end chamfer on linings; this used to be necessary with riveted woven linings, which sometimes tended to lift at the ends, thus causing grabbing. The use of bonding as a means of attachment overcomes the need for a chamfer with either woven or flexible moulded brake linings as lifting of the ends is entirely prevented.

Another feature of the riveting of woven linings was the application of 'draw' to the rivet hole spacing; the pitch of the holes in the lining was made a little less than that of those in the shoe so that, when riveted in place, the lining was tightly stretched on the shoe to prevent lifting between the pairs of rivets.

The best riveting practice, which has become established, involves the use of a semi-tubular rivet of either brass or copper (easier to clench but now more expensive); this is used in conjunction with a slightly smaller hole in the shoe than the lead hole drilled in the lining (Fig. 2.3(a)). When the rivet is clenched the tool is adjusted to bottom in the tubular bore, upsetting the shank of the rivet which then becomes a tight fit in the hole in the shoe; the remaining clearance around the rivet where it passes through the lining obviates any likelihood of splitting it.

At the same time, the riveting punch rolls over the end of the rivet so that, if the length is correctly chosen, it presses firmly against the under side of the shoe platform (Fig. 2.3(b)). Countersunk head rivets are most commonly used in the UK, but flat headed semi-tubular rivets, fully tubular steel ones and solid aluminium ones are sometimes used.

a

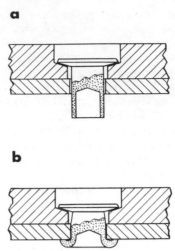

b

Fig. 2.3   Clenching semi-tubular rivets

2.4 Drum brake linings

As moulded drum brake linings (Fig. 2.4) came into wider use, those chemists engaged in formulation began to exercise their freedom to add inclusions of various kinds—both metallic and non-metallic—to the basic mix of asbestos fibre and resin; the object was to modify the properties of the materials in various specified ways to enhance their suitability for various types of duty. Attention was also turned to the resins which were used to bind the fibre and other constituents together, imparting strength and helping to determine the general friction level of the material; the research chemists were asked to find

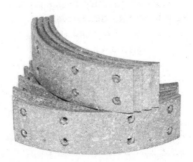

Fig. 2.4   Moulded asbestos based brake linings (courtesy of Ferodo Ltd.)

natural or synthetic resins with properties such as, on the one hand, greater temperature resistance or, on the other hand, improved flow during the liquid phase.

Whilst the resin and asbestos combination determined the general level of friction of a formulation, the added constituents could be selected to modify this level, either throughout the range of working temperatures or in a particular part of it. Not only was it necessary to determine which additive would best achieve the desired result, it was also necessary to discover the optimum amount to use and the necessary tolerances to achieve satisfactory control of quality; over several decades, considerable experience has been acquired by the manufacturers involved.

In addition to work on the formulation of drum brake linings, much has been done on production techniques in the endeavour to optimise the structure of the materials and reduce costs; although the companies concerned are reticent regarding their own achievements, it is known that moulding has progressed from the production of individual linings to the extrusion of roll (sometimes with a wire mesh backing, to impart extra strength) and to the manufacture of curved sheets from which linings of the same curvature and thickness, but of different widths, can be cut.

One of the expensive items in the production budget is the heat required to cure the resins used, so plant is designed to minimise fuel consumption and formulators are under pressure to use resins which require either a lower temperature or a shorter time (or both) to cure. Another large expense is the provision of dies in which products are subjected to heat and pressure; there is therefore a constant endeavour to simplify such tooling and maximise the utilisation of it and to develop materials which need to spend less time within the constraint of a die or other former.

Mention has already been made of riveting, but the European and American brake industries have for many years also used bonding as a means of attaching brake linings to shoes. Bonding is effective over the whole area of the lining so that the assembly is stronger than when riveted, it avoids the high cost of drilling jigs, it allows a greater volume of the friction material to be used (although it is still desirable to retain a certain minimum lining thickness as a thermal barrier), it saves the expense of riveting and it eliminates the trapping of abrasive material in the rivet holes of linings in service. On the other hand the removal of worn linings is somewhat troublesome, used shoes have to be prepared carefully with emphasis on the cleanliness of the shoe platform and precise control of temperature, time and clamping pressure must be exercised so bonding is not a job for the do-it-yourself motorist or small repair workshop.

One other aspect of the method of attachment of linings which is sometimes of interest is that it can affect the incidence of brake squeal; as is often the case with squeal, there are no hard and fast rules but it has been known for a change from riveting to bonding or vice versa to be associated with the onset of squeal. This is probably because of a difference in stiffness between the two types of assembly and the possibility that those parts of a riveted lining between rivets would, if vibrating, tend to damp out this vibration by their movement relative to the shoe platform with which they are in contact.

2.5 Disc brake pads

The conventional design of disc brake uses a lining which is only a fraction of the area and volume of the drum brake lining which would have been used had a drum brake been installed instead. When disc brakes began to become a popular option on cars a typical example used a pad approximately one quarter the area and one half the volume of the drum brake lining which was replaced (Fig. 2.5).

Fig. 2.5   Comparison of areas of equivalent drum brake lining and disc brake pad

From this relationship, it is apparent that for equivalent braking the same amount of energy is being dissipated over a much smaller area and that, ignoring other factors, the braking force generated per unit area is increased by a factor of four. However, three other factors combine to make the requirements for a disc brake pad lining particularly arduous.

Within a given size of wheel, a drum may be replaced by a disc of about the same overall diameter; the effective radius of the drum is clearly equivalent to its inside radius but that of a disc of the same outside radius is reduced by approximately half the width of the braking path (see Fig. 2.6), giving roughly 3/4 of the value for the

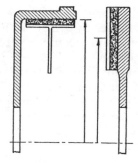

Fig. 2.6   Comparison of effective radii of drum brake and equivalent disc brake

drum. Because of this, lining loadings for equivalent braking are increased by the inverse ratio, a factor of 4/3.

Next comes the consideration that the option referred to above related to the replacement of a two leading shoe drum brake by a disc brake having no self-servo effect; this necessitated a further increase in operating pressure to produce the required equivalent torque output—an increase in the proportion of, perhaps, 3/2.

Finally, at the time at which the above option was current, the best available friction material for disc brake pads had a coefficient of friction of only about 3/4 of that of the good quality drum brake linings then in use so that this, also, made necessary an increase in operating pressures in the ratio of about 4/3. From these approximations it will be realised that the applied pressure on a disc brake pad is of a much higher order than that on a drum brake lining and that, even for equivalent braking duty, surface temperatures must be considerably higher; in fact, drivers soon took advantage of the more stable braking characteristics of the disc brake and the level of duty soon tended upwards, exceeding the expectation.

Although some drum brake lining formulations were at first also used in disc pad form, they were only suitable for light duty; at elevated temperatures their friction level soon fell and their wear rate rose dramatically. To withstand the much higher temperatures and pressures involved a superior category of friction material was needed, the principal difference being in the resin used; at first, however, there were moulding problems and it was necessary to avoid sharp corners and thin sections in order to ensure even density throughout.

In addition to the need for friction materials to 'bed in' to the profile of the mating surface with which they are in contact, they need to achieve a degree of surface conditioning in service such that the frictional properties, if not completely stable, are slow to change as the working temperature changes. This kind of conditioning is something which cannot be fully brought about in production, although it has been known for pads to be treated by contact with a heated plate, but careful formulation can take into account the need to minimise the time taken to achieve conditioning.

The surface appearance of a piece of friction material therefore changes considerably between the unused condition, the normally bedded condition and—in extreme cases—the condition brought about by severe overheating. In general, the colour of a brake lining darkens as chemical changes in the surface are brought about by elevated temperatures, applied over a period of time; only experience enables an observer to differentiate between the depth of colour due to normal duty and the slight charring which indicates that the recommended temperature limit has been exceeded by a small margin. This change of colour is accompanied by a change—usually a fall—in friction level due to the chemical changes at the lining surface; this is what is commonly called fade.

When temperatures go well beyond the maximum recommended value, the surface of the material is first completely charred, as the resin is carbonised, and then—in the case of asbestos based materials—changes through grey to white as the asbestos fibre is exposed. The latter change usually occurs first at the edges of the working surface, these being most exposed to the oxygen needed for the carbon to burn away; a study of the side faces also will often reveal evidence of the effects of prolonged high temperature.

It is of the nature of a friction material that, at the working surface, there is a continual breakdown to powdery wear products as heat is generated; by virtue of the skilful compounding of the material, this breakdown is at such a slow rate that the service life of the product is long and the conditioned surface is continually regenerated. A good lining behaves consistently throughout its life, the only effects of wear being that, as its thickness diminishes, the heat flow through it increases and the risk of contact between the steel shoe or backplate and the mating surface also increases.

The useful wear limit of a friction lining is reached either when, in the case of riveted material it is worn almost to the rivet heads or, in the case of bonded linings, the material is too thin to act as a heat barrier and to ensure that metal-to-metal contact will not occur. The usual recommendation with disc brake pads is that they should be replaced when the linings are worn to between 2.5 and 3 mm (0.1–0.12 in); if linings are worn beyond these limits, there is a serious risk that the heat transfer through the piston(s) will cause vapourisation of the brake fluid.

The majority of disc brake pads are supported by a steel back plate of about 3 mm (0.12 in) thickness, as with the examples illustrated

Fig. 2.7   An assortment of disc brake pads (courtesy of Ferodo Ltd.)

(Fig. 2.7); this usually serves to transmit the clamping force evenly over the lining material, to locate the assembly in the caliper and to support the reaction to the friction force developed at the working surface. Early pads were made as individual pieces which were usually bonded to the backplate, Girling using spigoted pads to ensure pad retention in the event of bond failure; rivets have also been used for a time as additional safeguards.

Present practice is for the friction material to be 'integrally moulded' to the plate, which has a number of holes in it (Fig. 2.8) which the material fills; adhesive is applied to the surface of the plate so that the lining is attached both by the adhesive and by the spigots which form in the holes.

One problem which has arisen with disc brake pads of conventional design when subject to heavy duty as in competitive motoring, is the differential expansion of the steel and the friction material; the 'bi-metallic strip' effect sets up a shear stress in the bond which tends to cause bond failure around the edges of the pad and separation of the pad from the plate so that greater reliance is placed on the integrity of the spigots. To minimise this effect, pads for competitive purposes are usually grooved almost to their full thickness (Fig. 2.9) so that the single pad is effectively replaced by two or more shorter ones; grooves have also been used at times when there was a particular problem of clearing a water film from the disc surface.

Other features affecting the design of brake friction surfaces will be

Fig. 2.8   Backplates for integrally moulded disc brake pads

Fig. 2.9   Competition disc brake pads with central groove (courtesy of Ferodo Ltd.)

referred to in later chapters when the various types of drum and disc brakes are considered.

2.6 Non asbestos friction materials

Asbestos—which is widely used for many purposes, in addition to the manufacture of brake linings—has been found to present hazards to health and its continuing use has been called into question. In particular, the blue variety of asbestos has been recognised as specially hazardous and is no longer used in friction materials; white asbestos is less dangerous and is still in use but with appropriate precautions in its handling.

It is the fibre itself which constitutes the danger, if particles of a particular size range are inhaled, so special care is needed in the factories where it is processed; once the fibre has been moulded into a product, only a very small proportion is ever released either by drilling or other machining or by the processes of wear. The wear products from a brake fitted with conventional linings consist of dust which includes carbonaceous material from the resin and fillers, metallic material from the mating surface and inclusions in the lining and silicaceous material from the breakdown of asbestos with heat; very little free asbestos is, however, to be found but as it is obviously inadvisable to inhale dust of any kind it is common now for workshops to use vacuum equipment when relining brakes.

In addition to the taking of additional care in the manufacture of friction materials, action has been taken to reduce the amount of dust adhering to products despatched from the factory so that they are cleaner to handle and any hazards are correspondingly reduced. Advice is available for workshops which handle or machine friction materials regularly; in recent years, the regulations relating to the presence of asbestos fibre in the atmosphere of a working environment have been increased in stringency very considerably.

There is, however, residual concern about the use of asbestos— even in a safety promoting activity such as braking—and legislation to limit or even, eventually, forbid its use is in existence in some countries (not at present including the UK). Manufacturers have for many years been looking for alternatives to asbestos because of its variability, limited availability and rising cost so, with the addition of pressure from those bodies and individuals worried about the possible risk to health, there has been a powerful incentive to develop friction materials having some alternative base.

The cotton based materials referred to earlier have too low a temperature resistance to be suitable for automotive brake purposes and this underlines the fact that, asbestos having proved to be such an outstanding substance for this purpose, there is at present no alternative which is as good in all functional respects, let alone superior. Amongst the alternatives which have been considered are glass fibre, mineral wools, steel wool and carbon fibre, either singly or in combination, as well as synthetic fibres.

After some premature claims for asbestos free brake linings, which proved to be less than acceptable in service, materials are now in production which are meeting requirements for original equipment purposes and their use may be expected to extend slowly as experience is gained and new plant capacity increased. Because of the present close control of asbestos and the consequent minimisation of the health hazards from its use, it is likely to be some years before it ceases to be used on automotive brakes altogether.

The development of asbestos free friction materials involves both formulation work and the determination of new production techniques. Disc brake pads have, in general, been considered before drum brake linings and clutch facings because they are relatively compact in form so that achieving homogeneity throughout is not difficult; experience has thus been accumulated before dealing with the combination of thin sections and large areas.

The manner of introduction of asbestos free friction materials is such that they must be compatible with conventional brake systems; that is to say their frictional, wear and physical properties must be of the same order as those of existing classes of asbestos based materials. This implies that the average driver may expect to find no greater difference in response or in lining life when his brakes are relined in the transitional period than he would before the change commenced.

2.7 Drum and disc materials

For a friction force to be generated there must be two surfaces in contact with a force applied to them to press them together. In automotive practice it is usual for the friction material—supported by an appropriate metal part—to be stationary with respect to the chassis whilst the other element in the friction pair is a rotating drum or disc.

It is accepted that the friction material will wear in service so provision is made in the design of the brake for its easy replacement; the mating member is metallic so that it can resist the stresses induced by its rotation, together with those due to the pressure on the friction material, and it can conduct away from the working surface much of the heat generated there whilst resisting abrasion by the brake linings.

Cast iron is the material which has been commonly used from the early days of motoring for the manufacture of mating surfaces; it is relatively inexpensive and easily formed into complex shapes, it is strong and able to resist thermal shock and it has good resistance to wear. In general it has been assumed that, with regard to the determination of friction levels, the cast iron played a minor part in contrast to the friction material and so any attention it has received has mostly been with regard to its strength, its thermal properties and its machinability.

For many years there was little reason to take a closer look at cast iron but eventually Ferodo scientists, convinced by anomalies of performance and wear in the test house and in service that there was a hitherto unrecognised factor, made a lengthy investigation. The outcome of this was the discovery that most supplies of cast iron contain trace elements—principally titanium and vanadium—which are present in the form of extremely small and very hard particles.

The exact part these particles play in determining the friction level and the wear rate of both lining and mating surface remains to be discovered; it has, however, been demonstrated that friction level and wear rate increase as the hard particle content decreases, the exact relationship depending on the particular friction material involved. In service, some problems have undoubtedly been created when, for whatever reason, discs or drums having differing hard particle content have been fitted to one axle of a vehicle.

The differences in braking due to this cause are of most importance when the front axle is involved, because front brakes are required to have the higher output and because steering geometry may enhance the effect. Problems with pulling caused by unbalanced braking due to differences in mating surface metallurgy have therefore most commonly occurred with disc brakes at the front of vehicles having a steering geometry with positive offset.

It has also been shown that the surface finish of new discs and drums plays a part in determining the coefficient of friction and, because the processes of wear which eventually reduce the effect of surface finish are related to the hard particle content, that this needs to be specified in conjunction with the general metallurgy. Directional effects from machining have been identified, as have those due to the use of different types of machining process; surprisingly a finish which, by accepted standards, is somewhat rough can initially give lower friction than is subsequently achieved when wear has smoothed the surface.

A very rough surface will initially give high friction and wear which will decrease rapidly as the roughness decreases with wear and stay relatively low for some time before it rises again, as the surface finish gradually becomes smoother; the rate of change of these effects and the friction level achieved will depend, amongst other things, on the hard particle content of the metal parts.

Consistency of performance of brakes in service from prototype to production vehicle and in prolonged service can only be achieved, it has been made clear, if brake drums and discs are of consistent quality in all relevant respects. The cast iron of which these parts are made therefore needs to conform to a recognised standard, such as BS 1452: 1977, and be of at least grade 200 to ensure adequate strength; the hard particle content needs to be controlled to a level appropriate to the friction material used and the desired frictional characteristics. In addition to these requirements, the surface finish must also be controlled.

Because of the directional character of turned surfaces, it is desirable that grinding or even honing should be used to achieve a finish with a roughness average (R_a value) of about 0.5 μm (20 μ in); when the surfaces cannot be ground or honed they should be finished by fine turning, making not less than 4 cuts/mm (100 cuts/in) and their quality should be the best that can economically be achieved. The ovality of drums and the runout and thickness variation of discs must be minimal and it is important that castings are treated to obviate distortion in service; the penalty for lack of care in these respects is paid by the user who has to endure unacceptable vibration during braking and—ultimately—to buy replacements.

The ideal would be the establishment of an agreed international standard or series of standards so that the purchaser of replacement parts from any source could be assured that they were compatible with the originals; unfortunately, although the necessary expertise has been available for some time, relatively little progress has been made in applying it.

Alternatives to cast iron have been considered and some motor cycle manufacturers use stainless steel for discs in order to avoid the unsightly effects of corrosion; light alloy discs with a sprayed iron coating on the rubbing surface are also sometimes used. The use of these other materials, however, limits the choice of friction material considerably because of their vulnerability to abrasion on the one hand or flaking of the applied surface on the other; their adoption represents a compromise between the opposing claims of function and appearance.

In addition to the importance of the material from which drums and discs are made, their form has an effect on such matters as heat dissipation and internal stresses, but this is more appropriately considered in connection with the associated brakes.

Clearly, there cannot be friction brakes unless there are drums or discs to act as one half of the friction pair and it must now be accepted that the metallurgy of the cast iron from which these are usually made is of greater importance than had hitherto been realised. It is now seen to be the case that the functional properties of a friction material cannot be stated satisfactorily without adequate reference to the exact nature of the mating surface.

3

Leading and trailing shoe brakes

3.1 Introduction

The early years of the history of the motor vehicle formed a period of innovation when there was no established practice and virtually all ideas were new ones and worth trying. Quite rapidly, however, the design of many components stabilised in concept and so it was with brakes; the majority of vehicles soon adopted drum brakes, each consisting of two shoes which could be expanded inside a drum (Fig. 3.1) which rotated with one of the rear wheels. Braking of all four wheels only became general towards the end of the 1920s and brought about such an improvement in braking standards that warning signs for the rear of cars so fitted became popular—akin to the warnings seen more recently on the rear of air braked trucks.

The concept of two shoes inside a brake drum with a means of pushing them outwards seems a simple one but the number of important variations is considerable, as is the effect of some of these on the performance characteristics of the brake; quite literally, there is more in drum brakes than meets the eye, especially when handbrake mechanisms and automatic adjustment are incorporated.

When dealing with friction between flat surfaces few complications are encountered, except in the case of automotive clutches which are a subject to themselves; curved brake shoes in a drum, however, are subject to considerations which have exercised the minds of theoreticians for many years. It is not the purpose of this book to go into drum brake geometry in any depth but some consideration of the matters involved is necessary if their many practical consequences are to be understood.

Although the contents of this chapter relate particularly to cars, what is said about leading and trailing shoes is true for brakes of all sizes; many of the brakes described in detail are also used on car derived vans and light commercial vehicles so, as with some of the later chapters in this book, there are no clear cut demarcations in the application of the equipment considered.

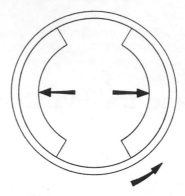

Fig. 3.1   The elements of a two shoe internal expanding drum brake

3.2 Leading and trailing shoes

The easiest way to incorporate two shoes into a drum brake with an axle passing through the drum is to pivot them at adjacent ends and expand them by means of some mechanical device located between the other adjacent ends (Fig. 3.2); what then is important is the direction in which the drum is rotating when the expander forces the shoe tips apart, so that the brake linings attached to the shoes contact the drum. In order that what happens can be considered easily, the two shoes are considered separately and the lining length has been reduced considerably to a nominal value.

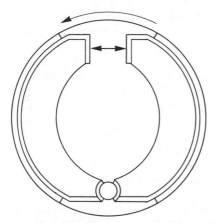

Fig. 3.2   The basic features of a leading/trailing   shoe   (simplex) drum brake

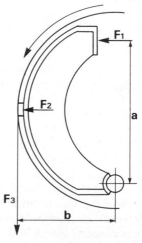

Fig. 3.3   A simplified leading shoe

The left hand shoe of Fig. 3.2 is considered first and the assumption is made that the brake drum is turning in the anti-clockwise direction (Fig. 3.3). The force F_1 is applied to the upper end of the shoe, at a distance a from the pivot centre, and so exerts a turning moment F_1a in an anti-clockwise direction causing the lining to be pressed against the drum by a force F_2; the coefficient of friction between the lining and the drum then causes a friction force F_3 to act on the drum and a reaction force to act on the lining at their point of contact and in opposite directions, only that acting on the lining being shown in the diagram.

The force F_3 acts on the brake shoe at a distance b from the pivot so that an anti-clockwise turning moment F_3b is generated and, being in the same direction as F_1a, augments it; the turning moment applying the shoe to the drum is therefore increased by the reaction which it produces, the increase being related to the value of the coefficient of friction between the two materials in contact. This effective increase in the applying force leads to a small increase in the reaction which, in turn, further increases the force on the lining; in practical cases (except when the condition known as 'grab' occurs, by mischance) the shoe and its lining are so designed that this augmentation of the force on the lining is restricted in its effect, so that the braking effect of the shoe is controllable.

A shoe which has a 'self-servo' characteristic such as is described above is popularly known as a leading shoe; it may be easily identified by noting that the arrow indicating the direction of drum rotation in the diagram is pointing the same way as that representing the shoe tip force. The ratio F_3/F_1 is known as the shoe factor; it relates the braking force acting on the drum, otherwise known as the drum drag (which is equal and opposite in direction to the reaction force acting on the lining), to the shoe tip force and, as will be seen later, there are a number of ways in which this can be varied.

Consideration is now given to the right hand shoe of Fig. 3.2, the direction of drum rotation still being assumed to be anti-clockwise (Fig. 3.4). Again a force F_1 is applied to the shoe tip, the distance from the pivot being as before, so that the same turning moment is exerted on this shoe as on the left hand one, but in a clockwise direction. Again, a force F_2 acts on the lining to apply it to the drum and a reaction force F_3 then also acts on the lining, as shown.

The line of reaction force F_3 is at a distance b from the pivot, so a turning moment F_3b is generated, acting in an anti-clockwise direction; this second turning moment, being in the opposite sense to that applying the lining to the drum, diminishes it and causes an effective reduction in the shoe tip force. The design of the parts concerned is normally such that, as in the case of the leading shoe, the

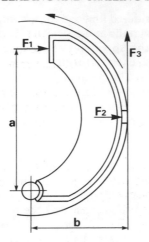

Fig. 3.4   *A simplified trailing shoe*

successive effects of this feedback diminish rapidly and for any set of conditions the drum drag is predictable.

The output of a brake shoe operating in the manner illustrated in Fig. 3.4 is less than it would be were there no opposing effect of the reaction force on the lining and this type is popularly known as a trailing shoe; it may easily be identified by noting that the arrow indicating the direction of drum rotation in the diagram is pointing the opposite way to that representing the shoe tip force. The names leading and trailing given to these two types of shoes have long been established but have no special significance; other names for types of brake shoe will be referred to later.

As with the leading shoe, the ratio F_3/F_1 for the trailing shoe is known as the shoe factor; for a trailing shoe this ratio is always less than one, for a leading shoe the ratio is always greater than one for practical values of the lining coefficient of friction. When these two shoes are considered together as forming part of a brake such as is illustrated diagrammatically in Fig. 3.2, this is called a leading and trailing shoe brake (L & T); the individual shoe factors may then be added together to give a ratio called the brake factor, which is the ratio of total drum drag to the shoe tip force applied to either shoe. An alternative name for this type of brake is Simplex.

The drum drag is the force which, acting at the drum inside radius, causes a braking torque to be applied to the wheels of the vehicles; it is therefore important to have some understanding of the dependence of this drum drag on the design of the brake shoes and the coefficient of friction of the brake linings. Lining arc length and position as well as friction level, have to be taken into account, in addition to shoe stiffness, position of shoe tip force, manner of support at the ends and direction of drum rotation; the methods of determining the output of a brake from a knowledge of these factors are beyond the scope of this book but the principal characteristics which can be determined are easily described.

A typical brake shoe sub-assembly (Fig. 3.5) has a lining of about 110° arc, displaced a little towards the trailing end of the platform (the end the drum passes over last during normal forward rotation), these

Fig. 3.5   A typical brake shoe

features being determined by the need to achieve a relatively high shoe factor; excessive lining length would cause problems owing to lack of clearance at the ends when the brake was released. Lining width is determined by the need to provide a sufficient area of lining over which to dissipate energy—so that temperatures are limited to an acceptable value—and the thickness by the need to provide a sufficient volume of friction material to give acceptable life. The choice of brake diameter and width is restricted by the space available within the wheel which the vehicle designer has chosen.

3.3 Shoe and brake factor curves

It can be shown that for brake shoes of conventional design, the biggest factor affecting output after shoe tip force and direction of drum rotation is the coefficient of friction of the lining. Shoe tip force is under the control of the driver and drum rotation for forward motion (the significant direction) is always the same for a given shoe or brake so lining friction level, which may be affected either by choice of material or—in service—by the working temperature, becomes the factor which is important as a basis of assessment of the characteristics of a brake.

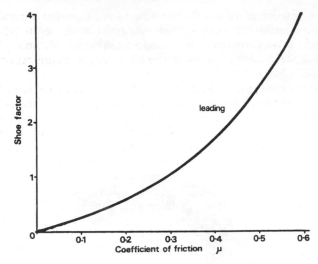

Fig. 3.6   A shoe factor curve for a typical leading shoe

Figure 3.6 shows a curve for a typical leading shoe which relates the shoe factor to the lining coefficient of friction; in fact, the range of values of friction shown, from zero to 0.6 extends way above and beneath the range of values available in practice, which is of the order 0.35 to 0.45, but this does not affect the usefulness of the curve.

It can be seen that, as might be expected, the value of the shoe factor depends on the friction level; however, this is not a constant relationship, as the shoe factor increases more rapidly as μ, the coefficient of friction increases. It is possible to design a leading brake shoe in such a way that, above a certain level of μ, its shoe factor curve rises almost vertically; such a shoe would be prone to sudden fierce engagement with the drum (grab) such as could easily lock the wheel concerned, this being a condition to be avoided.

Similar grab and associated problems can be caused in service by a lining which contacts the drum only at its ends (toe and heel contact), perhaps because its thickness is initially excessive. Conversely, a lining which contacts the drum only on an area about its centre (crown contact) gives a low shoe factor which would rise as bedding-in proceeded.

Since, in general, it is desired that shoe tip forces are kept to only moderate values, there is a tendency to achieve high shoe output by using leading shoe designs in conjunction with relatively high friction levels; there is, however, a penalty in carrying this policy to the extreme. At high values of μ with a high output design of leading shoe the shoe factor curve has a steep slope such that, for a quite small reduction in μ (due, perhaps, to high operating temperature), there is a relatively large drop in shoe factor; if a lower friction lining is used with a shoe designed for more moderate output, the same reduction in μ causes a lesser drop in shoe factor.

High output leading shoes are, therefore, said to be very sensitive—subject to considerable variations in output in service; although these variations may be initiated by lining fade at high temperature, their degree is out of proportion to the degree of fade actually occurring. The brake designer, knowing the class of car on which his product is intended to be used, has to compromise between the conflicting demands of high output and stability of output.

Figure 3.7 is for a trailing shoe of similar general design to the leading shoe considered above; the curve which is to be seen indicates very different characteristics to those just considered. Instead of rising with a slope which increases as μ increases, the curve for the trailing shoe rises less steeply as μ increases but the change is only slight and the line does not depart greatly from being straight.

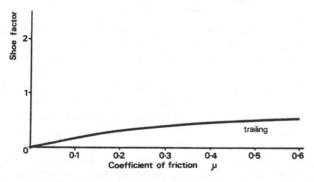

Fig. 3.7   A shoe factor curve for a typical trailing shoe

Clearly, the value of the shoe factor for a trailing shoe is quite low by comparison with a leading shoe—it is, in other words, less powerful—but it is also much less sensitive to changes in lining friction level. When, therefore, one leading shoe and one trailing shoe are combined to form a leading/trailing shoe or Simplex brake, as illustrated diagrammatically in Fig. 3.2, the good and bad features of the two tend to cancel each other out; the low output of the trailing shoe limits the overall power of the brake but its relative insensitivity to lining fade makes the brake reasonably stable in output (Fig. 3.8).

When a leading/trailing shoe brake operates in the reverse

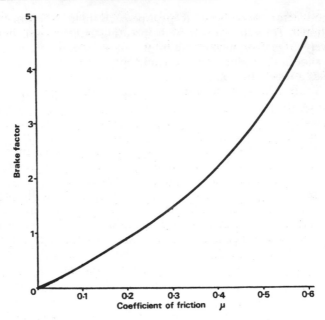

Fig. 3.8   A brake factor curve for a leading/trailing shoe brake incorporating the two shoes featured in Figs. 3.6 and 3.7

direction, the shoes exchange their characteristics; in some cases such brakes are so designed that the same brake factor is achieved in reverse but in others there is a difference, the factor then being lower. Since vehicles cannot normally be driven as fast in reverse as in the forward direction, this deliberate differentiation in favour of forward braking is a common design policy.

One side effect of the adoption of the leading/trailing shoe configuration of brake is that it promotes an unbalanced force on the drum, which affects the loading of the wheel bearings. Since the self-servo characteristic of the leading shoe causes it to be applied harder to the drum, the contrary being the case for the trailing shoe, there is a net force on the bearings which acts in a direction dependent on the mounting of the two shoes. If other considerations made it possible to mount a leading/trailing brake so that the leading shoe faced down and the trailing shoe upwards, this unbalanced force would act upwards and the load on the wheel bearings would then be reduced during brake application.

Because leading and trailing shoes dissipate different amounts of energy, their linings wear at different rates unless steps are taken to cause otherwise; in some few cases in the past it has been possible to interchange leading and trailing shoes at an appropriate stage of lining wear so as to achieve full lining utilisation.

3.4 Shoe expansion

As will be understood from a general knowledge of vehicle construction, the axle and the hub on which the wheel is mounted occupy much of the space at the centre of a drum brake so the means by which the shoes are expanded can only be situated at or near their tips. Early vehicles used cam or wedge mechanisms of similar type to those considered in Chapter 7 of this book, but these are not now current on cars although still found on light weight motorcycles; however it was not so much the mechanical expanders themselves, as the cable or rod systems by which they were operated, which were inefficient when these brakes were current.

The Austin A35 van which continued in production until 1962, used a mechanical expander (Fig. 3.9) at the rear until the end, but this was exceptional; in this design, operation of the lever 8 caused the tappet 3 to apply the leading shoe; the reaction on the pivot 7 caused the housing 1 to slide on the backplate and apply the trailing shoe. This reliance on a sliding movement to apply a second friction element, as a result of the reaction force from the direct application of the first, is a principle which has continued in the design of some hydraulic drum brakes and of some disc brakes; as long as the freedom to slide is maintained, all is well but severe maintenance problems are created if this freedom is restricted by corrosion.

Once hydraulic brake systems (considered in Chapter 5) had been introduced on vehicles, the means adopted most commonly to apply a

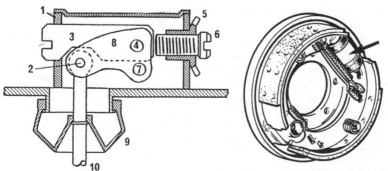

Fig. 3.9   A mechanical expander for a leading/trailing shoe brake

Fig. 3.10   A fixed double acting wheel cylinder (courtesy of Automotive Products PLC)

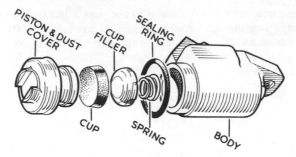

Fig. 3.11   A cup type pressure seal (courtesy of Automotive Products PLC)

leading/trailing brake was the fixed double acting wheel cylinder (Fig. 3.10), which is still widely used; the cylinder body and pistons may be either ferrous or of light alloy, the cylinder bore being machined to a high standard of accuracy and smoothness. Each piston is faced at its inner end with a synthetic rubber cup (Fig. 3.11), or has a groove into which is fitted a pressure seal (Fig. 3.12); in either case, the lip of the rubber component makes a light contact with the cylinder bore under zero internal pressure so that the fluid is retained and air excluded. In fact, the lips of cups and pressure seals are so designed that a very slight film of brake fluid is allowed to remain on the walls of the cylinder as motion occurs, to ensure lubrication of the sliding surfaces when under pressure and so minimise wear.

Wheel cylinders have two ports, threaded internally for the insertion of hydraulic brake system fittings; one is the feed port and the other, located at the upper part of the cylinder bore, is usually for bleeding off air through a bleed screw (Fig. 3.13), as referred to later. Sometimes the supply to both rear brakes of a car is taken by a single

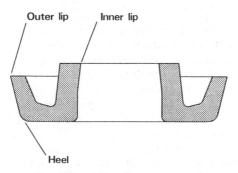

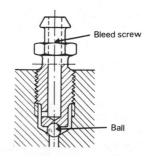

Fig. 3.12   A U section pressure seal   *Fig. 3.13   A brake bleed screw*

pipe; this is connected to the inlet port of the wheel cylinder of one brake and a further pipe is used to link the other port of that cylinder to the inlet port of the wheel cylinder of the second brake. Both brakes are then bled through the bleed screw fitted to the wheel cylinder of the second brake.

Those wheel cylinders which have a cup type pressure element usually incorporate a cup spreader, under the influence of a light spring, to keep the cup in place against the end of the piston and ensure that it effectively seals the cylinder at all times. The mouth of wheel cylinders is usually fitted with a rubber dust cover and this serves to exclude water and dirt from the cylinder bore; rubber lubricant contained within the dust cover lubricates the piston as it moves in the outer part of the cylinder bore. Other components sometimes found inside wheel cylinders will be referred to later in this chapter under automatic adjustment.

As an alternative to the double acting fixed wheel cylinder, the single acting sliding wheel cylinder (Fig. 3.14) is still found in large numbers, particularly on some Girling rear brakes; the piston

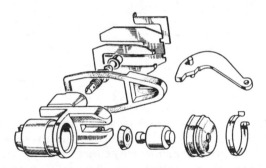

Fig. 3.14   A single acting sliding wheel cylinder (courtesy of Lucas Girling Ltd.)

operates the leading shoe directly and the reaction to the shoe tip forces causes the cylinder body to slide on the brake backplate and apply the trailing shoe, which abuts on the end of it, with an approximately equal force. The wheel cylinder moves in a slot in the backplate and is retained by thin steel plates, slid into grooves around the projection from the cylinder body; a rubber boot is fitted to exclude water and dirt and retain the special brake grease which lubricates the sliding surfaces (this brake grease is not for use with hydraulic components, which may only be lubricated with brake fluid or rubber grease). Defective sealing or lubrication of the sliding surfaces may lead to the cylinder seizing, with the trailing shoe then either rubbing continuously or else inoperative.

3.5 Brake shoes

Brake shoes for cars, vans and the larger motor cycles are nowadays mostly of sliding type, their tips resting on flat abutments instead of being pivoted on a fixed pin; it is important that the shoe tip contact points at both ends are lubricated with the brake grease referred to above so that the shoes have freedom to position themselves correctly in the drum. A sliding shoe loads its lining more evenly (and therefore wears it more evenly) and develops a higher shoe factor than a pivoted shoe, relatively few examples of which are now found in service on cars.

Many makes of leading/trailing shoe brake have an abutment for the shoes on which the relevant surfaces are parallel (Fig. 3.15);

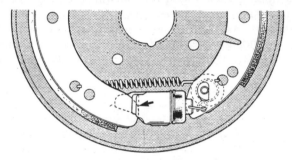

Fig. 3.15   A parallel brake shoe fixed abutment (courtesy of Automotive Products PLC)

Girling brakes commonly use abutments with these surfaces converging towards the centre of the brake, as this gives a higher shoe factor. The abutment for the shoes may either be a solid attachment to the backplate or, as considered later, may be combined with the means of adjustment.

Brake shoes may be formed from rolled steel Tee sections or, more commonly, may be fabricated from two steel pressings welded together, the shoe tip at the abutment end sometimes being ribbed for stiffness; the shoe platform is pierced with holes for rivets and often its edges are each formed with three 'nibs' (Fig. 3.16). When such a shoe is assembled onto a backplate, the nibs are in contact with machined platforms, the surfaces of which are lubricated with brake grease to facilitate free movement; the shape of the nibs makes it easier to keep this grease away from the lining surfaces.

The shoe web will be pierced with holes, some of which serve as locations during manufacture and which are therefore accurately sized and positioned; shoes may be used on more than one type of

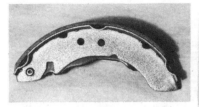

Fig. 3.16 'Nibs' on the edge of a brake shoe platform

Fig. 3.17   A brake shoe web gashed for flexibility

brake assembly and not all holes may be used at once. The holes are used in connection with pull off and other springs, shoe steady devices, hand brake (parking) mechanisms and manual or automatic adjusters; during the period of currency of a particular design of shoe, the number of holes may well be increased as its range of functions is extended, but any reduction may create problems on older vehicles to which it relates.

In the case of Lockheed shoes, the web is sometimes gashed (Fig. 3.17) so as to achieve a particular degree of flexibility. The way in which the force applied to a drum brake lining is distributed along its length is greatly dependent on the flexibility of the shoe and affects matters such as the shoe factor and the likelihood of squeal.

As well as being located at their tips, brake shoes are commonly held against their support points on the backplate by a shoe steady device; this takes one of a variety of forms, some of which are illustrated (Fig. 3.18), and permits the shoe to be expanded or to slide but not to lift away from the backplate. In some cases the ends of shoe return springs are so shaped that they exact a turning moment on the shoes when they are in place and steadies are not then needed (Fig. 3.19).

Pull-off or shoe-return springs are fitted, usually from shoe to shoe,

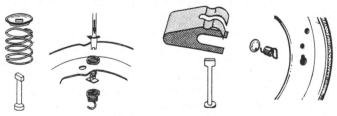

Fig. 3.18   Some types of shoe steady

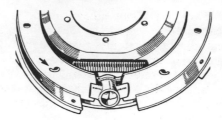

Fig. 3.19   A return spring designed to act also as a shoe steady (courtesy of Lucas Girling Ltd.)

to pull the shoes back to their off position when the brake pedal is released; usually these springs are of coil form but Volkswagen has commonly used a single large U shaped spring to return the shoes. These springs can be subject to considerable stress and it is necessary to ensure that the brake adjustment is fully retracted before attempting to fit or remove them; for trouble free servicing of brakes it is advisable to fit and remove parts in the order recommended by the manufacturer and to use any special tools which may be available.

Before an unfamiliar brake is serviced, it is good practice to make a diagram showing the positions of pull-off and other springs in relation to the holes in the shoes and other places to which they are hooked, also to note the order in which they are removed; it must be borne in mind that the brakes on opposite ends of an axle are mirror images of each other. Springs may be damaged if they are stretched excessively during the servicing of a brake; if this happens, new springs must be obtained and fitted.

3.6 Brake adjustment

It is desirable, as will be considered in a later chapter, to limit the brake pedal movement when an application is made; it is therefore necessary to provide a means of adjusting the clearance between the linings and the drum so that it can be set correctly when relined shoes are fitted and reset as lining wear takes place. Two modes of adjustment can be identified and each is associated with a variety of mechanisms by which it is effected.

On the one hand, the shoes are allowed to fall back from the drum only by the desired amount as the pedal is released, the components of the expander then adopting an appropriate position; on the other hand, an adjuster can be inserted at a convenient point between shoe tips and abutments, so that the piston(s) always traverse the same portion of the cylinder bore.

Most of the brakes made early in the period considered had manual adjustment which was carried out either at predetermined servicing intervals or when the driver considered the brake pedal travel to be excessive. Manual adjustment after the first mode mentioned above is either by means of (1) a 'snail cam' mounted on the backplate and turned by a square headed spindle; this contacts a pin which projects from the web of the shoe (Fig. 3.20) so that the expander end of the shoe can be lifted in distinct stages. (2) An eccentric pin, similarly mounted, which engages the edge of or an opening (which may have alternative uses) in the shoe web (Fig. 3.21) and which gives infinitely variable adjustment. In each of these cases the adjuster spindle is deliberately made stiff to turn, so that the adjustment is held, and it should not be lubricated; these adjusters have more than sufficient lift to permit the lining to be fully utilised in service.

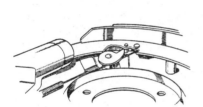

Fig. 3.20   A snail cam shoe adjuster (courtesy of Lucas Girling Ltd.)

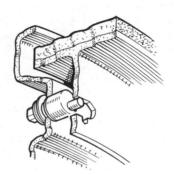

Fig. 3.21   An eccentric pin shoe adjuster (courtesy of Automotive Products PLC)

Manual adjustment of the second mode often takes the form of a cone and tappet mechanism (Fig. 3.22) which replaces the simple fixed abutment and which is so constructed that rotation of the threaded spindle forces the tappets apart, lifting the shoes in distinct stages; the components of such an adjuster, especially the threaded spindle, should be well lubricated with brake grease on assembly. An alternative method is the use of left and right hand threaded tappets which are screwed into toothed adjuster wheels and may be assembled to the hydraulic pistons (Fig. 3.23); this permits individual adjustment to each shoe and such a mechanism may, alternatively, be incorporated into the shoe abutment. A further method, still come across, is the snail cam mechanism which may be located at a shoe tip, locating in a suitable cut-out (Fig. 3.24). In all cases it is necessary to

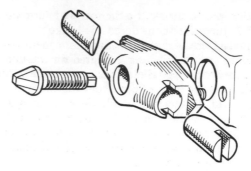

Fig. 3.22   A cone and tappet adjuster (courtesy of Automotive Products PLC)

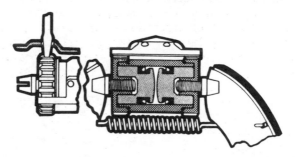

Fig. 3.23   A threaded tappet type adjuster (courtesy of Alfred Teves GmbH)

Fig. 3.24   Snail cam adjustment at the shoe tip (courtesy of Automotive Products PLC)

take up the adjustment with the wheel lifted until the drum is locked and then slacken off just sufficiently for the drum to rotate freely; the brake pedal is then operated hard a few times and the adjustment checked.

One consequence of the first of these two modes of adjustment is that as the piston(s) move to suit the newly set position of the shoes, the fluid level in the reservoir falls a little and—if the reason for this is not understood—may cause apprehension; a different consequence arising from the second mode is that, over a long period of service, there may be local wear in the cylinder bore (of which the same portion is always used), which is a reason why renewal at recommended intervals is desirable.

Automatic adjustment of brakes ensures that normal pedal travel is always minimal so that a full reserve of travel is maintained and a quick response assured; there is also the consideration that, all disc brakes (often fitted at the front of cars) being automatically adjusted, it is desirable to match this by eliminating the need to adjust manually the rear drum brakes likely to be fitted. There is, on the other hand, the consideration that the need to adjust brakes manually draws attention to them and may encourage more regular examination and servicing as may be found necessary.

When automatic adjustment of leading/trailing shoe brakes was introduced, the brakes concerned were generally for use at the rear where a parking mechanism was required, the adjustment was then arranged so that it took place during handbrake application or release; more recently, legislation in some countries has called for adjustment to be effected during service (foot) brake operation. All these mechanisms will be considered after the description of hand brake mechanisms which follows.

There are, however, methods of automatic adjustment sometimes found which are independent of the handbrake mechanism. In the one case, the necessary components are incorporated into the double acting wheel cylinder (Fig. 3.25), where they are ensured of a consistent environment and protected from contamination. In the example shown, a threaded bolt located in the back of each piston, where it is retained by a split ring, is threaded into the double ended split sleeve located at the centre of the cylinder bore; the thread is of a form which permits the bolts to move outwards, springing the sleeve open, one pitch at a time, but prevents inwards movement which, during brake servicing, is achieved by turning the pistons to screw the

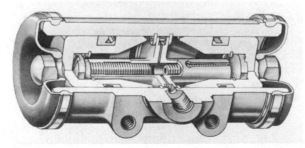

Fig. 3.25   Automatic adjustment housed inside the wheel cylinder (courtesy of Alfred Teves GmbH)

*Fig. 3.26   A friction shake back stop on a
shoe web*

bolts back in. Another mechanism located in the wheel cylinder utilises spring rings, assembled into grooves in the pistons, which grip the cylinder bore with sufficient force to prevent the pull off springs from retracting the pistons; operation of the foot pedal exerts sufficient force to move the pistons and apply the shoes and there is sufficient clearance in the grooves to permit the desired drum to lining clearance to be obtained.

Friction is also harnessed in the adjuster shown next (Fig. 3.26) which is assembled to the web of each shoe; friction washers under spring pressure grip the web so that only when the brake pedal is applied is enough force available to move the shoe relative to the adjuster. The hollow stem of the adjuster has sufficient clearance between its bore and a pin set in the backplate to permit the normal running clearance. There are a number of variations of this type of adjuster to be found.

3.7 The brake backplate

The component which forms the basis for a car drum brake assembly is the backplate, on which sub-assemblies such as wheel cylinders, fixed abutments and adjusters are mounted; the backplate transmits the torque reaction when the brake is applied and it also fits closely to the mouth of the drum, to exclude water and dirt from the brake, as far as is possible. A typical backplate is a complex steel pressing (Fig. 3.27), parts of which may support the shoe webs or may be machined to form locations on which the edges of the shoe platform rest.

The brake lining for any particular shoe is generally made a little narrower than the shoe platform, on which it should be centrally

Fig. 3.27   A typical brake backplate

positioned when being riveted or bonded in place; the lining material will, therefore, not touch the backplate. This ensures that the friction between the edge of the shoe platform and the backplate, under the pressure of the shoe steady device, results only from metal-to-metal contact; it also makes it possible to grease these contact points—as described earlier in this chapter—without the grease finding its way directly onto the lining surface.

Some brakes have had fixed or adjustable steady posts set in the backplate to support the shoe web and some have had pins or posts which anchored springs or engaged with adjusting devices attached to the shoes (referred to above); backplates are usually pierced with holes for the shoe steadies, as well as for attachment to the mounting flange and may have holes for other purposes.

One Girling leading/trailing rear brake had a snail cam mounted in the backplate which was not concerned with adjustment. The shoes were disposed horizontally and it seems that there was concern lest the sliding wheel cylinder used should allow the lower shoe to rub; this shoe was therefore biased upwards by a spring hooked into the backplate, its upward movement being limited by the snail cam which engaged a post set in the shoe web. In later years this arrangement was considered unnecessary so current replacement shoes commonly omit the post and the hole for the spring.

Because of the complex shape of brake backplates, the press tools required for their production in quantity are very expensive; backplates for prototype brakes are therefore likely to be machined from the solid. Although components made in this way will closely match the strength of the quantity-made parts used later in production, it is quite possible that their vibration characteristics may differ somewhat; in some cases, at least, this may be partly why drum brakes of production cars give rise to squeal problems not encountered in development.

The heat resulting from the dissipation of energy with a drum brake is generated at the inside surface of the drum; much of this is conducted through the drum to its outer surface, but some is radiated inwards and may, in extreme cases, cause vapourisation of the brake fluid in the wheel cylinder. Some drum brakes used on high performance cars before the introduction of disc brakes have, therefore, used ventilated backplates; air scoops (Fig. 3.28) caused cooling air to pass through the inside of the drum and reduce the temperature of the internal components.

Fig. 3.28   An air scoop used to encourage cooling air to flow through a drum brake

3.8 Handbrake mechanisms

Transmission type parking brakes, usually mounted behind the gearbox, have never been common in the UK, although standard on the Landrover and Rangerover; instead, an independent means of applying the rear brakes by using a hand lever is usually provided. It is easy to do this with a leading/trailing brake, such as is common at the rear, and is all the easier because the rear wheels of conventional vehicles do not have to be steered. Duo-servo drum brakes (referred to later) have also been fitted at the rear of cars but it is no more difficult to equip these with a handbrake mechanism and this will be described at the appropriate place. As has already been mentioned, automatic adjustment is often incorporated with part of the hand-brake mechanism but these more elaborate types will be considered after the simpler ones.

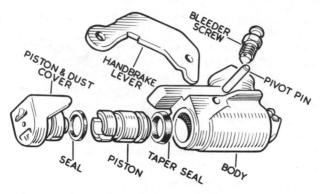

Fig. 3.29   A sliding, single acting wheel cylinder with handbrake mechanism incorporated (courtesy of Automotive Products PLC)

When a sliding wheel cylinder is fitted, it is possible to pivot a lever in the cylinder body and cause this to operate the leading shoe in parallel with the hydraulic piston. Figure 3.29 shows how Lockheed locate the operating lever in a slotted extension of the inner, hydraulic piston so that the separate outer piston can be operated either mechanically or hydraulically. Figure 3.30 shows how Girling arrange for the lever to engage an opening in the web of the leading shoe, a hardened steel wearing plate sometimes being clipped in place in the opening; the lever then acts directly on the leading shoe. In both of these cases, handbrake operation of the trailing shoe is caused by

Fig. 3.30   An alternative arrangement of the handbrake mechanism with a sliding wheel cylinder (courtesy of Lucas Girling Ltd.)

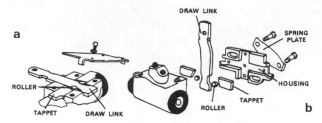

Fig. 3.31   Early and later wedge type handbrake mechanisms (courtesy of Lucas
Girling Ltd.)

the sliding of the wheel cylinder body as an effect of the reaction force
at the operating lever pivot.

The Girling wedge type handbrake mechanism was originally
housed in the wheel cylinder casting (Fig. 3.31(a)) but, in the latest
version (Fig. 3.31(b)), the cover has been modified to contain the
wedge, rollers and tappets. When the wedge is drawn outwards, the
tappets are expanded and contact the appropriately shaped shoe tips;
in order that equal forces are applied to both shoes the wheel cylinder
in the earlier version and the cover in the later version have limited
freedom of movement.

A very numerous class of handbrake mechanisms incorporates a
strut, situated close to the wheel cylinder, which operates in
conjunction with a lever to push the shoes apart. In one form (Fig.
3.32), the lever projects through the backplate where it is connected to
the handbrake cable or rod; the inner end is located in one of the
openings in the shoe web, and the strut is pin jointed to the lever. In
another form (Fig. 3.33), a lever pivoted on one of the shoes is
operated by the handbrake cable, which passes through an opening in

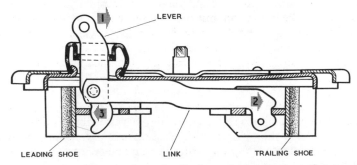

Fig. 3.32   One form of lever and strut handbrake mechanism (courtesy of Automotive
Products PLC)

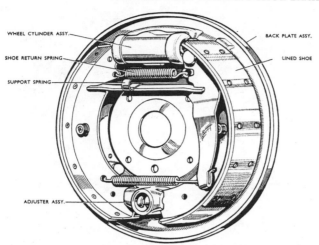

WHEEL CYLINDER ASSY.

SHOE RETURN SPRING

SUPPORT SPRING

ADJUSTER ASSY.

BACK PLATE ASSY.

LINED SHOE

Fig. 3.33   Handbrake mechanism with lever pivoted on trailing shoe (courtesy of Lucas Girling Ltd.)

the backplate; the strut is pushed against the second shoe by the lever and the reaction force on its pivot operates the first shoe.

Handbrake mechanisms need to be maintained in good order if vehicles are to be safely held on steep gradients and recommended lubricants should be used on all working parts; attention should be given to the cables and/or rods and the operating lever, or brake drag may be caused when the handbrake is supposedly released. Brake drag has sometimes been common in the past when vehicle manufacturers have relied upon the shoe return springs to return the cables or rods, as well as fulfilling their proper function.

Both Girling and Lockheed modified their sliding wheel cylinder type rear brakes to achieve automatic adjustment in conjunction with handbrake operation, but the two mechanisms differ considerably. The Girling brake (Fig. 3.34) has a ratchet wheel located at the rear of the cylinder, in place of the usual shoe abutment, and a threaded adjuster stem is screwed into this; attached to the handbrake operating lever is a spring steel blade which, as the handbrake is applied, sweeps over the teeth of the ratchet wheel until, when lining wear reaches a certain value, it is able to drop into the next tooth. When the handbrake is released, the return of the mechanism under the effect of the shoe return springs causes the ratchet wheel to be rotated by one tooth pitch and the adjuster screwed out by a corresponding amount.

In some versions of the Girling brake, the spring steel blade can be

Fig. 3.34   Automatic adjustment of threaded tappet by handbrake operation on a sliding wheel   cylinder   (courtesy   of   Lucas Girling Ltd.)

lifted onto a support provided (using a screwdriver inserted through a hole provided in the face of the brake drum) so that it is clear of the ratchet wheel; the latter can then be turned with the screwdriver to slacken off the adjustment to facilitate drum removal. This method of automatic adjustment, like others of a similar kind, takes up the same amount of clearance each time it operates; when relined shoes are fitted, it is usually necessary to operate the handbrake a considerable number of times to take up the excessive clearance.

The Lockheed type of mechanism (Fig. 3.35) has a ratchet wheel and adjuster screw incorporated into the outer piston and dust shield, adjacent to the leading shoe; the dust cover is extended so that a pin engages with a lever pivoted on a bracket attached to the cylinder body. As the brake is operated, either by the parking brake control or by the foot pedal, the lever is caused to sweep over the ratchet wheel until, as lining wear increases, it engages the next tooth; adjustment then takes place as the brake is released.

Another type of automatic adjustment which has been common, and which also uses a ratchet wheel operated by a lever sweeping across it, is incorporated into the type of handbrake mechanism which expands the shoes by means of a lever pivoted to one of the shoes and a strut; instead of the strut being a single component it is a sub-assembly, the length of which is variable. In the example shown (Fig. 3.36), the strut consists of a male and a female threaded component and a ratchet wheel; the lever or pawl which moves the ratchet wheel is pivoted on the shaft supported parallel to the backplate.

The lever which operates the handbrake mechanism enters the brake through a rubber dust cover and is attached to the shaft

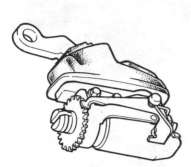

Fig. 3.35   Automatic adjustment of threaded tappet by footbrake operation on a sliding wheel cylinder (courtesy of Automotive Products PLC)

Fig. 3.36   Girling HAHC type rear brake; automatically adjusted by use of the cross pull type handbrake mechanism

referred to above; the shaft is supported on the backplate at one end and located in the end of the strut at the other, so that the lever operates the trailing shoe directly and the leading shoe by reaction, the shaft being able to swing a little. The shaft also carries the pawl but this is not rigidly attached to the shaft but is rotated through the medium of a coil spring wound around it.

The coil spring transmits sufficient force to enable the pawl to turn the ratchet wheel and adjust the brake (this happens as the brake is applied) but, should the threads become seized, it can be overcome to allow handbrake operation to take place, although with increasing travel. To facilitate drum removal, the operating lever rests against a stop (Fig. 3.37) behind the backplate which can be removed to allow extra shoe retraction; this stop must be replaced when servicing has been completed.

The line of action of the cable to this brake is parallel to the axle but a companion brake is designed for a forward pull cable, attached directly to a lever pivoted on the trailing shoe; the pawl is mounted on this shoe, not rigidly but on a pivot and loaded by a spring. As with the previous brake, adjustment takes place during application of the handbrake and the spring loading of the pawl allows for seizure of the screw threads. To facilitate drum removal in this case, a plug shaped stop can be withdrawn from behind the brake; this type of stop may not be re-usable.

Fig. 3.37   Removable stop to facilitate drum removal by increasing handbrake release

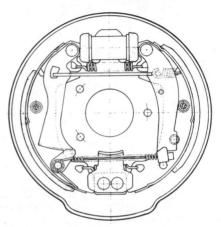

Fig.   3.38   DBA   leading/trailing (simplex) brake with automatic adjustment (courtesy of DBA SA)

3.9 Adjustment by service brake

Although the association of brake adjustment with the handbrake is reasonable—on the basis that this is applied at least at the conclusion of every journey, and that the lining wear during this period will be small—legislation relating to brake design has in some influential countries come to require that adjustment should be associated with the service brake. The one Lockheed brake already described above already satisfied this requirement but there are others which must be considered.

In the DBA brake shown (Fig. 3.38), the forward pull lever is pivoted to the trailing shoe and operates the leading shoe by way of the one piece strut shown; this strut does not contact the leading shoe itself but has a lug engaging an opening in an adjuster plate pivoted on that shoe, having ratchet teeth on its lower edge. A spring loaded pawl also pivoted to the leading shoe retains the adjuster plate in position but can lift to allow it to rotate towards the centre of the brake.

The strut is spring biased towards the trailing shoe; the lug has sufficient clearance in the opening in the adjuster plate to permit the shoes to be applied by the fixed double acting wheel cylinder without disturbing the adjuster mechanism. When, however, the brake linings wear, hydraulic operation of the brake causes the lug on the strut to take up all the clearance and pull the adjuster plate with it, lifting the pawl a little; when sufficient wear has taken place, the pawl advances by one whole tooth and the adjuster plate is retained in a new position.

Some brakes of this general type have a projection on the pawl to enable it to be pressed down, releasing the adjuster plate and allowing the shoes to retract for easy drum removal; not every vehicle manufacturer, however, provides access into the brake for this purpose and in difficult cases it may be necessary to drill a hole through the face of the drum.

A design made by Volkswagen (Fig. 3.39) has a wedge (Fig. 3.40) which is assembled between the strut and its point of contact with the leading shoe; the strut is biased towards the leading shoe by a spring so that the wedge, the angle of which is carefully chosen, is trapped in position. The strut has sufficient clearance in its location at the trailing shoe to permit normal service brake operation without affecting the strut until lining wear takes place; a lever pivoted on the trailing shoe acts in conjunction with the strut for parking.

With increasing wear, service brake operation causes the strut to be

Fig. 3.39   VW wedge type automatic adjustment

Fig. 3.40   The lever, strut and wedge from the VW brake

pulled away from the leading shoe so that the wedge can be pulled downwards by a light spring; on releasing the brake, the normal running clearance is restored and (as with all the brakes described in this section) the wheel cylinder pistons take up a new position.

A number of other designs of service brake actuated handbrake mechanism make use of a variable length strut, the Girling example shown (Fig. 3.41) serving as a basis for describing others. The illustration shows the forward pull operating lever, which is pivoted on the upper end of the trailing shoe, and the strut by means of which the leading shoe is operated; the end of the strut contacts the pawl, which is pivoted on the leading shoe, and when the handbrake is applied the strut prevents any movement of the pawl.

The pawl spring, which is anchored in the leading shoe web, tends to turn the pawl in an anti-clockwise direction so that during service brake operation, when the strut is not under load, it is able to push the strut away from the leading shoe by an amount which depends on the lining to drum clearance. As the pawl turns it rotates the ratchet by one tooth space to lengthen the strut; at the end of the service brake application, the shoes are then supported nearer to the drum by the strut. Successive applications of the service brake are necessary to take up excessive clearance left after brake servicing. Some of these

Fig. 3.41   The Girling HASF4 type rear brake; with forward pull handbrake and automatic adjustment during service brake operation

brakes have an aperture in the backplate through which a tool can be inserted to push the operating lever away from a stop so that it can move further towards the trailing shoe platform, permitting the shoes to contract further than usual to facilitate drum removal.

Cross-pull handbrake mechanisms are also found in combination with automatic adjustment by service brake; the first of these to be considered looks very similar to that illustrated in Fig. 3.36 but the pawl, although still turned by a spring attached to the spindle which is joined to the operating lever, has a projection shaped to match the operating lever and lies beside it in the slot in the trailing shoe web against a hardened steel insert (Fig. 3.42). As the handbrake operating lever turns, the pawl turns with it under the influence of the coil spring until it contacts one of the teeth on the ratchet wheel; the coil spring is, however, in this case, not strong enough to rotate the ratchet wheel while the strut is under load. During footbrake operation, as the shoe tips separate, the trailing shoe lifts away from the handbrake operating lever but the pawl is able to rotate by an amount which depends on lining wear; the strut is not now under load so the pawl is able to rotate the ratchet wheel by one tooth space and effect the adjustment.

Fig. 3.42   Girling HASC1 type rear brake having cross pull handbrake and automatic adjustment by service brake operation

A modified version of the brake just described dispenses with the spindle but works on the same principle; the pawl in this case lying between the wheel cylinder and the strut. These last designs of brake have a different type of removable stop, fitted externally, to provide for extra clearance when the drum is to be removed; they are, like those described just before them, of incremental type which require several brake applications to take up excessive clearance.

The last example to be described is of what is known as the 'one shot' type, which allows for the taking up of a considerable amount of clearance during a single service brake application, again with a

Fig. 3.43   Girling HASC3 type rear brake having cross pull handbrake and one shot automatic adjustment by service brake operation

cross pull type handbrake mechanism. This design (Fig. 3.43) uses a different type of strut to link the handbrake operating lever at the trailing shoe to the leading shoe; the contact with the leading shoe is made through the medium of a quadrant lever (at the left of the illustration). The quadrant lever can both pivot and slide with respect to the strut; it has teeth which engage with a toothed wheel rigidly attached to the strut, the teeth being held in contact by the curved leaf spring.

The surface of the quadrant lever on which the teeth are cut is at a varying radius from its pivot centre (after the fashion of a snail cam) so that as the quadrant lever turns on its pivot, which is attached to the strut, the effective length of the strut varies. Handbrake operation does not cause adjustment to take place but during service brake operation, the strut being held in contact with the trailing shoe (on the right) by the coil spring, the leading shoe moves away from the strut and takes up the clearance between the projection on the quadrant lever and the opening in the shoe web through which it passes.

With increasing lining wear, the leading shoe will draw the quadrant lever away from the toothed wheel, overcoming the tension in the leaf spring, until the teeth disengage; the quadrant lever will then be turned a little so that, when the brake pedal is released, contact with the toothed wheel is made at a slightly greater radius, holding the shoes in a new position but at the original clearance from

Fig. 3.44   The handbrake lever stop on the Girling HASC3 brake, removal of which facilitates drum removal

the drum. This mechanism can take up a considerable amount of clearance in one application of the service brake but the quadrant lever is so designed that adjustment cannot proceed beyond the limits of lining thickness; increasing pedal and handbrake lever travel is then a warning that this limit has been reached. Yet another type of removable external stop is provided for the handbrake operating lever of this brake, this one being attached to the lever by means of a pin (Fig. 3.44).

This somewhat lengthy section is indicative of the variety and complexity of automatic adjustment mechanisms, when combined with the handbrake mechanism; although it might be supposed that all of the principal possibilities have been exhausted there is little doubt that designers will continue to exercise their ingenuity on this aspect of brake application.

4

Other car drum brakes

4.1 Introduction

Having dealt in some detail with leading and trailing shoe brakes, attention is now to be turned to the other ways in which two shoes can be operated to provide a means of stopping a vehicle; first, however, it is relevant to recall that the leading/trailing type, whilst relatively stable in output over a wide duty range, does not develop a particularly high output—both of these characteristics being due to the effect of the trailing shoe.

In the days when it was usual to find leading/trailing brakes fitted at both axles of cars and operated mechanically, some action was taken (as will be briefly noted in the next chapter) to achieve a reasonable braking ratio so that the brakes of the more heavily loaded front axle might contribute their proper share to the total braking force. It was, however, at some stage realised that if both shoes could be caused to act as leading shoes, the output of the resulting brake would be some 50% greater than that of the established type, which would be of great benefit in the design of a complete brake installation.

4.2 Two leading shoe brakes

It is quite practicable to make a mechanical two leading shoe brake; some motocycles have used them, with an extended linkage (Fig. 4.1) to operate two cams, and in Chapter 8 those types used on heavy trucks will be considered. However, in the case of cars in the UK, the introduction of the two-leading-shoe or Duplex brake was generally associated with hydraulic actuation; it is a simple matter to operate two shoes by means of individual wheel cylinders in such a way that, for forward movement, they act as leading shoes (Fig. 4.2).

The Girling two leading shoe brake illustrated has many features described in detail in the previous chapter; the shoes are of sliding type with inclined abutments, adjustment is by means of snail cams

60

Fig. 4.1   *The operating linkage of a motor cycle two leading shoe drum brake*

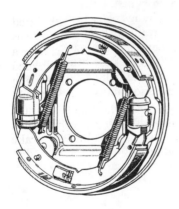

Fig. 4.2   *A Girling HLS/S two leading shoe brake (courtesy of Lucas Girling Ltd.)*

which contact cam posts set in the shoe webs, shoe steadies are fitted and coil springs are used to return the shoes to the off position. The hydraulic input is always to the lower cylinder, so that air in the system can be purged upwards through the bleed screw at the highest point of the upper cylinder; the two cylinders are linked by a pipe, usually shaped so that it presses against the backplate to reduce the likelihood of it vibrating.

When drum brakes were common at front and rear, it was usually—but not always—the case that they were of the same diameter; since, however, the front brakes were dissipating more energy than the rears, they were sometimes made wider. The increased width did not affect the torque developed by the brake but it gave a greater lining area; this reduced the rate of energy dissipation per unit area of the linings and helped to keep working temperatures within the acceptable range.

The use of two leading shoes avoided the setting up of an unbalanced load on the wheel bearings and drum and it led to even wear of the two shoes; some such brakes were, however, so designed that they were very inclined to grab if the lining friction level was unduly high or if, for any reason, the initial contact between the drum and the linings was at the ends only of the latter. Grab is characteristic of an excessively high level of shoe or brake factor, as referred to briefly in the previous chapter, such that brake application is abrupt and uncontrollable; in extreme cases, drum brakes lock on and cannot be released until, after the vehicle has come to rest, some reverse movement takes place.

The relatively high output of a two-leading-shoe brake is its desirable feature; there is, however, a much greater variability of brake factor with frictional variation (for instance, either with changes in working temperature or with a change of friction material) and when used in reverse both shoes act as trailing shoes, with a large fall in brake output. Used at the front of cars in combination with a rear leading/trailing shoe brake, the two leading shoe brake at once contributed to the achievement of better brake balance; it was well suited to the saloon cars of the day, the performance of which was much more sedate than has since become acceptable.

Two leading shoe drum brakes are still made by all the proprietary drum brake manufacturers; by contrast with the great many noteworthy variations of the leading/trailing shoe brake, the only differences between two leading shoe brakes for cars relate to minor features.

4.3 Duo-servo brakes

A rather more dramatic way of increasing the output of a two-shoe brake is to couple the shoes to form the type formerly extremely common on American cars but only occasionally considered in Europe; this is the duo-servo or 'self wrapping' brake, also often known as Bendix brakes from their American parentage. Mechanically operated versions and truck versions will be referred to in later chapters; those found on recent European cars—with one minor exception—have all been hydraulic.

The geometry of a leading shoe is such that, not only is the drum drag greater than the shoe tip force, the same is true of the force with which the shoe presses on its abutment; if there is no abutment to such a leading shoe but, instead, an articulated link coupling this first shoe to a second shoe, then what would have been the abutment or reaction force from the first, becomes the input to the second. The second shoe also necessarily acts as a leading shoe and so its reaction force is greater still; Fig. 4.3 shows the essential features of such a brake in simple form, including the fixed anchor pin which forms the abutment for the second shoe when the brake operates, as well as locating both shoes when the brake is off.

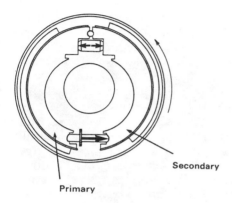

Secondary

Primary

Fig. 4.3 The principal features of a duo-servo brake

The two shoes are usually given the names 'primary' and 'secondary' and there are various ways in which they can be designed; the brake factor curve (independent shoe factor curves are not featured for a duo-servo brake) is very steep, giving a typical value of 6 for a lining coefficient of friction of 0.4, about 1.75 times as much as for a typical two leading shoe brake.

If the primary and secondary shoes were designed with similar features, the secondary shoe would do considerably more work than the primary shoe, would get correspondingly hotter and wear its lining faster; it is therefore usual for the linings to differ in dimensions and, often, in material. The secondary lining is often longer than the primary one and may be of a lower friction material, to even out the work done by the two shoes, or of a higher friction material to enhance the 'self-servo' effect.

The very high output of this type of brake is only achieved at the price of much greater sensitivity to lining friction changes than the two leading shoe brake, which is why it has seldom found favour on European cars. The minor exception, referred to earlier, is a mechanically operated brake of this type, used as a parking brake on cars with disc brakes front and rear; the rear discs are designed with a cylindrical portion between the mounting face and the braking path which serves as a brake drum. When used in this way, the high output of the brake is of great benefit while the sensitivity is of little consequence as (although the braking surface will be hot, from the use of the service brakes) the linings will not normally be heated to the point at which fade occurs.

The illustration of a typical duo-servo rear brake (Fig. 4.4) shows the principal features clearly. The shoes are shaped to locate closely

Fig. 4.4   A typical rear duo-servo brake (courtesy of Automotive Products PLC)

around the anchor pin, to which the return springs are attached; between their opposite ends is fitted the adjuster assembly, consisting of a sleeve in which is housed a threaded spindle, on which is an adjuster wheel. A coil spring holds the shoe tips into contact with the adjuster and also rests on the adjuster wheel to prevent it from being rotated by vibration; shoe steadies hold the shoes against the brake backplate.

A fixed, double acting wheel cylinder is located just below the anchor pin so that when the brake is operated equal forces are applied to both shoes; because of this, the brake operates in a similar manner whichever way the drum rotates. It is for this reason that this design of brake is called a duo-servo brake; a few cases have been made with a single acting wheel cylinder, so that the high brake factor was only obtained for forward drum rotation, this type being known as a uni-servo brake.

The duo-servo brake only gives identical output for both directions of drum output if it is designed to do so; usually the linings are dimensioned and positioned and their respective friction values are such that there is a considerable difference in the forward and reverse brake factors.

The lever and strut type handbrake mechanism seen is the only feature which differentiates the rear brake shown from a front brake; the brake operates in a similar manner with either the mechanical or hydraulic means of actuation if the drum is moving but the shoes operate more in the manner of leading and trailing shoes if the vehicle is stationary on a level road. Because the secondary shoe is held firmly in contact with the anchor pin, when the brake is operated with the vehicle moving, the effort applied to it by either the adjacent piston or the handbrake mechanism serves merely to reduce the amount of force transmitted to the pin.

Duo-servo brakes with automatic adjustment are rare on cars and have been known to cause problems in service; one such mechanism was operated when the vehicle was braked in reverse and when the amount by which the secondary shoe (acting in reverse as a primary shoe) moved away from the anchor pin exceeded a pre-determined limit due to lining wear. A lever coupled to the anchor pin moved a pawl across a ratchet wheel incorporated in the adjuster assembly, turning it by one tooth pitch as adjustment took place.

As with two leading shoe brakes, the very many individual duo-servo brakes differ only in matters of detail and no further description is needed in this chapter.

4.4 The search for stability

The combination of two leading shoe front and leading/trailing rear drum brakes became extremely common on new models in the UK during the early post war development period; however, with a rapidly growing interest in high performance, there was a call for better braking than this combination could give. Better, that is, not in terms of brake balance or torque output, but as regards the ability to withstand high working temperatures without suffering an appreciable fall in output. The rising generation of high quality and high performance cars had better road holding and acceleration than had been common ten years previously, so a corresponding standard of brake performance was needed.

Girling approached the problem by making use of the characteristic, noted in the previous chapter, of the trailing shoe—low but stable output; the company made a brake with two such shoes, like a

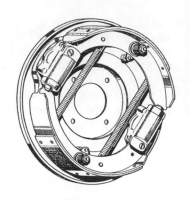

Fig. 4.5   A Girling HTS2 two trailing shoe brake with friction shake back stops (courtesy of Lucas Girling Ltd.)

two-leading-shoe brake used in reverse, which fulfilled a useful function for a number of years (Fig. 4.5). However, although a simple description may liken this brake to the reverse of a two-leading-shoe brake, there were important differences.

Because the basic concept of the brake was different, the lining dimensions and positions (there were variations) differed from those used with leading-shoe brakes; the shoes themselves were stronger, to match the heavy forces to which they were subjected, and were of pivoted type. To obtain the required drum drag from trailing shoes, much larger wheel cylinders were needed, which raised a problem in having to provide for a sufficient displacement of brake fluid at an appropriate pressure (see Chapter 5).

This problem was minimised by providing automatic adjustment, of the shoe web mounted friction type, as described in Chapter 3; this ensured that the lining/drum clearance was held to a constant, limited amount, so that only a small piston movement was necessary. A vacuum servo unit, as described in the next chapter, was used in all the brake installations concerned. In reverse, of course, these brakes reverted to leading shoe characteristics.

A two trailing shoe brake was also used by Rolls-Royce on various of their post-war models, being similar in general appearance to the Girling brake; at that time Rolls-Royce used a gearbox driven mechanical servo, which augmented the input to the brake master cylinder. On some Bentley models, the same manufacturer used a design, probably unique, which had four shoes per front brake; these were pivoted in pairs on shoe carriers arranged like shoes of a trailing-shoe brake (Fig. 4.6). Because the shoes were pivoted, they gave a neutral characteristic, imparting the desired stability to the output, and their tendency to tilt with drum rotation was counteracted by the overlapping of the adjacent ends.

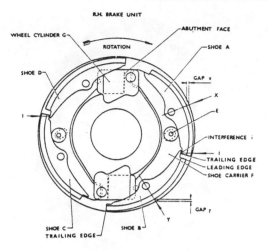

Fig. 4.6   The arrangement of a Rolls-Royce four shoe brake (courtesy of Rolls-Royce Motors Ltd.)

Another Rolls-Royce special type was a modified leading and trailing-shoe rear brake; this used a linkage, adjacent to the double acting wheel cylinder, which connected the two shoes near their tips in such a way that the net force applied to the trailing shoe was increased at the expense of that applied to the leading shoe, so that the duty (and wear) was more evenly shared between the two and the output stabilised (see also the description of the Lockheed Brakemaster brake, below). The linking of the shoes permitted the use of a single shoe web friction adjuster on the trailing shoe (in most—but not all—cases) to adjust both shoes automatically.

The two trailing shoe type of brake was also made in France by DBA, whose design (Fig. 4.7) differed from others in two ways, apart from the use of pressed steel shoe steadies which clip into the backplate. Both ends of each shoe have an elongated hole which locates over a fixed anchor pin so that, whichever way the drum rotates, the shoes move with it when the brake is applied until restrained at the trailing end; the reaction force on the linings then sets up a moment about the effective anchor pin contrary to that applying the shoes which, therefore, act as trailing shoes. To match the two trailing shoe characteristic for both directions of drum rotation, the brake has two double acting wheel cylinders.

The final example to be described in this section is the design produced by Lockheed, which was given the name Brakemaster (Fig. 4.8); this is a leading and trailing shoe type brake, but is operated by a

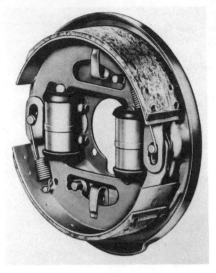

Fig. 4.7   The DBA two trailing shoe Thermostable brake (courtesy of DBA SA)

Fig. 4.8   The Lockheed Brakemaster leading/trailing shoe brake (courtesy of Automotive Products PLC)

fixed double acting wheel cylinder having a stepped bore. The larger piston operates the trailing shoe and the small one the leading shoe so, the relative piston areas being chosen so that the output of the two shoes is approximately equal, the same is true of lining wear. With the leading shoe contributing only half of the initial total output of the brake, its sensitivity has a lesser effect if friction varies for any reason;

the trailing shoe, in its more significant role, is able to exert an enhanced stabilising influence on the output.

The fluid displacement requirement of the Brakemaster brake is increased by the large area of the piston which operates the trailing shoe; there is, however, an automatic adjuster which maintains a limited clearance between the linings and the drum, so that piston movement is minimised. This adjuster takes the form of a strut between the two shoes, this having an elongated hole at one end and a plain hole at the other.

A stud attached to the leading shoe passes through the elongated hole in the strut and a nut then applies pressure to friction pads which grip the stud; the plain hole has clearance around a pin set in the trailing shoe, a spring clip being applied to keep the strut in place, the clearance being sufficient to permit the normal movement of the shoes during brake application. As lining wear takes place, the forces applied to the shoes cause the strut to be moved through the friction pad; as a guard against failure of the friction device, a pawl in the friction pads housing engages ratchet teeth on the edge of the strut.

As will be described in Chapter 6, it was not long before the advent of disc brakes for production cars put an end to attempts to use drum brakes to dissipate energy at ever increasing levels of intensity.

4.5 Brake drums

Car brake drums differ little in design, most being entirely of cast iron although a small proportion use a steel pressing for the mounting face with an iron rim cast on; in a very few cases a cast aluminium alloy drum having a ferrous braking path insert has been used in the endeavour to promote better heat dissipation. Being of the form of a cylinder open at one end, a brake drum tends to distort both to a bell-mouthed form under the internal pressure of the brake shoes and to an oval form; its open end is therefore usually strengthened by a substantial rib.

It is desirable to exclude from the inside of the brake any water thrown up from the road by the wheels; the edge of the drum and of the backplate are therefore mutually designed so that no direct path of entry is offered. On the other hand, the fit between these components must not be so close that water which has entered when passing through a flood or a ford cannot drain out quickly.

The greater part of the heat generated inside a brake drum has to be dissipated from the outer surface of the cylindrical portion; it is therefore the responsibility of the vehicle designer to ensure that there is an adequate air space between the drum and the wheel and that air is caused to flow through this space when the vehicle is in motion. If the cooling is inadequate the temperature of the wheel and tyre may reach unacceptable levels and the heat flow through the face of the drum into the hub bearings will be likely to increase, possibly causing problems.

It has been customary to retain the drum in place with two countersunk screws, independently of the ultimate retention by the wheel and wheel nuts; sometimes, recently, a single screw only has been used. In some cases the drum and hub have been combined in a single casting so that, unless tapered roller bearings are used, a special drawer is needed to remove the drum. In a few cases, the face of the drum is pierced by a hole suitably placed to give access either to the brake adjusters or, when a certain type of automatic adjustment is incorporated, to the means of releasing it to facilitate drum removal.

Brake drums usually locate over a closely dimensioned spigot machined on the hub to ensure concentricity; if left in position for an extended period, corrosion at this point can make drum removal difficult and slight easing of the fit by careful use of abrasives may be necessary. If a good grade of iron is used for the manufacture of brake drums, they should outlast many sets of linings; there is, however, the likelihood in the present age that replacement will be necessitated after relatively few years, because of exterior corrosion due to winter salting of roads, rather than because of interior wear.

As has already been noted, the metal mating member—in this case the drum—is expected to withstand the interior forces acting upon it, to transmit much of the heat generated at the braking path to its outer surface and to resist abrasion by the friction material. That the greater proportion of all brake drums achieve these aims satisfactorily is a measure of their quality, but there are various possible faults that can develop if this quality is lacking or for other reasons; these matters will be considered and illustrated in Chapter 12.

With the wide adoption of front disc brakes for cars, drum brakes are now seldom found at all four wheels but continue to be the normal choice at the rear for low and medium price cars; their design changes little in principle but it is to be expected that development and refinement in matters of detail will continue for the foreseeable future.

5

Basic hydraulic systems

5.1 Introduction

Consideration having been given to drum brakes for cars and light vehicles, attention is now turned to the means of operating these—the brake actuation or braking system. As the chapter heading indicates, hydraulic systems form the main subject, but before beginning to examine these it is useful to consider briefly what came before.

Mechanical actuation which preceded hydraulic systems used either rods or cables to transfer the effort applied at the brake pedal to the brakes themselves, the effort applied to the rear brakes sometimes being reduced by the interposition of a relay lever so as to yield a sufficiently accurate braking ratio; in many cases these systems worked reasonably effectively while they were new, but when they had been in use for some time their shortcomings became apparent. The illustration (Fig. 5.1) shows a portion of a fully compensated rod operated system for a car; in this portion alone there are no less than six pivots, each needing periodic lubrication and each subject to friction and wear.

Those early systems which lacked compensation needed to be precisely adjusted or they would apply the brakes unevenly; cable operated systems in some cases applied the front brakes unevenly if they were used whilst the car was being steered. Even though salt was not used on roads in winter when these systems were made, corrosion of the pivots with resulting increased wear was inevitable; much of the force applied to the brake pedal was therefore dissipated and a considerable proportion of the available brake pedal travel was used to take up the excessive clearances which developed.

5.2 Column of fluid

When hydraulic systems were introduced, they replaced the rods and cables previously used in tension with a column of fluid in compression, contained in tubing; equalisation of the pressures applied to

71

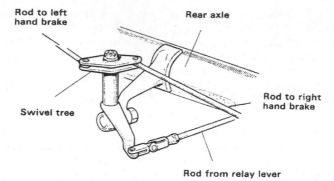

Fig. 5.1   Rod operation of brakes (courtesy of Lucas Girling Ltd.)

the brakes was then automatic and, with appropriate use of flexible hoses, it was easy to allow for wheel deflections or steering action when on the road.

Brake fluid—considered in more detail later in this chapter—when used with pipes of appropriate diameter, can transfer force with virtually no frictional losses; at the working pressures used, the compression of the fluid is very small (and the expansion of the pipelines is similarly negligible) so there is no wastage of pedal travel. The result is that a force applied at one point in a hydraulic system is transmitted to any other part of the system virtually instantaneously, without any appreciable lessening of the force itself or any reduction in the volume of fluid displaced.

The pipes used to form a hydraulic brake system have sometimes been of copper but, more usually, they are formed from copper coated mild steel strip, brazed to give the strength required and then coated with a thin layer of zinc or other metal to increase the resistance to corrosion. Such piping has proved to be very vulnerable to the effects of the salt which is now used in large quantities in the UK and elsewhere during the average winter so that an alternative—an alloy called Kunifer 10, consisting mainly of copper and nickel—has become of increasing interest to both car designers and those concerned with maintenance and repair, while plastics coated piping has been developed and is also coming into use.

In addition to the need for the hydraulic piping to be highly resistant to corrosion, so that the likelihood of a sudden disastrous loss of pressure during a brake application is minimised, the material used must be suitable for forming easily to the required shapes at its ends, where it is connected to the system components with pipe nuts, and must be easily bent to the curves which the layout requires. In view of the importance of the piping to the reliable functioning of a hydraulic brake system, its unavoidable exposure to a corrosive environment, the consequences of a failure in service and the practical difficulties of replacement, it is a little surprising that steel tubing is still so commonly used.

The brake pipes are used to link hydraulic cylinders which operate the brakes to another—called the master cylinder—which is operated by the driver; the master cylinder contains a piston fitted with a pressure seal, usually of synthetic rubber, which can drive fluid out at a pressure which may reach a normal maximum of about 100 bars (1500 lbf/in^2). Girling have in the past produced a master cylinder, the piston of which was directly coupled to the brake pedal pad (which therefore moved in a straight line instead of the more usual arc) but the general arrangement is for the pedal to be operated by a pivoted lever such that the effort exerted by the driver is multiplied by a factor of the order of 4–4.5:1.

Figure 5.2 shows diagrammatically how the pedal effort f is multiplied by the pedal ratio r so that a larger force F, is applied to the

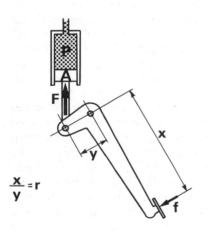

$$\frac{x}{y} = r$$

Fig. 5.2   The pressure generated in a hydraulic system

master cylinder piston. Necessarily, the hydraulic force on the piston must equal the external force so, if its area is A and the fluid pressure P,

$$F = PA \qquad (5.1)$$

Hence, for a given force F and known piston area A, the resulting fluid pressure is given by

$$P = F/A \qquad (5.2)$$

It can therefore be seen that to increase the fluid pressure without changing the input force, it is necessary to reduce the piston area A; it will, however, be realised that a further consequence of this action will be a reduction in the volume of brake fluid displaced for a given amount of piston movement.

In the hydraulic cylinders which apply the brakes, the fluid acts against pistons fitted with pressure seals which transmit force to the working parts of the brake; in accordance with Equation 5.1, the force developed by these pistons is the product of the fluid pressure and their area. The force exerted by brake cylinders can, therefore, be increased by increasing their area but, necessarily, with the penalty of an increase in the volume of brake fluid involved in a particular value of piston movement.

When considering the specification of the dimensions of the braking system for a particular vehicle, the designer is concerned with the pedal effort and travel in relation to the braking efficiency achieved, and with the braking ratio; this latter he will aim to have correct for a chosen value of braking efficiency (ignoring the effect of certain system refinements to be considered in a later chapter). The variables at his disposal are the pedal ratio, the diameter of the master cylinder, the diameters of the cylinders which apply the front and rear brakes and, of course, the output characteristics of the brakes themselves.

Varying the pedal ratio will directly affect the pedal effort for a given value of braking efficiency, but will also affect pedal travel; varying the master cylinder diameter will also affect pedal effort but will, in addition, affect fluid displacement (and hence, again, pedal travel). A similar effect to that achieved by a change of master cylinder diameter can also be obtained by an appropriate change to the size of both front and rear brake cylinders, but with the same consequences. Finally, braking ratio can be varied by making a change in the relationship between the sizes of front and rear cylinders, but again with an effect on fluid displacement and pedal travel, or by making an appropriate change to the brakes.

There is often, therefore, an element of compromise in the drawing up of a system specification because of the consequences of any change; additionally, the range of sizes of the various cylinders which are available to the designer is not always large enough to cater for his needs. In practice, although it is relatively easy to change the choice of brake linings at front or rear or both, a change of brake design is not always practicable for reasons of cost.

5.3 Brake fluid

The fluids used in brake systems have evolved considerably over a period of more than fifty years and, at best, are highly complex substances. The principal requirements which a fluid has to satisfy are that it should be stable under the pressure normally used and only boil at a temperature which is high enough to be acceptable; at the other end of the temperature scale, its viscosity must not increase excessively at low ambient temperatures and its freezing point must be such as to ensure functioning under the worst conditions likely to be experienced. The fluid must have lubricating properties, to assist the smooth working of moving parts in the system, and it must not attack any of the materials with which it is likely to come into contact; finally, it must inhibit corrosion.

Although reference has been made only to brake systems, the same fluid is used in hydraulic systems for clutch control; the requirements for the two systems are very similar but while clutch systems are not normally subject to high temperatures and pressures are only moderate, lubrication is of special importance because of the greater distance of travel of the pistons concerned and the frequency of clutch operation.

For many years, brake fluids commonly used have been principally constituted of a mixture of an oil and a solvent, the oil contributing lubricity and the solvent ensuring suitably low viscosity; castor oil (a vegetable product) and petroleum derived mineral oils were the alternatives for the greater part of the period, but the former has now been replaced by synthetic products. The choice now is therefore between petrolum based and non-petroleum based fluids, both of which are in production; it is important that for any brake system only the correct class of fluid is used.

The greatest drawback of fluids of the above types is that the solvents which form such an important part of them are hygroscopic——they absorb moisture from the atmosphere; so strong is this affinity for moisture that it is accepted that not only is it absorbed at the exposed surface in the reservoir, but that it is also absorbed through the micro-porosity of flexible hoses and past the lips of pressure seals. The principal effect of this moisture is on the boiling point of the fluid, the value of this falling appreciably as the moisture content rises to some 2–3% of the total volume.

Before illustrating this, it is useful to differentiate between boiling point and vapour lock point. As has been mentioned, brake fluid is a mixture of substances, each of which has a different boiling point to the others; the vapour lock point is the temperature at which the constituent having the lowest boiling point boils while the boiling

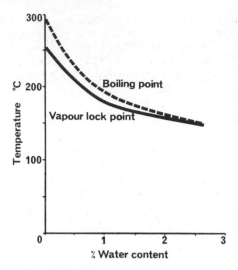

Fig. 5.3   The effect of moisture content on brake fluid

point is, effectively, the temperature at which the whole mixture is boiling. The vapour lock point is the maximum safe operating temperature at which the fluid can be used; at higher temperatures bubbles of vapour form which prevent the proper transmission of force by the fluid.

Figure 5.3 illustrates, for a typical general purpose brake fluid, the difference between the two temperatures with new fluid, how they fall with increasing moisture content and how, as the moisture content increases, the difference between them reduces to zero. Attempts to develop fluids with enhanced high temperature properties over the expected range of moisture content values have met with only limited success; raising the dry boiling point generally also raises the freezing point but has little effect on the wet boiling point, which is the critical one.

Standards for brake fluids have mostly come from the USA; formerly the SAE (Society of Automotive Engineers) 70R3 specifications was widely adopted and this was succeeded by their J1703. It must be emphasised that these documents, which detail the properties to be examined, the test procedures to be followed and the minimum standards to be achieved, are only laying down minimum requirements which the more reputable manufacturers regard as the starting point from which they have progressed. As with the pipelines in which the brake fluid is contained, the fluid is of such importance in both operating the brakes and keeping the system components in good order, that the extra cost of using the best is surely money well spent.

Supplementing the SAE standard, the American DOT (Department of Transportation) has issued a series of standards for brake fluid, of which DOT3 corresponds to J1073; European manufacturers have since encouraged the ISO (International Standards Organisation) to issue a standard based more on European practice, which is now published as ISO 4925.

As part of the search for higher wet boiling points, a new American specification designated DOT4 has been drawn up; the difference between the requirements of this and DOT3 is shown in Fig. 5.4. Under the test conditions specified, the wet boiling points for fluids to DOT3 and 4 are, respectively, 140°C and 155°C. Although satisfying DOT4 has been difficult and there is a cost penalty, several manufacturers produce such fluids but they are more widely accepted on the European mainland than in the UK.

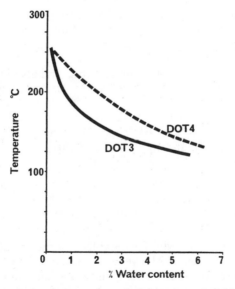

Fig. 5.4   A comparison between vapour lock temperatures of different brake fluids

A further specification, DOT5, has been prepared and requires—amongst other things—a wet boiling point of 180°C, the most commonly pursued line of development being the use of silicones as a base. Silicones are not hygroscopic, they have good viscosity characteristics at low temperatures and they do not harm paintwork like conventional fluids do; their lubricity is, however, the subject of some doubts, as is their compatibility with rubber, while their compressibility is greater than that of the more usual fluids. The viscosity of silicone based fluids is higher than that of conventional fluids at summer ambient temperatures and leads to concern that difficulties could occur when filling and bleeding systems, either on assembly or in service.

It is principally because of the fall in boiling and vapour lock point temperatures with increasing moisture content that fluid, brake and vehicle manufacturers advise replacement at regular intervals; the recommendations vary between twelve and eighteen months as the interval between replacements in normal service and are, necessarily, on the conservative side. It is a tribute to the quality of both fluids and system components that in so many cases they continue to function satisfactorily for years without attention; however, lubricity and corrosion inhibition also decline with age so it is wise to take notice of the advice which is given.

The conditions which are most likely to promote brake fluid vapourisation other than driving at and braking from high speeds are the towing of trailers (with over-run operated trailer brake actuation, the duty on the towing vehicle brakes is increased somewhat), the descent of long steep hills with hairpin bends and also high altitude; often, it will be realised, the three occur in combination, as when a caravan is towed on a holiday in the mountainous regions of the continent. The maintenance of high average speeds on twisting and undulating roads, as well as participation in many kinds of motor sport, will also cause high temperatures in parts of the brake system such as could cause fluid vapourisation.

5.4 Master cylinders

There are types of master cylinder suitable for installing at a variety of angles, to suit the particular vehicles concerned, so this has a considerable effect on their design; there are also tandem master cylinders which are used with divided or duplicated systems (described in Chapter 11), so these also differ in various ways. All of these cylinders have to fulfill the same function, however, whether for one or two circuits, so they have similar features which are used in a variety of combinations.

Mention has already been made of the fact that the master cylinder piston drives brake fluid under pressure through the hydraulic pipelines to operate the brakes; this piston is returned to the off position by a coil spring in compression and it is necessary to ensure that, no matter how quickly it returns, the master cylinder remains full of brake fluid. The problem arises because after a brake application, the brake fluid previously expelled from the master cylinder returns to it relatively slowly, owing to the limited strength of the shoe return springs and the small diameter of the brake piping.

If, during brake release, the pressure inside the brake master cylinder were to fall much below atmospheric, because of the rapid return of the piston, air might be drawn in and have much the same effect on the braking system as a bubble of vapour (but with permanent effect). As soon, therefore, as the brake pedal is released, provision must be made for brake fluid from a reservoir to be able to flow into the master cylinder and keep it full; this fluid must then be able to return to the reservoir—except for what is needed to make up for losses or as adjustment occurs—during the later stages of brake retraction. Brake fluid reservoirs, which at one time were often separate components, are now usually an integral part of master cylinder assemblies for cars.

Recuperation of the system, as it is called, may be achieved by means of a piston with twin seals as in the Lockheed example (Fig. 5.5), in conjunction with twin ports between the cylinder and the reservoir; the annular space between the seals is always full of fluid which enters through the larger of the two ports. When the cylinder is operated, the lip of the primary seal passes the smaller port and pressure is generated in the fluid trapped.

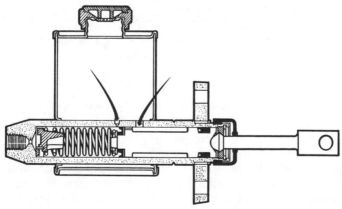

Fig. 5.5 A master cylinder which uses seal recuperation (courtesy of Automotive Products PLC)

During brake release, as the piston returns rapidly, the fluid between the primary and secondary seals (which is subject to atmospheric pressure) is able to pass through drillings in the piston face and around the primary seal in order to keep the cylinder full; this supply is replenished from the reservoir by way of the large port. This design is commonly referred to as AS (American Standard), the US company which originated it.

As brake retraction continues, any excess fluid is returned to the reservoir through the small port. Because of the regular movement of fluid out of and back into the reservoir in this way, usually with an overall gradual drop in level as fluid is permanently displaced because of brake adjustment, the reservoir cover is provided with a small air vent, blockage of which would impair normal operation; reservoirs for vehicles such as motot cycles, which are subject to considerable tilting in service, may have a flexible diaphragm fitted under the cover so that changes of level may occur but loss of fluid through the air vent is prevented.

Another method of recuperation which has been common is the centre valve (CV) as used by Girling (Fig. 5.6); as the piston returns to its off position, it withdraws the centre valve from its seat, opening direct communication with the reservoir. If the master cylinder piston

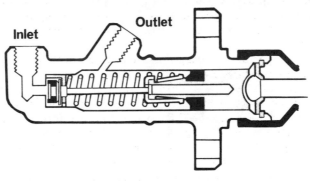

Fig. 5.6   Centre valve recuperation of a master cylinder (courtesy of Lucas Girling Ltd.)

returns faster than the corresponding fluid flow from the brakes, atmospheric pressure acting in the reservoir lifts the centre valve from its seat prior to its being lifted by the returning plunger. The drilling in the plunger, which accommodates the valve stem during brake application, is difficult to purge of air when the system is being bled; rapid agitation of the brake pedal is necessary to entrain the air so that it can be dispelled.

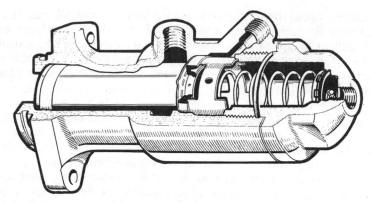

Fig. 5.7   A master cylinder with a fixed pressure seal (courtesy of Lucas Girling Ltd.)

The Girling CB or compression barrel type (Fig. 5.7) has a stationary pressure seal, through which passes a tubular plunger which is closed at the outer end and in which is housed the return spring; a second seal, situated in a groove at the outer end of the barrel, retains the low pressure fluid from the separate reservoir. Bypass holes, drilled around the plunger just within the lip of the main seal, allow fluid to pass freely between the reservoir and cylinder when the pedal is released; movement of the plunger carries these bypass holes under the seal so that further plunger movement builds up pressure.

System recuperation during brake release is achieved by lifting of the main seal lip by the fluid from the reservoir; this system, however, does not lend itself to tandem layouts so its use is now declining. This cylinder has been made in quite large sizes, some of which have been equipped with their own bleed screw to facilitate purging them of air.

The fourth way of allowing for the recuperation of the fluid in a master cylinder is by the use of a tipping valve (TV) shown in Fig. 5.8, a part drawing of a Girling unit; as seen, the piston is in the off position and is displacing a spring loaded valve by tipping the valve stem to one side, so that the port between the fluid reservoir and the

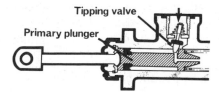

Fig. 5.8   A tipping valve used in a master cylinder (courtesy of Lucas Girling Ltd.)

cylinder is open. The tipping valve stem is behind the piston flange, so that when the brake pedal is operated and the piston moves forward, the light spring above the valve draws it upwards against its seat; during brake release, if recuperation needs to take place, atmospheric pressure acting on the fluid in the reservoir causes it to unseat the valve and flow through.

A master cylinder for a vehicle having a single hydraulic system could be of either AS, CV or CB type and might be made either of cast iron or light alloy, its bore being machined to an extremely high standard of surface finish; its piston would be retained in the cylinder by a spring ring located in a groove machined just within the open end or, sometimes, both the piston and the push rod are retained in this way. The push rod connects the piston to the brake pedal but when the master cylinder is installed there should always be a little clearance between the end of the rod and the piston; this ensures that the piston can return completely to the off position when the brake pedal is released. There is always, therefore, a little free movement of the brake pedal before the master cylinder piston begins to move (equivalent to the amount of clearance multiplied by the pedal ratio) and a further small amount of unopposed movement before the fluid in the cylinder is isolated from the reservoir and pressure begins to rise.

Figure 5.9 shows a typical Lockheed master cylinder of a type which was popular before divided brake systems became common; it

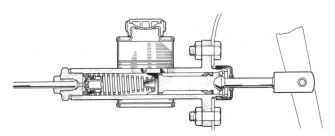

Fig. 5.9   A Lockheed master cylinder (courtesy of Automotive Products PLC)

is for horizontal installation and the push rod and part of the brake pedal can be seen, as well as the bulkhead to which the cylinder body is bolted. This unit is of AS type and all its principal features can be seen together with one not so far mentioned, a trap line pressure valve or check valve at the fluid outlet.

A check valve is sometimes included because it makes bleeding of the system easier; it discourages the return of the fluid pumped out during the down stroke of the pedal when the pedal is subsequently

BASIC HYDRAULIC SYSTEMS 83

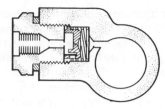

Fig. 5.10   A trap line pressure valve
(*courtesy of Automotive Products
PLC*)

released. An enlarged view of such a valve (Fig. 5.10), from a unit of
different configuration to the one illustrated above, shows that the
valve consists of a cup held against the face of the outlet by a light coil
spring; a flap in the side of the cup allows fluid to be expelled into the
brake pipeline and its return from the brakes is effected by lifting the
valve off its seat—there being insufficient pressure differential during
bleeding for this to happen. A very small diameter port in the centre of
the valve ensures eventual equalisation of pressures.

Check valves are not usually incorporated in clutch master
cylinders because they would be likely to interfere with the control of
the clutch during engagement; in installations which incorporate disc
brakes, it is important that there is no likelihood of there being a
residual pressure which could cause brake drag.

When hydraulic braking systems became established, it was usual
for many years for them to incorporate a stop light switch; this was
commonly inserted in the fourth arm of a fitting which divided the
supply from the master cylinder between the front and rear brakes. In
recent years, however, with the introduction of divided hydraulic
systems, the stop-light switch has reverted to a mechanical type,
operated by the brake pedal; this helps to limit the number of
connections—each of which is a potential leakage point—in the
hydraulic system.

5.5 Servo assistance

Consideration has already been given to the way in which the diameters
of the various cylinders in a hydraulic system and the pedal ratio are
chosen; this is so as to ensure that sufficient force is applied to the
brakes without exceeding a reasonable limit of pedal effort and travel.
When larger vehicles are considered there comes a point—although it
cannot be exactly defined—beyond which physical limitations make
it impossible to achieve the required braking characteristics without
assisting the driver in some way.

It has been shown that the fluid displacement of the master cylinder
has to be adequate for the brakes fitted to the vehicle; it has also been

shown that as the cylinder diameter increases, either the input force must be increased in proportion to maintain the same output pressure or—if the input force remains constant—the output pressure will fall. Assistance has therefore been made available for the drivers of the larger vehicles and two principal ways of providing it have been used during the period reviewed; in the earlier years it was usual to boost the hydraulic pressure delivered from the master cylinder while, more recently, it has become the practice that the input force to the master cylinder should be boosted.

In both of the cases mentioned above, the usual source of energy utilised (one exception will be considered later) was the partial vacuum which exists in the carburettor venturi of a petrol engine; because compression ignition (diesel) engines—which are increasingly common on cars as well as on light commercial vehicles—do not have a venturi in their air intake system, they have to be equipped with an engine driven vacuum pump (sometimes known as an exhauster) of diaphragm, piston or rotary vane type when this form of assistance is to be used. The partial vacuum only exists when the engine of the vehicle is running—although there is usually a limited reserve of assistance provided in the system—so a vehicle which is coasting or being towed with the engine idle would be very much more difficult to stop than would normally be the case.

The important thing about giving assistance is that at all times the response to pedal effort should be predictable so that, as is usually the case, the driver of a vehicle does not need to know whether the system is boosted or not; a servo is a device which augments an effort applied to it and so the name 'vacuum servo' is applied to the devices with which this section is concerned. With such a device, another important consideration is that should it cease to function, the driver is still able to apply the brakes, even though a great deal more effort may be required.

In describing what a vacuum servo does, before coming to how it does it, two diagrams are helpful. The first (Fig. 5.11) is intended to illustrate in a simple way the relationship between pedal effort and pipeline pressure; although no units are given against the horizontal and vertical scales, line A shows that for every value of pedal effort on the horizontal scale, there is a corresponding value of pipeline pressure determined by the pedal ratio and the master cylinder diameter. Line B is much steeper than A and shows that the need for servo assistance exists when a higher pipeline pressure is required for the same value of pedal effort as indicated by line A. The task of the designer of a vacuum servo is, therefore, to provide a means by which the differences indicated by lines A and B can be achieved.

Figure 5.12 is similar to the previous one as regards the horizontal

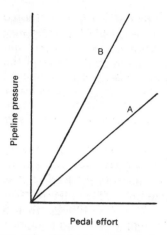

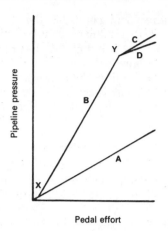

Fig. 5.11   The basic requirement for a brake servo; to boost hydraulic pressures from level A to level B

Fig. 5.12   Alternative characteristics for vacuum servo units

and vertical scales and the position of line A, but line B is now different; Fig. 5.11 showed line B as starting from the origin of the scales but, in practice, this cannot be so. Whatever the design of the servo may be, it takes a certain minimum applied force (whether in the form of an external physical force or an internal fluid pressure acting on a moveable element) to initiate its operation; this force must correspond to a particular value of pedal effort so, up to that value, no servo assistance has yet been developed. A point X may therefore be indicated on line A as the point from which line B is to start; this point is commonly named the crack point and, occurring as it does at a very low pedal effort, in practice it is impossible to detect when it has been reached.

At pedal efforts greater than that corresponding to the crack point, the servo gives assistance and boosts the pipeline pressure so that the required characteristic, indicated by line B in diagram 5.11, will be matched very closely. There is, however, a limit to the assistance which is available from the servo because there is a limit both to its size and to the pressure difference (commonly of the order of 0.67 bar) (10 lbf/in²) which it is harnessing; this upper limit is represented by point Y on line B and at pedal efforts higher than that which corresponds to this point, the driver receives no additional assistance to that which is already being given.

Beyond point Y the line continues, but at a slope which depends on the nature of the servo fitted; with hydraulic units, to be described shortly, the slope (line D) is somewhat less than that of line A but with direct acting units it is the same (line C) as that of line A. The driver is able to develop pipeline pressures higher than that which corresponds to point Y, but he then has to exert proportionally more effort. Point Y is popularly known as the knee point, from the shape of the line on which it lies. The braking system into which a servo is incorporated will be so designed that very rarely will a driver need pipeline pressures beyond the knee point.

5.6 Hydraulic units

For many years the servo units generally in use were inserted into the hydraulic system between the master cylinder and the brakes; they incorporated a slave cylinder which had at one end an inlet from the master cylinder and at the other an outlet to the brakes. In this cylinder was a slave piston having a central fluid port and a plunger entered the cylinder through a pressure seal; when actuated by an external force, the plunger could seal the fluid port in the slave piston and drive the piston before it (Fig. 5.13). The force on the slave piston was then that exerted by the plunger plus that due to the incoming hydraulic pressure acting on the annular area of the piston exposed to it; this generated an outlet pressure which was greater than the inlet one.

The plunger referred to above was actuated either by a piston or by a diaphragm of fabric reinforced rubber contained in an appropriately shaped pressed steel chamber; pistons were usual in earlier days but were subject to frictional losses, especially when the viscosity of the lubricant used was high in cold weather, and have since given way to diaphragms in most cases. A difference in the air pressure in the two regions of the chamber caused the piston or diaphragm, the latter supported by a push plate, to exert the force on the plunger referred to above.

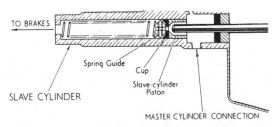

Fig. 5.13   The slave cylinder of a hydraulic servo unit (courtesy of Automotive Products PLC)

Early servos, when at rest, had air at atmospheric pressure in both regions of the chamber (atmosphere suspended), some of the air in one region being sucked out when the unit operated, so as to create the required pressure difference; this, however, gave a slow response under some conditions of engine operation. Present practice is for both regions of the chamber to be partially exhausted as soon as the engine is started (vacuum suspended), air from atmosphere then being admitted to the appropriate region as the unit operates; this method of operation gives a very rapid response so that it is virtually impossible to 'beat the servo'.

It used to be common for there to be a vacuum tank connected between the tapping into the carburettor and the servo unit (and having a non-return valve at the engine end); this improved the response with atmosphere suspended servos and gave a reserve of assistance if the engine were to fail. Vacuum tanks are not now usual but there is still a non-return valve in the suction line to the carburettor or exhauster; the capacity of the servo unit is such that, even if the engine stops, the driver still has ample assistance available for four or more stops.

There is an easy way of confirming that a vacuum servo is working, although this is not a very searching test. The driver sits in the car with the engine stopped, operates the brake pedal a number of times to ensure that air at atmospheric pressure is present in both regions of the chamber, then maintains heavy effort on the brake pedal; the engine is then started and the driver will note a small increase in pedal travel as the servo assistance takes effect.

The amount of force which a servo develops depends on the area of the piston or diaphragm which, in turn, depends on its diameter; as there is a practical limit to the size of unit which can be accommodated in the usually crowded engine compartment of the average car, the need for greater assistance cannot simply be met by increasing size. It is, however, possible to arrange for two pistons or diaphragms to be appropriately housed and to operate a single push rod, as described later in this chapter; by this means a ratio of up to 5:1 or so can be provided with units for use in cars and light commercial vehicles.

5.7 Precise control

Having described the slave cylinder and the means by which the external force was developed in a hydraulic servo, it is now necessary to consider the way in which the admission of air from atmosphere to the servo chamber was controlled. It will be seen that the two mechanisms commonly found in hydraulic servos each incorporated

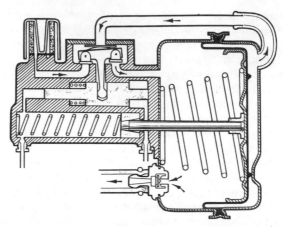

Fig. 5.14   A Girling vacuum/hydraulic servo unit (courtesy of Lucas Girling Ltd.)

a way of balancing two forces, one against the other, action being taken automatically to relate the augmented pressure fed to the brakes to a control signal.

A typical Girling unit (Fig. 5.14), in this case utilising a diaphragm, compares the pressure from the master cylinder with that fed to the brakes by using a compound piston, housed in a cylinder adjacent to the slave cylinder. The master cylinder pressure acts both on the back of the slave piston and on the large diameter face of the compound piston; the small diameter face of the compound piston is acted on by fluid from the output end of the slave cylinder. Movement of the compound piston operates an air valve which connects the servo chamber either to atmosphere (a filter cleaning the incoming air) or to the vacuum source (via the servo casing and the non-return valve).

Operation of the brake pedal by the driver causes a rise in the fluid pressure acting (initially) on both faces of the compound piston which, under the influence of its return spring, would be in the position shown, so that both regions of the servo would be connected to the vacuum source; this same pressure, acting on the differing areas of the compound piston faces, would cause the piston to move to the left and operate the air valve to isolate the servo chamber from the vacuum source.

A further increase in pressure would move the piston a little more, so that the air valve now admitted air from the atmosphere; this would pass through the pipe to the servo chamber and act on the back of the diaphragm, causing it to move the push rod. Only a small movement of the push rod would be needed to close the orifice in the slave piston, trapping the brake fluid beyond it so that its pressure could rise above the inlet pressure, as described above. The increased outlet pressure would now act both on the brakes and on the small end of the compound piston, moving it to the right (with the assistance of the return spring) until—when the pressures were in the correct ratio—the valve returned to the mid position, maintaining constant servo assistance.

Any change in the brake pedal effort would now unbalance the compound piston and cause it to operate the air valve one way or the other. An increase would lead to further air being admitted, while a decrease would lead to air being exhausted; in either case the change would continue until the piston was again in balance. A very heavy pedal effort, leading to admission of full atmospheric pressure, would bring full servo assistance and leave the piston unbalanced with the air inlet open; releasing the brake pedal would cause the partial vacuum in the servo chamber to be restored to its initial value, leaving the piston unbalanced (as it was at first) with the vacuum inlet open). Changes were made to the design of the slave piston of this unit (shown in simplified form in Fig. 5.14) but did not affect its operating principles.

In contrast with the Girling unit, a typical Lockheed unit of this period is shown (Fig. 5.15), this example incorporating a piston having a seal around its periphery instead of a diaphragm; the slave

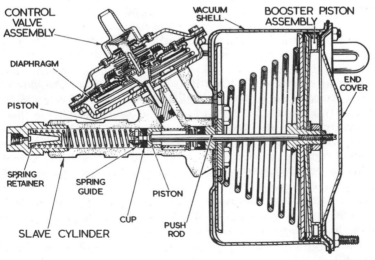

Fig. 5.15 A Lockheed vacuum/hydraulic servo unit (courtesy of Automotive Products PLC)

cylinder and piston are similar to those just considered, but the valve mechanism differs considerably. The control system now balances the pressure of the fluid delivered from the master cylinder against the pressure of the air admitted from atmosphere; the latter pressure determines the effort exerted by the servo piston which, in turn, determines the pressure of the fluid discharged to the brakes, so the desired result is achieved in this way. A simplified diagram, Fig. 5.16, shows the essential features more clearly.

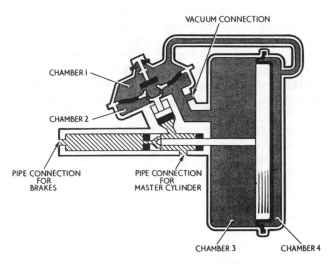

Fig. 5.16   *The Lockheed servo valve mechanism simplified (courtesy of Automotive Products PLC)*

The valve chest is divided into two regions by a diaphragm, the upper region being connected to the servo chamber by an exterior pipe and the lower to both the vacuum source and the servo casing; in the centre of the diaphragm is an annular valve seat which is linked to a small control piston, acted upon by the low pressure fluid. Located in an opening in the valve chest cover is a double valve, which seats either on the valve chest cover or on the central port in the diaphragm; movement of the diaphragm from the position shown, when the brake pedal is applied and low pressure fluid acts on the control piston, first seats the valve cover over the central or vacuum port then lifts it to open the air valve in the valve chest cover.

The initial movement of the diaphragm, which closes the vacuum port at its centre, isolates the upper part of the valve chest—together with the servo chamber—from the vacuum source; further movement then opens the air valve and admits air from atmosphere. This flows both into the valve chest and the servo chamber; in the first, it acts on the exposed area of the diaphragm while, in the second, it acts on the servo piston and causes an effort to be exerted on the slave piston. The air pressure on the control diaphragm acts in opposition to the low pressure fluid behind the control piston and, as it increases, pushes back the piston so that the air valve closes and no more air enters the valve chest; the servo unit then develops constant assistance for the driver as he maintains his pedal effort.

Any variation in the pedal effort will now unbalance the control mechanism either one way or the other; if the air valve is re-opened, more air will be admitted and the assistance increased; if the vacuum port is opened, some of the air already admitted will be extracted and the assistance will be reduced. With either of these types of unit, a failure of the servo to act for any reason simply left the driver to develop the required fluid pressure without assistance, the fluid passing freely through the slave piston to the brake pipelines.

Hydraulic servos became very popular as do-it-yourself optional extras for cars, in addition to their use on certain models as standard equipment; provided space could be found under the bonnet or in some other compartment adjacent to the engine, they could easily be piped into the hydraulic brake system. One drawback of these units was, however, the additional number of potential fluid leakage points which they introduced into the hydraulic system; this was one reason for the transition to the purely mechanical types to be described.

5.8 Direct acting servos

The alternative approach to the application of servo assistance, which has displaced the hydraulic unit, is the direct acting type which augments the physical effort applied to the master cylinder piston; this involves no complication of the hydraulic system which (subject to the inclusion of pressure limiting or modifying valves, to be considered in a later chapter) therefore is at the same pressure throughout.

The example illustrated first (Fig. 5.17) is by Lockheed; it consists of a pressed steel casing in which is a combined diaphragm support and valve body, a diaphragm, a primary push rod (operated by the brake pedal) and a secondary push rod (coupled to the master cylinder piston). The vacuum source is connected to the servo casing which, by means of a passage cast in the diaphragm support, is in communication with the inside of the valve body; in the 'brakes off' condition, there is then communication with the servo chamber by way of an annular vacuum valve and a radial port in the valve body.

The primary push rod passes into the valve body through an

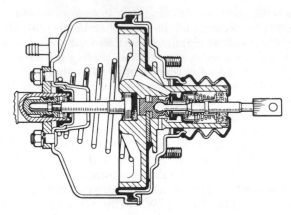

Fig. 5.17 A Lockheed direct acting vacuum servo (courtesy of Automotive Products PLC)

annular air filter and through the centre of the control valve; it is connected to a plunger having the air valve seating on its rear face and a flat face at the front, which is a little distance from a rubber reaction disc. The control valve is pressed by its spring either into contact with the air valve seating or with the concentric vacuum valve seating, depending on the relative positions of the primary push rod and the valve body.

At its forward end, the reaction disc is in full contact with the flat end face of the secondary push rod while, at its rear end, an outer annular portion is in contact with the diaphragm support. Where the valve body passes through the servo casing a seal is fitted and an exterior rubber gaiter keeps dirt away from the sliding surface.

Initial movement of the brake pedal causes the vacuum valve to be closed, isolating the servo chamber from the vacuum source, and takes up part of the clearance between the plunger and the reaction disc; further movement opens the air valve, allowing air to pass through the filter, around the push rod and into the servo chamber, while the face of the plunger presses against the reaction disc. When this happens, the combined diaphragm support and valve body moves forward with the push rod, the total force which is transmitted to the secondary push rod through the reaction disc then consisting of the driver's direct effort acting on the central circular portion and the servo output acting on the outer annular portion.

The rubber of which the reaction disc is made behaves somewhat like a fluid and, as the servo assistance increases while the air valve remains open, the force on the annular portion of the disc causes the central portion to be extruded, thrusting back against the plunger and primary push rod until the air valve is closed and the system maintained in balance. Any variation in the pedal effort will now cause either the vacuum valve or the air valve to be opened and the unit will give a corresponding response. The boost ratio of this design of servo is determined by the ratio of the area of the circular portion of the reaction disc to that of the annular portion.

When the degree of servo assistance which is required is greater than can be obtained from a single diaphragm of the maximum diameter which can be accommodated, two diaphragms of equal size can be incorporated into a tandem unit (Fig. 5.18); the integral valve body/flange assembly is extended to a second flange or diaphragm plate and a centre plate separates the two diaphragms. Passages through the centre of the valve body and around the periphery of the rim of the centre plate connect the pairs of chambers so that identical pressures are present on the corresponding sides of the diaphragms which then operate together.

The next example (Fig. 5.19) is of a Girling Flexing Diaphragm type of servo; in this case, although air enters the unit around the primary push rod, passing through a filter, the valve mechanism is directly associated with the diaphragm which, as well as rolling inside the

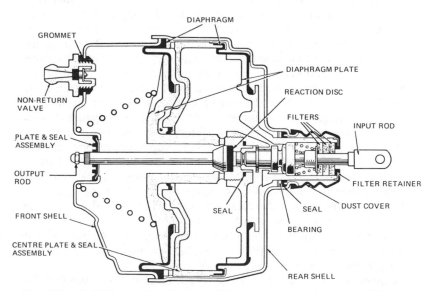

Fig. 5.18 A Girling tandem Supervac direct acting servo (courtesy of Lucas Girling Ltd.)

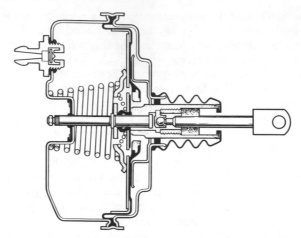

Fig. 5.19   The Girling flexing diaphragm vacuum servo (courtesy of Lucas Girling Ltd.)

casing at its periphery, can flex over its central area where it is stiffened by a number of metal fingers. The metal fingers are in contact with an annular fulcrum plate, assembled to the secondary push rod, and—like the fingers—this is pierced with holes to permit air to flow freely to the vacuum connection, in which is situated a non-return valve; the diaphragm is in two portions, inner and outer.

The primary push rod is directly coupled to a valve body which is integral with a flange to which the outer diaphragm is bonded; the secondary push rod is assembled into the valve body, but has a small amount of free movement in the longitudinal direction. The front face of the valve body has the air valve seating closely positioned around the push rod and the vacuum valve seating at a larger radius.

In the 'brakes off' condition as shown, the large return spring, acting through the medium of the fulcrum plate, presses the outer portion of the diaphragm back against its support; the inner portion of the diaphragm is held against the air valve and the vacuum valve is open. Initial movement of the brake pedal takes up the clearance between the valve body and the secondary push rod; at the same time, this relative movement also causes the centre of the diaphragm to flex forward until the vacuum valve is closed.

Further movement of the brake pedal causes the pressure of the vacuum valve seat to flex the diaphragm even more so that the inner portion lifts away from the air valve seating and air enters the chamber behind the diaphragm; the diaphragm then exerts a force on the secondary push rod through the fulcrum plate. The area of the diaphragm outside the radius of action of the fulcrum plate is greater than that which is within so, when the servo operates as described, there is a turning moment on the metal fingers which makes the diaphragm flex back until, at a pre-determined air pressure, the air valve is closed and the system then remains in balance until disturbed by a further movement of the brake pedal.

With this design, the boost ratio is decided by the radius of the fulcrum on the fulcrum plate relative to the outside radius of the diaphragm; this can easily be varied if required, when the manufacturer wishes to apply the unit to a different vehicle, by making an alternative pressing with the fulcrum at a different radius.

A later Girling servo, called the Servac, retains the flexing diaphragm in a simplified form, with the air and vacuum valves inside the valve body (Fig. 5.20); the primary plunger incorporates a poppet valve, which seats against the flexible rubber seal to close the air valve, under the influence of the light return spring. Initial movement of the primary plunger allows the seal to extend and close the vacuum valve whilst the air valve remains closed; further movement then causes the air valve to open, admitting air from atmosphere through the filter and into the servo chamber, as the flat face of the primary plunger contacts the end of the secondary plunger.

The build up of air pressure over the rear of the diaphragm, acting on the unequal areas within and beyond the circular fulcrum, causes

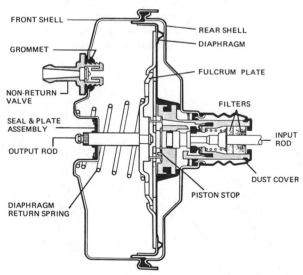

Fig. 5.20   A Girling Servac direct acting servo (courtesy of Lucas Girling Ltd.)

the metal fingers to be deflected backwards so that they press the valve body back until the air valve is closed; the brake application is then sustained by the sum of the forces in the primary plunger and on the diaphragm which together act on the secondary plunger. Any change in the pedal effort then opens one or other of the two valves to vary the servo assistance, within the range available, in appropriate manner.

With each of the direct acting servos described above, loss of the vacuum assistance leaves the driver still able to apply the brakes; his effort on the primary plunger is transmitted directly to the secondary plunger and thence to the master cylinder piston without any loss, as indicated by line C in Fig. 5.12.

5.9 Other forms of assistance

Earlier in this chapter, it was stated that an alternative source of energy to the partial vacuum generated either in the carburettor venturi or by a vacuum pump would be considered; this is, in fact, the engine itself. Rolls-Royce and Bentley cars built in the earlier part of the period reviewed used a mechanical servo (Fig. 5.21), driven from the gearbox output shaft at approximately one fifth of the propeller shaft speed, and therefore continuously rotating while the car was in motion; when actuated, the unit operated the master cylinder by means of a rod linkage.

The device consisted of a plate clutch, contained inside the casing mounted on the side of the gearbox; relative motion between the two outer levers caused an axial load to be applied to this clutch so that the rotating drive shaft transmitted motion to a pressure plate, part of

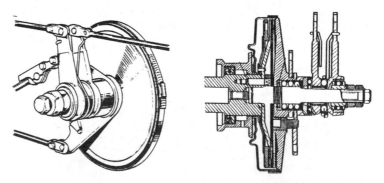

Fig. 5.21 The Rolls-Royce mechanical brake servo (courtesy of Rolls-Royce Motors Ltd.)

the face of which was exposed. A pin set in this face then contacted one or other of the two inner levers—depending on the direction in which the drive shaft was rotating—which were linked by rods to another lever; this lever, in turn, operated the hydraulic system, a balance beam being incorporated on cars with twin master cylinders.

The brake pedal was linked to the innermost of the two longer levers which, on initial movement of the pedal, transmitted this movement to the outermost lever by means of the torsion spring, thus applying the rear brakes mechanically; either 30 or 40% (depending on the model) of the force to apply the rear brakes was transmitted in this way, the handbrake linkage being also coupled to this system. The ensuing resistance to further movement of the outermost long lever then caused the other to move relative to it; the adjacent faces on the bosses of these levers were formed with opposed inclined surfaces, between which steel balls were assembled, so that the axial load referred to above was then developed and the servo assistance generated.

One disadvantage of this mechanical servo was that, because its effect depended on the road speed of the vehicle, its speed of response varied; additionally, it did not give assistance when stationary, as when holding the vehicle on an incline.

The final device to be described is not a servo, since it does not make use of an external source of energy, but is a hydraulic intensifier; this is the Baldwin brake booster (Fig. 5.22) which, for a short time, was incorporated into the braking system of Mini Coopers until the adoption of a higher friction disc brake lining material made it unnecessary. It was also offered for sale as an optional do-it-yourself fitment at about the same time.

The unit consists of a compound piston sliding in a cylinder with a stepped bore; an axial fluid passage has a check valve at the input end which, with the piston returned to its off position by the return spring, is held off its seat by a pin. When the brake pedal is first operated and the fluid in the system is at a low pressure, unobstructed fluid flow

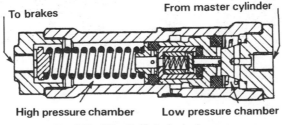

Fig. 5.22   The Baldwin brake booster

through the axial passage occurs whilst clearances are taken up; as fluid pressure then starts to rise, it acts equally on the larger piston face at the input end and the smaller face at the output end, the annular space between the steps on the piston and in the cylinder being vented to atmosphere.

At a relatively low pressure, of the order of 10 bars (150 lbf/in^2), the unbalanced force on the compund piston is sufficient to move it to the left, compressing the return spring a little and allowing the check valve to close; any further increase in the pressure of the fluid from the master cylinder then causes the unit to intensify the output pressure in the ratio of the areas of the large and small pistons. Typically, at an input pressure of about 55 bars (800 lbf/in^2), the output pressure was stated to be about 83 bars (1200 lbf/in^2); the direct penalty of the unit was a reduction in the volume of fluid displaced in the output circuit, this being in inverse proportion to the boost ratio, resulting in a slight increase in pedal travel during the effective part of its stroke.

In conclusion, the vacuum servo seems to be here to stay but is subject to ongoing development to reduce weight and cost but without affecting reliability. Girling, for instance, are working on the use of thinner steel for the pressings which form the working chamber, this involves passing two long studs right through this chamber, to transmit the reaction force between the master cylinder and the bulkhead, bellows being used to contain the pressure difference where the studs pass through the diaphragm. On the other hand, DBA are seeking to shorten the length of the servo/master cylinder assembly (and thus reduce installation problems) by recessing the cylinder body into the servo chamber. Similar minor developments are likely with other components described in this chapter but the more significant future developments in hydraulic braking systems are likely to relate more to those components considered in Chapter 11.

6

Car disc brakes

6.1 Introduction

Whereas drum brakes have a relatively long history, much of which has only briefly been touched on in this book, the story of the disc brake as a practicable means of stopping production cars goes back only to 1956. It is true, and has been widely noted, that Dr F.W. Lanchester patented a design of disc brake in 1902, but this appears not to have been followed up; he also fitted a design of oil immersed disc brake to a Lanchester car marketed between 1906 and 1914, but this brake made little impact at the time. Even the introduction in 1952 of disc brakes on certain racing cars, these being very largely based on wartime aircraft brake experience, did not have an immediate effect on brake design practice for quantity produced cars.

It was not until 1956 that disc brakes were established as a viable alternative to drum brakes; Dunlop units then became standard equipment on the Jensen 541 de luxe saloon and Girling ones on the Triumph TR3 sports car while Citroen, in France, put their own design of disc brake into production on the DS19 (a car with very many advanced features when it was introduced). Lockheed in the UK followed in 1959 with initial equipment on the Alvis TD21, Teves in Germany began production (at first making a Dunlop design under licence) in 1961 and DBA in France added disc brakes to their production programme in 1962.

Before proceeding to consideration of the various types of disc brake and their evolution, it is relevant to pose two questions and then set down brief answers, the questions being 'What is the difference between drum and disc brakes?' and 'What is the difference between the performance characteristics of drum and disc brakes?' In this context, it must be understood that the comparison is made between the conventional quantity production designs of drum and disc brake; various alternative designs of each have been proposed from time to time by ingenious inventors which fall into a different category.

The common automotive drum brake consists essentially, as noted

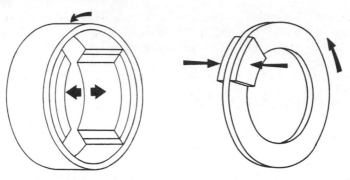

Fig. 6.1   A schematic drum brake   Fig. 6.2   A schematic disc brake

in Chapter 3 (Fig. 3.1), of two shoes which may be expanded against the inner cylindrical surface of a drum (Fig. 6.1). The greater part of the heat generated when a brake is applied has to pass through the drum to its outer surface, in order to be dissipated to atmosphere, and the drum material is at the same time subjected to quite severe stresses due to the distortion induced by the opposed shoes, acting inside the open ended drum.

The conventional disc brake on the other hand, consists essentially of a flat disc on either side of which are friction pads; equal and opposite forces may be applied to these pads to press their working surfaces into contact with the braking path of the disc (Fig. 6.2). The heat produced by the conversion of energy is dissipated directly from the surfaces at which it is generated and the deflection of the braking path of the disc, due to the clamping forces on the pads, is very small so that the stressing of the material is not so severe as with a drum.

The difference between the two types of brake, then, lies in the difference between the shapes of the friction and mating surfaces; on the one hand the surfaces are of cylindrical form while on the other they are flat. From this difference follows the answer to the second question.

Consideration has already been given in Chapter 3 to some aspects of the geometry of drum brake shoes and it has been shown that, because of geometrical effects, the output of the brake will depend on the detailed design of the shoes and other components. In most cases, the design of the brake is such that its output is related to the input force by a curve which rises with increasing steepness as μ, the lining coefficient of friction increases (a non-linear relationship).

The disc brake described, however, is not subject to geometrical considerations except to a very minor extent; its output is, in simple terms, the product of clamping force, coefficient of friction, mean radius and the number of working surfaces (usually two per brake). Because of this, the relationship between brake factor and coefficient of friction for such a disc brake is illustrated by a straight line (a linear relationship).

A disc brake, therefore, is particularly insensitive to changes in the coefficient of friction of the lining material, for whatever reason they occur, but is not by its nature a powerful type of brake; it lends itself to use on high performance cars, for which consistent braking is important and which are in such a price category that the cost of including a servo in the specification is acceptable. In the later 1950s and early 1960s, disc brakes were applied to a variety of models, some of which were far from being in the high performance category, as a sales feature which has continued to find favour; a number of the smaller models on the market have, however, retained drum brakes at the front as well as at the rear. It may be accepted that any car which covers a high annual mileage and/or is driven at high average speeds will benefit from having disc brakes at least at the front; for use on low mileage family cars there is, however, still a strong case for the use of a good drum/drum installation because of its expectation of long, trouble free service, with economy of maintenance and good all-round performance.

6.2 Possible configurations

Enlarging on the simple basic concept of a disc brake illustrated in Fig. 6.2, there are a number of configurations which have been or are being used (Fig. 6.3), some of these being of the nature of deviations from what has been subsequently seen as the principal line of development.

The first example (i) of the ten illustrated relates to a relatively short

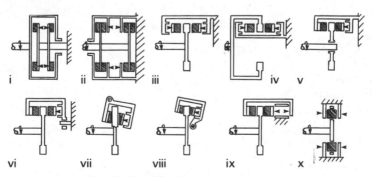

Fig. 6.3   Possible disc brake configurations

lived installation adopted by the American Chrysler company in 1950. This consisted of an enclosed brake which used stationary full disc type friction surfaces in a rotating casing; the friction surfaces could be forced apart, so that they rubbed on the inside faces of the casing, which was ribbed externally for strength and heat dissipation. The hydraulic operating cylinder was between the friction discs, so avoidance of fluid vapourisation must have been difficult and, apart from one other little known case, mentioned later, it was a number of years before disc brakes again appeared on American cars.

Example (ii) is an inversion of the first, in which the casing is stationary and encloses two double sided rotating friction discs, with a stationary member between them; the central member exerts an axial force against the friction discs to generate a braking force. This type of brake has not been used on cars, although a slightly different version forms a notable exception, but is common on tractors; it therefore receives consideration in Chapter 10. The exception was an early Lockheed disc brake, fitted in 1937 to the land speed record breaking car, Thunderbolt, which had a single rotating friction disc which could be clamped by hydraulic pressure between two stationary cast iron mating surfaces.

Example (iii) in Fig. 6.3 is of a fixed, opposed piston caliper and, like all the subsequent examples, incorporates friction pads whose working area is only a fraction of that of the braking path; this type has been widely made from 1956 onwards and its many variations will receive attention in the sections which follow. The opposed pistons apply equal and opposite forces to the pads and move as appropriate as wear of the linings takes place; the disc is not free to move axially. An unusual variant of this type (iv) was made by Teves in small numbers in 1963 for a Porsche model; the disc was connected at its periphery to an extension of the hub while the caliper straddled the bore of the disc (Fig. 6.4). Both assembly and maintenance of this type must have been difficult, whilst no benefits can be identified; it has, however, recently been reintroduced for motor cycles by another maker.

As will be considered in detail, there have been many approaches to the design of calipers with a single hydraulic cylinder, the first of these shown (v) being included for record purposes only; it has a fixed, single acting caliper and an axially sliding disc. Calipers of this type were fitted to the late Donald Campbell's land speed record car Bluebird, designed in 1959/60 (the brakes were operated by compressed air), but the axially movable disc is not really a practicable feature for production cars.

The obvious inversion of this last type is to have a disc which is fixed and make the caliper slideable and example (vi) is of a single

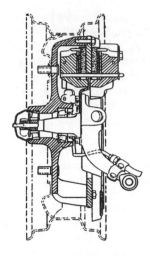

Fig. 6.4   A rim mounted disc with internal caliper

acting caliper configuration, such as has been used ever since 1962 by DBA; the problems of ensuring axial freedom were much less formidable in the case of the caliper than they would have been had the disc needed to slide and this type has given good service on cars of a number of makes. Various other manufacturers have developed sliding calipers which can be classified under this same heading, the differing ways in which the pads are supported and the forces transmitted being considered below; this type is now extremely popular and seems likely to become the most widely used in the foreseeable future.

A variant of the fixed disc and movable single acting caliper is to arrange for the caliper to pivot, instead of sliding. Two different positions for the pivot axis (vii) and (viii) have been used by Lockheed and Girling respectively and, allied to other features, have resulted in very different looking brakes; this class of configuration has, however, not found extensive application any more than the next. Example (ix) has a single, rigidly mounted cylinder and an axially constrained disc but the cylinder is double acting; the outboard (furthest from the centre line of the car) piston applies the inboard pad directly, while the inboard piston applies the outboard pad by means of a sliding yoke plate.

Lastly, example (x) shows a rotating carrier plate, with openings into which fit double sided brake pads, this assembly running between stationary mating plates; the brake is applied by means of axial pressure on the mating plates and the design lends itself to multi-plate arrangements. This configuration has similarities to example (i) but does not use full area facings and the actuation mechanism is remote from the friction surfaces; it has for some years been used in certain large industrial clutches but has not made much progress in the automotive brake field since first being tried some twenty-five years ago as a prototype commercial vehicle brake.

It is not claimed that this is an exhaustive list of all possibilities but it is thought to be a practical basis for classifying those brakes likely to be encountered; many considerations are involved in determining which of the various types is most favoured at any particular time. Most of the disc brakes found in service are of type (iii) or types (vi)–(ix) from the above classification and it is these which are particularly considered in the sections which follow.

6.3 Disc design

A complete disc brake consists essentially of the disc, the caliper and the friction pads and it is convenient to consider the disc first, there being relatively little difference between discs for all the models of car produced in quantity since 1956. As dealt with at some length in Chapter 2, the generally recommended material for the manufacture of discs is cast iron; chromium plated discs have been tried for sports cars with spoked wheels, while motor cycles often use stainless steel, but for heavy duty applications there is at present no practicable substitute for cast iron. Before castings are machined, it is desirable that they are suitably stress relieved or distortion will occur in service; this would certainly lead to localised wear and consequent judder as well as to other problems.

The principal dimensions of a brake disc are the outside and inside diameter of the braking path and its thickness, the design of the mounting face and the offset between the braking path and mounting face; the width of the braking path naturally has to be considered in conjunction with the design of the disc brake pads. As soon as the design of a disc is undertaken, it is found that some compromise is unavoidable because of the number of factors to be considered and the conflict between their requirements.

The thickness of the disc will largely determine its ability to absorb heat quickly, without the material reaching an excessive temperature, and the offset—as well as relating to the problem of fitting many components into a very confined space—determines the length of the heat flow path between the working surfaces and the wheel bearings. Discs are commonly quite deeply dished (Fig. 6.5) and in some cases, at the rear of disc/disc cars, the inner cylindrical surface so formed is used as the mating surface for a small shoe brake—usually of duo-servo type—used as a parking brake, as referred to in Chapter 4.

Fig. 6.5   Dishing the disc lengthens the heat flow path to the wheel bearings

The outside diameter of the brake disc is necessarily limited by the inside diameter of the wheel rim; sufficient space must be left for the brake caliper to straddle this disc, with appropriate clearances, and for air to circulate to conduct heat away. There is also a limit to the inside diameter of the braking path, because— particularly in the case of front brakes—of the shortage of space, but there is another consideration to be kept in mind. There is a diminishing benefit when attempting to increase pad area by extending radially inwards, because the mean radius (which as noted above, has a direct bearing on the torque developed) is thereby reduced; mean radius, it will be appreciated, is equal to the sum of the inside radius and half the braking path width (Fig. 6.6), so is affected by any change of the latter. It should, however, be noted that the actual mean radius, which depends in part on the centre of pressure and the contact pattern, may not correspond to the geometrical value.

Another compromise exists with regard to disc thickness; not only does this affect the heat capacity of the disc, it directly affects its weight which, being unsprung in most cases, needs to be kept to a

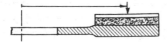

Fig. 6.6   The mean radius of a disc brake

minimum. A thicker disc also encroaches on the limited space which is available to accommodate the thickness of the disc brake pads which, determining their volume in conjunction with their area, sets a limit on their life.

Based on the above considerations, a thickness of the order of 10–13 mm ($\frac{3}{8}$–$\frac{1}{2}$ inch) has been common for brake discs on cars, vehicles with all-disc installations often having thicker discs at the front than at the rear; for some years, however, certain of the larger cars have used a ventilated type of disc of 22–24 mm (approx. 1 in) thickness in order to improve heat dissipation. The disc casting is formed with air passages between the two braking surfaces (Fig. 6.7), air circulation being promoted by the rotation; despite the extra mass and bulk (a spacer is assembled between the two halves of an otherwise standard caliper in some cases, in order to accommodate the extra thickness), it is accepted that a worthwhile improvement is achieved and the number of such installations is likely to increase, particularly on commercial vehicles.

Fig. 6.7   A portion of a ventilated brake disc

Contrary to expectations, it was found in the early days of disc brakes that when the rotating disc is wetted in bad weather conditions it retains a thin film of water; until this film is penetrated by the lining material, no appreciable braking force is developed and the delay in response can be potentially dangerous. Disc shields are now usually fitted on cars to deflect water from the inboard faces of the disc (they may also impair cooling) and the wheels protect the outboard faces to a large extent, but motor cycle discs have no such protection so they sometimes have the braking path either drilled, with a considerable number of holes of some 7–10 mm diameter, or grooved with a small number of shallow grooves, tangential to a circle of small diameter. These measures are thought to have some beneficial effect but will also increase the lining wear rate slightly; an alternative expedient is the use of one or more transverse grooves in the lining, but a suitable choice of friction material is the most effective remedy.

In a few cases, particularly of high quality cars, the brake disc is damped to reduce the incidence of squeal; a groove in the outer edge of the disc contains a close fitting welded ring or is filled with wound-on wire, the groove then sometimes being closed with a steel strip. Vibration of the disc in the circumferential direction causes relative motion of low amplitude between it and the damping material; this dissipates energy and limits the vibration to prevent it from being audible.

6.4 Disc brake pads

The first disc brake pads to appear on production cars in 1956 could hardly have differed more in shape (Fig. 6.8); the circular Dunlop pad would have been relatively easy to make while the segmental Girling pad was, in theory, the shape that would wear evenly in service. Both pads were attached to steel backplates with adhesive, the Girling pad having a spigot located in a recess in the plate whilst the Dunlop pad was recessed to fit over a spigot on the plate; both backplates served to locate the pad in the caliper and distribute the applied force over the pad area. Extensions on the Dunlop plate were coupled to retraction devices which positively withdrew the pad from the disc when the brake pedal was released.

Before continuing, it is as well to clarify the nomenclature which is being used in this book. A typical friction assembly, such as the Girling one shown in Fig. 6.8, is here called a disc brake pad—or pad, for short—and consists of a backplate (or plate) and a disc brake pad lining (or lining); in America, however, the metal plate is usually called a shoe, as for a drum brake, the assembly being a lined shoe or shoe assembly.

The original Dunlop circular pad was subsequently dropped in favour of one rectangular pad and one square one which, between them, were used to cover a variety of applications; these had a recess in the rear face into which was bonded a metal retraction plate (Fig. 6.9) which secured the withdrawal of the pad after the conclusion of an application. The Girling segmental pad was one of a range which, within a short time, was redesigned to incorporate backplates with part circular locating surfaces (Fig. 6.10), instead of parallel ones, so that caliper production was simplifed.

Unlike these Girling and Dunlop pads, which had linings of compact, simple geometrical form, Lockheed pads have usually been of less easily defined shape—both as regards the plate and also the lining attached to it; they have, however, remained relatively few in number. Teves, after at first using Dunlop designs under licence and

Fig. 6.8   The contrasting shapes of
early Girling (left) and Dunlop disc
brake pads

Fig. 6.9   The Dunlop series II pad

Fig. 6.10   A Girling pad for a turned
gap caliper

Fig. 6.11   An early design of Teves
disc brake pad

briefly making the unconventional caliper for Porsche already
referred to, settled on a pad shape (Fig. 6.11) which—in a variety of
sizes, all of similar proportions—they have used for some time;
Girling have also returned to the use of backplates with parallel
locating edges so, although these often have linings with inclined
flanks and the upper edge of the plate is sometimes straight, there is a
great general similarity.

Citroen, manufacturing brakes only for their own cars, have never
needed a range to offer on the market, their pad designs therefore have
tended to be individualistic from the first one, with a light alloy
backplate, to which the lining was bonded without any secondary
means of support, to the more recent ones; the unusual large Citroen

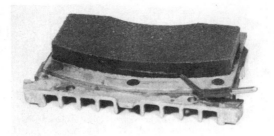

Fig. 6.12 A large Citroen pad assembly

Fig. 6.13 A Citroen pad backplate designed to facilitate removal

pad has the steel backplate proper attached to a light alloy carrier (Fig. 6.12), heavily ribbed for stiffness and to reduce heat conduction, whilst one of the smaller ones (Fig. 6.13) has a tail-like extension to the backplate to make it easier to cope with the limited accessibility of the brake when replacing pads.

DBA in France have, from their first design, favoured pad assemblies which were narrow in the radial direction by comparison with their circumferential length; for a given outside diameter of disc, this gives a greater effective radius than a wider pad and this manufacturer seems to have had no difficulty in achieving an even distribution of pressure over the lining area.

At the time when the American car industry began to give serious consideration to the use of disc brakes, the cars concerned were commonly much larger and heavier than they are now so the pads tended to be large by European standards; whereas the common British or Continental pad has a relative simple backplate of flat steel, although attachments to this may be made, American backplates have often been rather complex pressings (Fig. 6.14) to which the linings, in some cases, are riveted. American practice has often favoured the elongated lining form but a considerable variety of shapes is to be found.

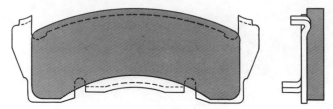

Fig. 6.14   American disc brake pads are sometimes quite large with complex backplates

In addition to the complications of outline to be found amongst the several hundred disc brake pads which have, by now, been in production, there is also the matter of tapered thickness, to which brief reference has been made; this, however, is most conveniently dealt with when the rather individualistic calipers concerned are considered. Chamfering or other relief of lining surfaces helps to ensure freedom from noise during bedding and early service; by initially moving the centre of pressure in a preferred direction it avoids the chance of it being unintentionally displaced in the opposite direction.

It will be realised that no mention has been made of the products from Japan so far in this chapter; these are, in general, based on European designs and made under licence or other arrangement so, although the number of differences in detail is increasing, the same broad principles are followed.

Bonding and riveting of linings to backplates have both been mentioned, the two having sometimes been used together, but the most common process is now what is often known as integral moulding; the backplate is produced with two or more holes in it so that, under the considerable moulding pressure used when the lining is formed, some of the friction material flows into these holes and forms spigots, which are able to resist the expected tangential reaction to the braking force. In addition, adhesive is spread on the surface of the plate so that a bond—also strong enough to withstand the force generated—is formed; unlike the rubber based adhesives commonly used for attaching linings to drum brake shoes, the platforms of which often have irregularities to fill, adhesives for disc brake pads are usually of synthetic resin type, having superior temperature resistance.

From the early days of disc brakes, some manufacturers have commonly used asymmetrical or handed backplates, usually because of a feature relative to the lining which necessitated ensuring that the pads could only be inserted in certain positions. Some Lockheed assemblies have the lining offset to reduce the likelihood of

Fig. 6.15 Lockheed pads with offset linings to prevent brake squeal

squeal (Fig. 6.15), the backplates having an associated projecting corner; the pads are therefore left and right handed and may be fitted in the same position in either caliper, the projection fouling the caliper body if wrong assembly is attempted.

The first DBA backplates had asymmetric recesses in them to locate them either to the single piston in the inboard part of the caliper or to the fixed outboard part of the caliper beyond the disc; the pad assemblies also had an unusual feature at the trailing end—a thickening which gave an increased area to transmit the braking reaction force to the caliper—so that all four assemblies were different. Subsequent DBA designs have a simpler, symmetrical shape of pad so that, although it is sometimes found that only the inner pad has a central recess on the back, the extreme complication of all pads being different is removed; such handing as exists is now in terms of inboard and outboard, as compared with the left and right of the Lockheed pads. The small steel discs sometimes attached to the rear of the backplate at the trailing end fulfil the same function as the thickening of the early linings and, again, affect the positions in which the pads must be placed.

Disc brake pad assembly retention is closely associated with caliper design and a variety of methods have been used; details of some of these methods will become apparent when a description is given of the calipers concerned, but the most common method is easily described. The many designs of pad having parallel sides like the Teves example shown in Fig. 6.11 are both located radially and retained in position by (usually) two pins which pass through elongated holes in the upper edge of the plate; the pins may be split for opening out, they may have a spring steel locking ring (Fig. 6.16) or they may be drilled or grooved for a wire clip. Other methods of retention are used for pins which assemble different parts of the caliper together and which may also locate the disc brake pads.

Fig. 6.16   Teves pad retaining pins with spring sleeves

6.5 Disc brake squeal and rattle

Some disc brake pads have spring clips attached to their back, which locate in the open end of the caliper piston, but most of the attachments and miscellaneous parts—as well as some features of the lining itself—are concerned with the prevention of squeal, already mentioned briefly above. This has been a particularly troublesome problem with disc brakes and, it having been accepted that it is not just the fault of the brake lining material, a great deal of work has been done by the brake and vehicle manufacturers, in addition to that which the lining makers had already been doing to develop friction materials which damp vibration.

An early approach to squeal prevention in fact involved the caliper rather than the pad assembly; Lockheed found that offsetting the centre of pressure on the pad by grinding a shallow step on the face of the piston (Fig. 6.17) had a markedly beneficial effect; this could be introduced relatively easily and different settings of the piston could be used for different applications, but there is the possibility of wrongly setting the piston in service.

Another way of achieving a similar effect to the use of a stepped piston is to insert a specially shaped thin steel plate between the pad backplate and the piston face; the particular feature of this is that it is cut away in such a manner as to give clearance between the plate and the piston over part of the annular face of the latter, thus moving the centre of pressure. These plates or anti-squeal shims, as they are often called, are often pierced with holes for the pad retaining pins to pass through and are sometimes formed with an integral arrow to indicate forward disc rotation, to simplify correct insertion; in other cases they are assembled to the pad as supplied (Fig. 6.18).

Squeal can often be suppressed by the judicious use of a suitable high melting point grease at the contact area between the piston and the backplate; there are a number of proprietary greases on the market which may be used for this purpose—and which should be

Fig. 6.17 A Lockheed caliper piston
with a step ground on the face; this
offsets the centre of pressure on the pad
to prevent squeal

Fig. 6.18 A Lockheed pad with an
anti-squeal shim assembled to it

applied also to shims when these are fitted—as well as other
substances which cushion the contact in one way or another.

Certain pad assemblies incorporate a thin layer of friction
material—or an allied substance—on the back as a squeal deterrent
and it is possible to incorporate thin base layers of suitable
compounds between the friction material and the backplate; such
layers, as well as being relevant to noise suppression, may be used to
reduce the heat flow through the pad assembly into the piston.

In addition to the reduction or elimination of brake squeal, it has
proved necessary to include an elastic element in the means of pad
retention so that pad rattle is prevented; the springs which have been
developed for this purpose take many forms. Some springs are
assembled between the pads and the retaining pins (Fig. 6.19), some
between the pads and the caliper, while others are formed integrally
with the anti-squeal shims; in addition to the use of spring steel sheet
components, many are made of spring steel wire and may be either
loose or attached to the pads.

6.6 Wear indication

Although it is usually possible to inspect the state of wear of disc
brake pads visually, without disturbing the caliper, this cannot be
done adequately—if at all—without removing the wheels; in at least
one case provision is made for checking lining thickness with a special
gauge without removing the wheels, but this has to be done with the
car on a lift or from an inspection pit. Since servicing intervals have
been considerably extended for most components and systems on
vehicles, this has increased the likelihood of excessive pad wear being

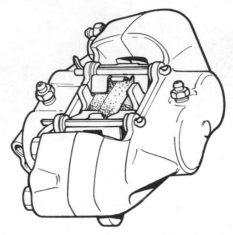

Fig. 6.19   *Anti-rattle springs in place between a disc brake pad and its retaining pins*

overlooked until contact between discs and the steel backplates has caused damage to the former.

Vehicle and brake manufacturers have, for a number of years, therefore, been developing electrical warning systems which, by illuminating an indicator (another similar indicator will be referred to in Chapter 11) on the instrument panel, alert the driver to the need to have his pads replaced. Early systems used a live element, energised from the car's electrical system, which completed a circuit when it contacted the disc; most recent ones employ a different type of live element in such a way that the process of wear breaks the circuit to energise the indicator.

The first type of system has used two types of element, the first being exclusive to DBA. This made use of a plastics button which could be inserted into a hole pierced in one end of the backplate (Fig. 6.20); an electrical lead could be plugged into a metal insert moulded into the button. As the limit of wear for the lining material was approached, the head of the button would contact the disc and itself wear away until, at the intended thickness of the remaining lining material, the metal insert would contact the disc and earth the warning circuit. The alternative type used an insulated wire bonded into a hole drilled into the lining parallel to the backplate and a short distance from its face (Fig. 6.21); again, the circuit would be earthed when, at the recommended wear limit, the wire contacted the disc.

The more recent systems use a detector of the second type, except that a loop of insulated wire is inserted into the pad; a plug type connector is used to give rapid separation and reconnection

Fig. 6.20   A DBA wear indicator

*Fig. 6.21   A pad wear indicator
inserted in the lining*

of the detector leads when pads are renewed. Because it is considered
that inboard pads are likely to wear more quickly than outboard
ones—although, for various reasons, this may not necessarily be the
case—and to limit the complication and cost of the system, it is
usually only the inboard pads which are fitted with wear detectors.

6.7 Disc brake calipers

The principal functions of the disc brake caliper are to contain and
support the pad assemblies, to apply a clamping load to them when
necessary and to withstand the reaction to the braking force
generated. However, before describing many of the ways in which
these functions have been fulfilled, it should first be noted that the
braking force on the rotating disc and its reaction on the caliper have
the effect of varying the load on the wheel bearings, depending on
whether the caliper is mounted at the front or at the rear, on or just
above the horizontal axis. If the caliper is at the front, the load on the
wheel bearings is increased when the brakes are applied while if it is at
the rear, the load is decreased; for intermediate positions the vertical
effect is less but an element of horizontal loading is introduced. When
twin caliper installations are fitted on heavy vehicles, this effect is
cancelled out.

The fixed opposed piston caliper (Fig. 6.3(iii)) has been the most
numerous type, having been in quantity production since 1956 and
will be considered first; it has been manufactured by all of the leading
suppliers, including those in America, and the differences in detail are
too numerous to be considered in full.

The simplest form of such a caliper was the single piece casting used
by Girling in 1956 (Fig. 6.22); to give access to machine the cylinder
bores, the outer end of the inboard cylinder was closed by a threaded
plug and the rectangular opening was finished to size by broaching.

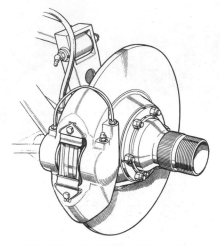

Fig. 6.22   The Girling B type caliper

Production was simplified and the need for the plug eliminated by the early introduction of a two piece design, split down the centre; in place of the original external bridge pipe linking the two cylinders, this type used linking ports drilled through the halves of the bridge to achieve the same result. Internal porting avoided the vulnerability to damage and corrosion of the external pipe but its proximity to the edge of the hot disc created a chance of brake fluid vapourisation instead. Girling experimented for sime time with calipers having part circular seatings for their pads as mentioned above, but then reverted to the parallel gap type with pin location of the pad assemblies.

Early Lockheed calipers were of heavy construction and had to be dismounted in order to remove and change the pads, whereas all Girling calipers of the period allowed inspection and removal of the pads through the open gap; the Lockheed H type (Fig. 6.23), for larger cars, had a completely closed bridge but the medium duty M type had a small opening which facilitated inspection of lining thicknesses. Lockheed subsequently changed to the open gap type of caliper with part circular or parallel sided seating for the pads and retention by means of split pins. Lockheed have in a number of cases used asymmetric pad backplates, usually in connection with anti-squeal features as mentioned above, and the caliper body has had to be machined to correspond.

Dunlop aimed from the first to ease both manufacture and maintenance by using a three part construction employing a cast steel bridge and brake mounting, to which were attached individual

Fig. 6.23   The Lockheed H type caliper

cylinders of light alloy linked by an external bridge pipe. In the case of the series I (Fig. 6.24), the cylinders and pad assemblies formed a subassembly whereas with the later series II (Fig. 6.25), the pads were partly located by the bridge, to which a pad retainer was assembled.

After a period when the Dunlop series II design was made under licence, Teves widely used the two piece parallel gap design (Fig. 6.26), very similar to that of Girling; DBA have also used such a design, but only to a very limited extent.

At this point it is convenient to digress and note that Girling have consistently followed the 'hydrostatic' principle established by certain of their early hydraulic drum brakes, which allowed the linings to remain very close to the working surface, but not under load; the pressure seals are designed to grip the piston closely and, when the brakes are released, retract the pistons by about 0.1 mm (0.004 in). Lockheed in their earliest designs included a positive retraction device inside the caliper pistons, so that the pistons were retracted by a similar amount to the above, leaving the pads free from load, they have since then always relied on seal retraction to achieve the same result. Dunlop used positive retraction with both series I and II: in the former case a twin friction and spring device operated on the pad assemblies to withdraw them and the pistons; in the latter case an

118

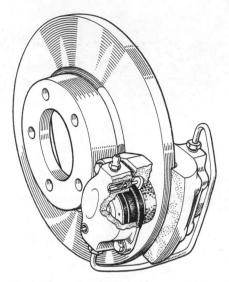

Fig. 6.24   The Dunlop series I caliper (courtesy of Lucas Girling Ltd.)

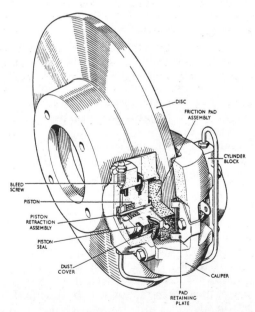

Fig. 6.25   The Dunlop series II caliper; versions were made fitting both square and rectangular pads (courtesy of Lucas Girling Ltd.)

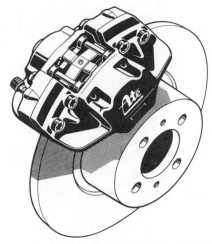

Fig. 6.26   A Teves opposed piston caliper (courtesy of Alfred Teves GmbH)

internal mechanism withdrew the pistons, the pads being coupled to them by means of the retractor plate seen in Fig. 6.9. Teves at first used internal positive retraction but soon turned to seal retraction, on which DBA have always relied.

All proprietary manufacturers have employed a range of cylinder bore diameters based on a series of metric or inch dimensions and designated in various ways; Teves identify their calipers by a number corresponding to the bore diameter in mm, Lockheed by a number corresponding to the bore diameter in sixteenths of an inch and Girling by an unrelated number.

Caliper castings have usually been of steel, protected against corrosion by an electro-plated coating in most cases; light alloy has, however, sometimes been used. Pistons are of chromium plated steel and are commonly protected by means of a rubber dust cover which extends from the mouth of the cylinder bore to the piston face; such covers are filled with a suitable lubricant when fitted and facilitate pushing the pistons back into their bores when new pads are to be fitted.

The pressure seals used are of high grade synthetic rubber which has to withstand the considerable operating temperature involved, retain pressures in excess of 100 bars (1500 lb/in^2) in service (three times this under test) and have the strength and resilience to perform the piston retraction function referred to above. These seals are of approximately square or rectangular cross-section and are housed in grooves of appropriate form near the mouth of the cylinder bore.

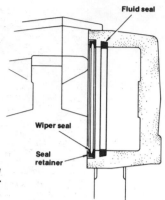

Fig. 6.27   A wiper or scraper seal protecting the pressure seal in a Lockheed caliper (courtesy of Automotive Products PLC)

Lockheed, who do not use a rubber dust cover over their pistons, fit an extra seal—a scraper seal—nearer the mouth of the cylinder bore than the pressure seal (Fig. 6.27) to prevent the ingress of dirt to the vicinity of the pressure seal; it is advisable, when this is the case, that the exposed surfaces of the pistons are cleaned with brake fluid or ethyl alcohol before returning them into their bores.

The inlet port through which fluid under pressure is fed is commonly on the body of the inboard cylinder, the fluid transfer port passing through the upper bridge of the more or less horizontally mounted casting; a bleed screw is situated on the upper bridge, its tapping communicating with the transfer port, so that air can be bled from both cylinders. Older calipers having external bridge pipes had these leading from the top of the inboard cylinder with a bleed screw on the top of the outboard cylinder. When problems in bleeding are found to occur at the development stage, manufacturers use detailed clear plastics facsimiles to enable them to observe the location of air pockets.

One unusual variant of the fixed, opposed piston caliper unique to the Girling range is the three piston type (Fig. 6.28); in this type, the single inboard piston is opposed by two smaller ones of combined equal area; all three cylinders are fed by one hydraulic circuit, so that equal forces are applied to the two pads, and normal feed and bleed arrangements still apply. The practical advantage of the three cylinder caliper is the reduced swept outline of the outboard part of the casting; this has eased installation problems in difficult cases.

The obvious further extension of the opposed piston caliper is to have two pairs of opposed pistons (Fig. 6.29); by using separate hydraulic circuits to supply each pair of opposed pistons, it is easy to enhance safety by ensuring continued brake operation in the event of

Fig. 6.28   *A Girling 3 cylinder caliper*

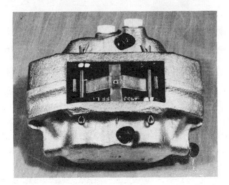

Fig. 6.29   *A Teves 4 cylinder caliper for dual hydraulic circuits*

the loss of either circuit. There have to be individual feed ports for the two inboard cylinders and individual transfer ports—one in each bridge; a total of three bleed screws is necessary, one on the upper bridge for the upper pair of cylinders and one on the top of each of the lower cylinders.

Although it is common for both pairs of cylinders in a four cylinder caliper to be of the same diameter, there are a number of cases where—because of the way in which the two separate circuits are arranged—this is not so; the reason for this will be considered in Chapter 11.

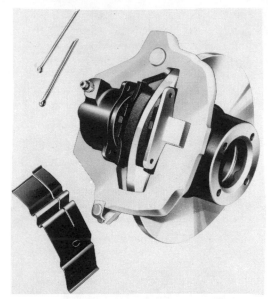

Fig. 6.30   One version of the Lockheed swinging caliper (courtesy of Automotive Products PLC)

6.8 Some other caliper designs

Although not next in importance, it is convenient to consider here two of the branches of caliper design which have not been as popular as their proponents hoped; although differing considerably, they have in common the aims of using only a single hydraulic cylinder and thereby reducing cost, weight and the likelihood of fluid vapourisation.

First, there are what have been popularly known as the 'swinging' calipers, of which there are two designs, both using tapered linings on their pads. The Lockheed design (Fig. 6.3(vii)) employs a pressed steel caliper of more or less flat form, located on its mounting by a vertical pivot; the cylinder body is assembled into the caliper in the inboard position (Fig. 6.30). The pad backplates are identical but, as can be seen, bear linings which taper in opposite directions so that the plates remain parallel during brake operation. As the cylinder applies the inboard pad directly, the reaction against its location in the caliper causes the latter to pivot and apply a force to the outboard pad which, ignoring frictional losses, is equal to that exerted by the piston.

The position of the vertical pivot is so chosen that as the linings wear, so the degree of taper reduces until, when the pads are due for replacement, the linings are of approximately constant thickness. With this design, one caliper might be used with a number of alternative cylinders of differing bore diameter to serve a variety of applications; the manufacture of tapered pads however, has not been without its problems, nor has it been easy to ensure location of the plate at right angles to the disc whilst retaining free movement of the unsealed pivot.

The Girling swinging caliper (Fig. 6.31) (Fig. 6.3(viii)) incorporates pads which are tapered radially so its pivot or hinge pin is appropriately positioned; a sectional view (Fig. 6.32) shows that the moving pad is operated by a pushrod, containing an adjustment mechanism, by either a hydraulic piston or a handbrake mechanism, each of which moves a 4:1 lever through the medium of a balance beam. The hinge pin and the operating mechanism are sealed to retain lubricants and exclude water and dirt; the caliper pivots, in a similar manner to the Lockheed example, to apply the fixed pad to the disc when the plunger applies the moving pad. When new pad assemblies are fitted to this caliper, it is necessary to screw in the plunger instead of pressing it in, a fact not always understood at first by mechanics

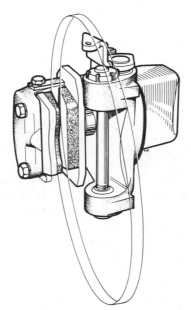

Fig. 6.31   The Girling swinging caliper, with hand operation for use at the rear (courtesy of Lucas Girling Ltd.)

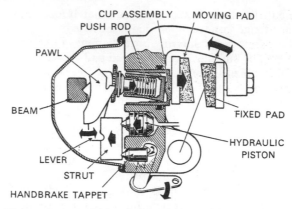

Fig. 6.32   The mechanism of the Girling swinging caliper (courtesy of Lucas Girling Ltd.)

who had not made themselves familiar with the working principles.

The second class of calipers to be considered under the above heading is peculiar to Girling and has been known as the 'Annette' or 'A' type (Fig. 6.3(ix)); it employs a single hydraulic cylinder, integral with the brake mounting, but this is double acting. A yoke plate slides in grooves machined on the cylinder body, and, in conjunction with a pad retainer or individual retaining pins, locates and supports the pad assemblies (Fig. 6.33); the outboard or direct piston operates the inboard pad directly while the inboard or indirect piston operates the outboard pad by way of the yoke plate.

Fig. 6.33   An example of the Girling A type caliper for front axle fitment

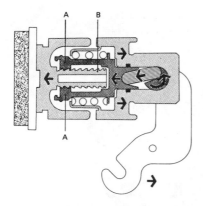

Fig. 6.34   One method of automatic adjustment for a hand brake mechanism incorporated into a Girling A type caliper   (courtesy   of   Lucas Girling Ltd.)

This caliper has been modified for dual hydraulic and mechanical operation, to provide for parking; the handbrake mechanism has been incorporated into the indirect piston in such a way (Fig. 6.34) that all the working parts are protected. When the handbrake lever is moved, an internal cam and push rod operates the direct piston by way of the two part strut; the reaction on the camshaft operates the indirect piston and the separation of the two pistons draws in brake fluid from the reservoir. Hydraulic operation of the brake causes part B of the strut to move with the indirect piston so that, when sufficient lining wear has occurred, the pawls A lift over the flanks of the teeth on part B, thus extending the strut automatically.

The way in which the pistons are retracted when new pads are to be fitted has changed during the life of this caliper; early examples have had a groove in the face of the direct piston, by means of which it could be turned 45° to disengage the adjustment mechanism and subsequently be turned back, later ones have had four shallow holes in the direct piston face by means of which the piston can be screwed back in as far as necessary.

The obvious drawback with this type of caliper is the unwanted friction which all too readily is likely to occur at the sliding contacts between the cylinder body and the yoke plate; this is liable to cause drag of the outboard pad, with consequent rapid wear. The use of different friction materials in the outboard and inboard positions is an expedient which is occasionally adopted to counter this and other problems.

6.9   Sliding calipers

Figure 6.3(vi) illustrates the principle of a sliding caliper of a type which, with many variations, is now very common; it has a fixed

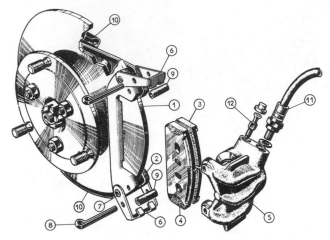

Fig. 6.35   The DBA series I caliper (courtesy of DBA SA)

mounting bracket and a sliding member which incorporates a single acting wheel cylinder. The first British brake of this kind is though to have been a Lockheed design, shown at the 1952 London Motor Show, but the first such design to go into production in quantity was the French made DBA Series I (Fig. 6.35) which appeared in 1962. It can be seen from the illustration that the pressed steel frame and mounting bracket locates the pad assemblies (which are all four slightly different, as referred to earlier in this chapter), while the caliper (which is of light alloy) only applies the clamping load to the pads; the pads are assembled into the caliper before this is placed in position in the frame and retained by the hinged clamps. Sliding calipers generally make little demand on space around and outboard of the disc, so may be easier to instal than opposed piston types in difficult cases.

Handbrake operation of this caliper is provided for by adding an external lever on the side of the cylinder body (Fig. 6.36) which presses on the inboard pad; the reaction through the caliper causes the outboard pad to be applied. To avoid excessive clearance between pads and disc of both front and rear calipers, the cylinders incorporate a friction device (Fig. 6.37) to limit the return movement of the piston under 'knock-back' conditions and maintain the desired pedal travel.

DBA series II calipers were generally similar to the earlier type but series III (Fig. 6.38) includes notable differences; the pads are now placed in the frame before the caliper is positioned and the caliper is then retained by sliding keys of anti-corrosion treated steel. One

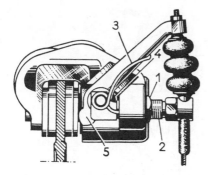

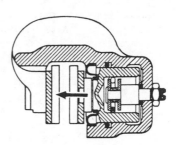

Fig. 6.36 Hand brake operation of the DBA series I caliper (courtesy of DBA SA)

Fig. 6.37 An 'anti knock-back' device used by DBA in a caliper piston (courtesy of DBA SA)

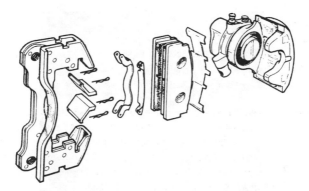

Fig. 6.38 The DBA series III caliper (courtesy of DBA SA)

development of this design uses light alloy for the cylinder which slots into a spheroidal graphitic cast iron caliper bridge, a handbrake mechanism (Fig. 6.39) is available and a two cylinder version of the composite construction allows for use with dual hydraulic systems.

A Teves design of sliding caliper seen in the early 1970s (Fig. 6.40) is similar to the series III DBA design in some ways; it has a frame combined with the mounting, which supports the pads and carries the reaction to the braking torque, while the caliper merely applies the clamping load. The caliper is, however, a steel pressing which houses the cast iron hydraulic cylinder and the grooves in which it slides on the frame are not parallel, but are circular arcs, so that the sliding member can freely align itself with the pads during brake operation.

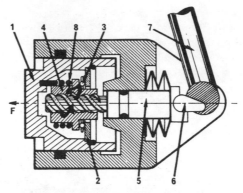

Fig. 6.39   The hand brake mechanism used by DBA in their series III caliper (courtesy of DBA SA)

Fig. 6.40   A Teves single cylinder sliding caliper (courtesy of Alfred Teves GmbH)

Sliding calipers, often of considerable size and with either one or two hydraulic cylinders, are also common in the USA.

All of these sliding caliper designs suffer more or less from the effects of friction, as contamination and corrosion affect their freedom of movement; a significant step forward, therefore was the introduction of an alternative design basis, wherein the relative location of the two major components is by two pins which can slide in holes with sealed-in lubrication. A Girling caliper of this type, designated Colette. but more generally known as a fist type, from the form of the sliding member, is shown (Fig. 6.41) with the two major components separated.

Fig. 6.41   *The major components of a Girling 'Colette' pin sliding caliper*

The combined mounting and frame which houses the pads also incorporates the two blind holes in which the pins locate; the caliper can be of two part construction, as shown, to benefit from the use of different materials, such as grey iron or light alloy for the cylinder and spheroidal graphite cast iron for the bridge, or may be in one piece. The pins on which the caliper slides are attached to it by cap screws so that, by unfastening one of these, the caliper can be swung back from the disc when pads are to be renewed, without exposing the sliding surfaces of the pins.

One of the pins is a close fit in the associated precisely machined bore and provides the principal location of the unit; the other pin may be rubber sleeved and provide secondary location whilst allowing for any deflection of the support bracket and preventing rattling. A special grease is used to lubricate these sliding surfaces and rubber dust covers are fitted to exclude dirt and water.

The provision of an integral handbrake mechanism is a straightforward matter with the Girling Colette design, the components being virtually identical with those illustrated in Fig. 6.34, but associated with a removable end cover to the hydraulic cylinder.

Other manufacturers also now produce pin sliding calipers which have between them, a considerable number of variations which need to be borne in mind when they are serviced. In some cases the pins have hexagon sockets and are screwed into the frame member; to exclude dirt and retain the lubricant, a rubber seal will usually be

Fig. 6.42   A Volkswagen single cylinder sliding caliper, part sectioned

fitted in the inner end of the open bore in the caliper and a rubber sleeve at the outer end (Fig. 6.42), the example shown being a Volkswagen design. The inboard pad of a Teves caliper of similar design (Fig. 6.43), has a spring clip which engages in the open end of the piston while the anti-rattle spring for the outboard pad is designed to hold it in place at the end of the fist; the pads can therefore be easily moved with the caliper once the pins have been removed, although their location is mainly achieved by the frame member.

In other cases, the pins fulful a dual role; besides being the means by

Fig. 6.43   A Teves pin sliding caliper

*Fig. 6.44   Another type of Teves pin sliding caliper, showing the clamp bolt which locks
the pins*

which the caliper slides with respect to the frame, they extend across
the frame and assist in locating the pads (Fig. 6.44). In this design, also
by Teves, the pins are retained in place by a pinch bolt but are also a
slight interference fit in the frame member; they therefore have to be
drawn out from the far end by the use of a slide hammer, screwed into
a threaded hole in the end of the pin, and subsequently driven back in
by the same means.

Sometimes the frame member is reinforced at the outboard side of
the disc (Fig. 6.45), sometimes it is not; as with all calipers, it is
necessary to ensure that, even when the maximum intended clamping

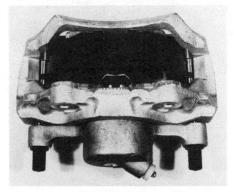

*Fig. 6.45   The same caliper as seen in Fig. 6.44, showing the reinforcement of the frame
member on the outboard side*

load is applied, the pads remain parallel to the disc. Various types of anti-rattle springs may be used and it is necessary to note carefully the manner in which these are fitted before the components are separated. Most—but not all—types of pin sliding caliper have an opening in the bridge through which the lining thickness can be easily inspected once the wheel has been removed; in one case at least, as referred to above, a gauge is supplied for checking lining thickness with the wheel still in place.

6.10 Parking

Already, mention has been made of a number of cases of a handbrake mechanism which is integral with the disc brake caliper and applies the same pair of pads as are used for service braking; there are, however, many other cases where the means for parking or braking in an emergency, such as hydraulic brake failure, is by the use of a self-contained mechanical brake, attached to the hydraulic caliper. One such brake, the second design produced by Girling, is shown (Fig. 6.46) and it can be seen that a lever assembly, operated by the

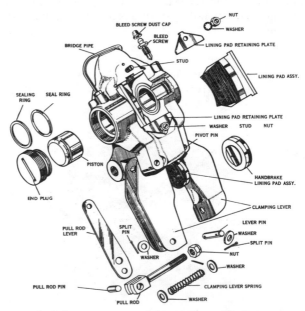

Fig. 6.46   An early Girling one piece parallel gap caliper with a lever operated parking brake attachment (courtesy of Lucas Girling Ltd.)

handbrake cable, clamps a pair of pad carriers against the disc to develop the required braking torque.

Disc handbrake mechanisms of this general type were notoriously poor in performance and great difficulty was often experienced in satisfying the examiner when a statutory annual test had to be passed; there were a number of reasons for this, including the following.

The small linings used for parking brake purposes were usually made of friction material chosen particularly for its high friction level; the material, however, not being in normal use, did not get bedded in to the disc or conditioned by heat in the usual way, so seldom performed as expected and could easily be overheated if used from a high speed in an emergency. The lever system needed regular maintenance of a high standard if it was to remain efficient, particularly in view of its exposure, and to ensure that a reserve of handbrake lever travel was retained close adjustment of the linings to the disc was necessary.

Dunlop brought out a self-adjusting parking brake (Fig. 6.47), in succession to an earlier one of simpler type; with this design it was possible to use a high mechanical advantage since the free travel never exceeded a very small amount. Enclosure of the levers and the pawl and ratchet type adjustment mechanism ensured that the lubricant was preserved and contamination prevented so the unit was much more effective than earlier types; it has been adopted by Girling, who

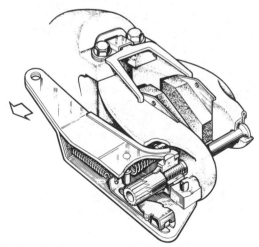

Fig. 6.47   The later form of Dunlop automatically adjusted hand brake mechanism (courtesy of Lucas Girling Ltd.)

acquired this and other designs from Dunlop, and is used by them in connection with all-disc installations of opposed piston type.

Reference has already been made, in the section on disc design, to the use of a small duo-servo drum brake housed in a disc of 'top hat' section for parking purposes; provided proper maintenance is given, this also is an effective means of fulfilling this requirement on an all-disc installation. The other way of using a drum brake for this purpose, found rarely in Europe but more commonly in the USA, is to mount it in the drive line, usually at the rear of the gearbox; since the torque developed is multiplied by the final drive ratio, holding power is not lacking but stresses in the drum are increased by the high rotational speed and a drive line failure makes the brake ineffective.

6.11 Motor cycle disc brakes

In 1966, fourteen years after disc brakes were first seen on racing cars, they brought success to a racing motor cyclist who used a light alloy version of the Lockheed PD26 opposed piston caliper, mounted on the left hand leg of the front forks of his machine. Subsequently, as with cars, disc brakes became established in production for road-going machines and their use steadily extended to most models in each manufacturer's range; it is convenient to include a description of them in this chapter.

Although opposed piston calipers were used for a time, they never found such wide application as on cars; instead, single cylinder calipers of pin sliding type found wide favour, anticipating their growing popularity on cars. The motor cycle market is currently dominated by Japan, but the four leading disc brake manufacturers in that country have, for a number of years, had licensing arrangements with Girling and their products show signs of European influence.

A typical small brake unit (Fig. 6.48) consists of a mounting plate, attached by means of two bolts to the fork member, and the caliper itself which is a light alloy casting; the outboard pad is applied directly by the piston and the reaction force causes the caliper to slide on the two pins on which it is carried, which are adjacent to the mounting bolts, so that the inboard pad also is applied.

The pads used in this caliper have rectangular backplates onto which anti-squeal shims are clipped; they are supported in the caliper on two bolts which pass through holes in their upper edge. Access to these pad retaining bolts, which are inserted from the inboard face of the caliper, is gained by dismounting the caliper and mounting bracket together from the fork leg. The reduced bulk of the inboard part of a single cylinder caliper, such as this, facilitates installation of the brake just as is the case with a car.

Fig. 6.48   A small single piston motor cycle disc brake

Other calipers used are more akin to car practice, in having an open gap through which the pads can be inserted or withdrawn; the example shown (Fig. 6.49) has a dirt shield in position over the gap, but this incorporates a clear plastics insert to permit inspection, and the underside of the cover is fitted with an anti-rattle spring which bears on the pads when it is in position. The pads are retained by conventional pins and an anti-squeal shim is often fitted; the linings sometimes have grooves, which may be either parallel or radial, across their surfaces to help disperse water.

The third example (Fig. 6.50) is of advanced design, and is based on the Girling Colette type brake; a frame which is integral with the mounting bracket supports the pads and resists the reaction to the braking force developed while the single cylinder caliper, which slides on sealed pins, only has to apply the clamping load. Disc brakes such as this are commonly used in pairs at the front, but it is then necessary to dismount one of the brakes when the wheel has to be removed.

The final example (Fig. 6.51) is of a Honda mechanical brake, as used on certain of their smaller models; it is operated by a cable which actuates an enclosed ball and ramp mechanism in the outboard part of the caliper to apply the adjacent pad directly. The inboard pad is fixed in the caliper body but this is pivoted to its mounting on the fork leg so that, under the reaction force, the caliper swings to equalise the

*Fig. 6.49   A medium size motor cycle caliper, having a single cylinder and a dirt shield
over the gap through which the pads may be removed*

forces on the two pads. An automatic adjustment mechanism is built
into the expander so that most of the hand lever travel can be utilised
for operating the expander and a high mechanical advantage can be
incorporated.

Motor cycle disc brake pads sometimes have a shallow groove
around their edge, parallel to the backplate, to indicate the point at
which lining wear necessitates replacement.

6.12 Trends

Returning to consideration of car disc brakes, the pin-sliding type of
caliper is—as stated above—steadily becoming more widely
established, with considerable variation in matters of detail; enclosure
of the slides minimises the force required to move the caliper so the
chance of drag is reduced and equalisation of the forces on the pads is
more nearly achieved. Because the caliper is better able to respond to
any disc run-out which may be present, 'knock-off' of the pads is
reduced and free travel of the brake pedal is not increased.

In conjunction with the above trend, linings for pads are tending to
become narrower radially and longer circumferentially; this seems to

Fig. 6.50   A large motor cycle disc brake modelled on the Girling Colette type

Fig. 6.51   A Honda mechanically operated caliper, pivoted on the suspension unit

be associated with an increased tendency to judder (low frequency, high amplitude vibration) which is receiving considerable attention from the vehicle and component manufacturers. It is thought that, although the compression of the disc when the brake is applied is very small in amount, the tangential forces may cause a wave-shaped deflection of the disc in the circumferential direction which the longer pads cannot conform to. There may, therefore, have to be developments to eliminate this judder which will affect one or more of the components involved in ways which cannot yet be foreseen.

As has been noted, calipers can often be made of combinations of materials each chosen for its particular properties; weight is a major consideration (especially since most brakes, being adjacent to the wheel, are unsprung), which has led Girling and others to make appropriate use of light alloy, and cost is another—either in terms of the direct cost of the material or perhaps in relation to the forming or machining costs involved.

Because sliding calipers with the hydraulic cylinder(s) contained only in the inboard position eliminate the brake fluid passage in the caliper bridge, maximum brake fluid temperatures are reduced and the likelihood of fluid vapourisation has been diminished; the introduction of asbestos-free linings has, however, somewhat increased the heat flow through the pad and piston so work on thermal insulation layers is in hand.

7

Braking medium weight vehicles

7.1 Introduction

The smallest commercial vehicles—light delivery vans—have braking installations based on car practice, although brake sizes may be a little larger than for cars; there is, however, a considerable class of somewhat larger vehicles which is fitted with brakes specially made for the purpose, but which does not approach the maximum permitted gross weight for the number of axles involved. In general, these vehicles are hydraulically braked, with servo assistance for the driver, so any exceptions will be ignored; direct air braking equipment will be considered in Chapters 8 and 9.

At the light end of the range, drum brakes continue to be used on both axles in many cases, with two leading shoe (duplex) units at the front and either leading/trailing (simplex), full two leading (duo duplex) or duo-servo ones at the rear; although exactly similar in concept to those fitted on cars, brakes for these vehicles are more sturdily constructed, because delivery duty and urban running—the common conditions of usage—involve a higher than average number of brake applications per mile at a higher load factor than most normal car duty. Brake backplates will therefore be stronger, as will the shoes, expanders and adjusters, to resist repeated heavy loadings (including frequent reversing), whilst the location of components and their attachment to each other will be designed with this same thought in mind; in matters of detail, however, there are some interesting differences from the brakes already described.

One brake that serves as a good example of how much difference details make is that long made by Vauxhall Motors Ltd. and used on Bedford trucks (Fig. 7.1); this is a leading and trailing shoe brake, but the shoes are articulated to an anchor pin by means of pairs of links, instead of pivoting directly on the pin or sliding on a fixed abutment. This articulated type of shoe mounting originated from the USA, its use by Bedford stemming from General Motors' ownership of that company; the Huck brake, as it is called, is made by Bedford in large

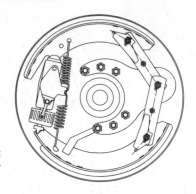

Fig. 7.1   A Bedford Huck type truck brake (courtesy of Bedford Commercial Vehicles)

numbers and incorporates Lockheed wheel cylinders—double acting at the front and generally of transverse type (operating a wedge and roller expander) at the rear, as in the example shown.

For a lining coefficient of friction of 0.38, the Bedford Huck brake is designed to have a brake factor of 2.5, the work rate for the leading shoe being considered to be four times that of the trailing shoe. Design features which contribute to this factor are the considerable angle through which the expander has been moved, relative to the line through the anchor pin and the brake centre, and the lining positions; of necessity, the two shoes differ considerably and the individual shoe return springs are of different stiffnesses.

The Huck brake offers the benefits of even lining wear and an enhanced brake factor usually associated with a sliding shoe type brake, but without the problems of variable abutment friction; the lining thicknesses when new are related to the work rates mentioned and the thick and thin paired linings are a characteristic feature. The general use of a transverse wheel cylinder at the rear makes it easy to provide for parking; either a mechanical connection can be made through the cylinder or a spring brake unit can be fitted. The spring plates assembled to the shoe links are to provide frictional restraint under the influence of inertia forces on the shoes and they should not be lubricated.

One variant of this brake which is commonly found in service has a Huck type leading shoe with a fixed pivot type trailing shoe.

7.2 Automatic adjustment

As with car drum brakes, automatic adjustment is becoming more common, either to comply with legislation or to reduce maintenance costs, and Fig. 7.2 shows a neat approach to the design of a

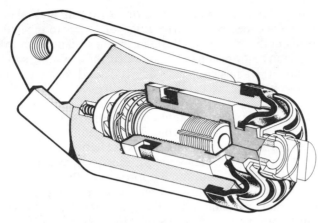

Fig. 7.2   The Girling drive ring type automatic adjuster (courtesy of Lucas Girling Ltd.)

mechanism for this purpose. This example is by Girling and it is situated entirely within the wheel cylinder, where it is lubricated by the brake fluid and protected from outside contamination; it 'is equally suitable for leading and trailing shoes, so may be used at either front or rear.

The illustration shows a part section of a complete wheel cylinder and it will be appreciated that there is no external indication of the internal complexity. The piston, to which a manual adjuster ring is assembled, is hollow and is threaded so that it can be screwed onto the adjuster shaft; the thread on this shaft is grooved and it has a longitudinal drilling, these features being designed to facilitate bleeding. A tappet, slotted to accept the shoe web, locates in the outer end of the piston and a rubber dust cover protects the cylinder bore.

Attached to the inner end of the adjuster shaft is a component having a cone surface, which seats in the counterbore at the end of the cylinder, and an adjuster helix; assembled onto this helix is an internally grooved drive ring, coned on its outer surface and also seating in the counterbore, being biased into contact with this seat by the load spring. Between the end of the adjuster shaft and the end of the counterbore is another spring; this ensures that an axial load is maintained on the threads which couple the piston and the shaft.

When hydraulic pressure operates the wheel cylinder, the piston and adjuster shaft assembly move together, the latter lifting away from its tapered seat; the drive ring, however, is made with a pre-determined clearance between its spiral grooves and the flanks of the adjuster helix so that, unless the normal lining-to-drum clearance is exceeded, it is not disturbed. When excessive piston movement occurs because of lining wear, the helix lifts the drive ring and relieves the pressure on the cone seat; the drive ring is then free to unwind along the helix under the influence of the load spring until piston movement ceases. As soon as the piston starts to return, the drive ring seats again and it is now the adjuster shaft which is caused to rotate, once the clearance between the helix and the drive ring has been taken up, and thus wind out the piston.

The helix angle is so chosen that only a proportion of the excessive clearance is taken up on any one occasion; the adjustment is therefore made most quickly when the clearance is greatest—as when the brake has been stripped and rebuilt—and progressively reduces in amount as the normal running condition is approached. By this means, over-adjustment is avoided, even when high working temperatures have caused the drum to expand. When the adjustment has to be slackened off, the manual ring is used; access to this when the drum is in place being gained through an opening in the backplate, normally sealed by an adjustment grommet.

A two leading shoe brake which incorporates this adjustment mechanism (Fig. 7.3), uses sliding type shoes; these do not need steady springs because of the design of the return springs, the ends of which press the shoes against the backplate. As can be seen, the cylinder body castings are shaped so that an angled abutment for the shoes is readily formed, so as to achieve the advantage of a high shoe factor, as referred to in Chapter 3. The brake backplate has openings through which the lining thickness can be examined, opposite the mid point of

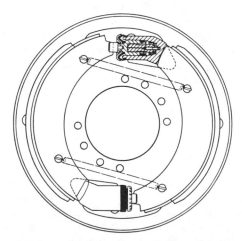

Fig. 7.3   A two leading shoe (duplex) Girling truck brake incorporating the drive ring type of automatic adjustment (courtesy of Lucas Girling Ltd.)

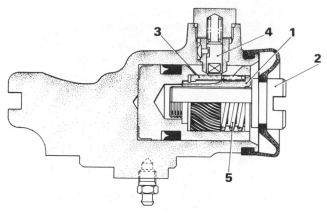

Fig. 7.4   A Lockheed design of automatic adjustment incorporated inside the wheel cylinder (courtesy of Automotive Products PLC)

the shoe platforms, as well as openings through which the manual adjuster rings can be turned.

Another type of brake using this same adjustment will be described later in this chapter.

Lockheed provides automatic adjustment on similar brakes by means of a mechanism also located within the wheel cylinder (Fig. 7.4); the piston is hollow and contains an assembly of adjuster nut 1 and sleeve 3, into which is screwed the threaded adjuster screw 2. The adjuster nut has longitudinal splines on its outer surface, on which the adjuster sleeve slides; an overload spring 5 is compressed by the sleeve, which is retained by a spring ring. A spring loaded adjuster pawl 4, housed in a boss on the wall of the wheel cylinder, passes through a slot in the piston to engage steeply angled helical grooves of asymmetrical cross section, formed on the outer surface of the adjuster sleeve.

During movement of the piston and adjuster assembly, the pawl is lifted against its spring as it rides up the flank of the helix; only when the clearance is sufficient to necessitate adjustment does the pawl drop into the next helical groove so that, when the brake is released, it causes the adjuster sleeve and nut to turn and wind out the adjuster screw. Should piston return occur under load, as when rolling back on a hill with the brakes on, when damage could be caused to the pawl and grooves, the overload spring compresses a little to relieve the load.

This mechanism can be incorporated into each cylinder of a two leading shoe front brake; the associated rear brake which is produced

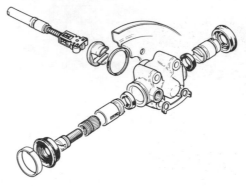

*Fig. 7.5   The Lockheed in-piston automatic adjustment used in a wedge type brake
expander (courtesy of Automotive Products PLC)*

is of similar two leading shoe design, but has an alternative upper
wheel cylinder. This is double acting (Fig. 7.5), with a solid piston
adjustment to the rear shoe and a wedge type expander between the
pistons which is operated by a spring brake unit; when the parking
brake mechanism is operated, this brake reverts to leading/trailing
shoe characteristics.

7.3 Duo-servo brakes

Duo-servo drum brakes have been widely used on vehicles of the
category considered for some years and there are some noteworthy
variations. In many cases, adjustment is carried out by varying the
length of the strut which links the primary and secondary shoes, by
turning a toothed wheel attached to the threaded female portion; this
may be done manually, as for the Lockheed example shown (Fig. 7.6),
or automatically. The corresponding brake with automatic adjustment has a number of additional components associated with the
secondary shoe (Fig. 7.7); these link a pawl plate, which rests on the
ratchet toothed adjuster wheel, to the anchor pin and function when
the vehicle is braked in reverse. When this happens, the roles of the
two brake shoes are interchanged and the secondary shoe lifts away
from the anchor pin by an amount which depends on the lining-to-
drum clearance, operating the linkage referred to as it does so; as
lining wear increases, the pawl plate eventually drops into the next
tooth on the adjuster wheel and rotates it when the brake is released,
to effect the adjustment.

Differences are seen in the next example (Fig. 7.8), which is a
manually adjusted duo-servo brake for industrial vehicles, made by

Fig. 7.6   A Lockheed duo-servo brake for light CVs, with manual adjustment (courtesy of Automotive Products PLC)

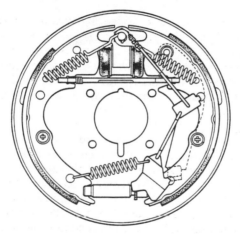

Fig. 7.7   Automatic adjustment on a small Lockheed duo-servo brake, otherwise as seen in Fig. 7.6 (courtesy of Automotive Products PLC)

Deutsche Perrot-Bremse GmbH of Mannheim, in West Germany; the products of this company are noted for their robust construction and a number of their characteristic features can be identified here. The backplate is of cast steel, with an integral abutment for the shoes of full width, against which the ends of the platforms rest; this abutment also anchors the shoe return springs and acts as a heat shield for the double acting wheel cylinder.

The brake shoes are of cast construction and the adjustment mechanism is located within the cast housing bolted to the backplate; it functions as a link between the primary and secondary shoes as in

Fig. 7.8   A Perrot manually adjusted duo-servo brake (courtesy of Deutsche Perrot-Bremse GmbH)

the previous examples and incorporates a centralising spring to hold the shoes clear of the drum when the brake is released. Larger versions of this brake sometimes have an adjuster stem protruding behind the backplate, instead of using a toothed wheel.

Perrot also make an automatically adjusted duo-servo brake of particularly neat design (Fig. 7.9), which is suitable for either road going or industrial vehicles; the principal feature of interest is the adjuster assembly which, whilst being free to slide and transmit force between the primary and secondary shoes, also incorporates two adjuster screws each having a toothed adjuster wheel. Mounted on the unit is a symmetrical adjuster plate loaded by twin return springs; this plate is so shaped that at either end the face of the adjuster wheel can contact it after a pre-determined clearance has been taken up.

The unit operates equally for either direction of wheel rotation, the primary shoe at the moment causing the adjuster assembly to slide in its frame, thus taking up the clearance between the adjacent adjuster wheel and the adjuster plate; the adjuster assembly continues to slide until the secondary shoe is in full contact with the drum, this movement being related to the lining-to-drum clearance. During this further movement, the adjuster wheel adjacent to the primary shoe presses against the adjuster plate, causing it to turn on the near pivot and ride up the flank of a tooth on the further adjuster wheel; if the clearance from the drum is sufficient, the plate will then drop into the next tooth space. When the brake is released, the adjuster plate will be

Fig. 7.9   An automatically adjusted duo-servo brake made by Deutsche Perrot for light CVs (courtesy of Deutsche Perrot-Bremse GmbH)

returned by the springs and the adjuster wheel will be rotated one tooth pitch, taking up the adjustment as the sliding assembly is centralised.

It is convenient at this point to describe another Perrot brake (Fig. 7.10), which is of interest; this is a hydraulically operated leading/ trailing shoe brake for rear axles. Adjacent to the fixed double acting wheel cylinder (which is protected by a shield from heat radiated from the braking path of the drum) is a self-adjusting strut which maintains the shoes at a constant clearance from the drum; this incorporates a spring loaded pawl which drops into successive teeth on one of the members as lining wear takes place. The shoe platforms are in contact with an abutment cast integrally with the backplate, as seen above (Fig. 7.8), but their tips rest against a flat cam which can be rotated by the parking brake mechanism but which also has limited freedom to slide circumferentially; when the parking brake control is operated and the shoes are expanded, any tendency of the drum to rotate causes the abutment force of what is at that moment the leading shoe to be transmitted through the strut to the other shoe, the pistons meanwhile sliding within the sheel cylinder without any displacement of fluid. This brake therefore acts as a duo-servo brake for parking purposes, giving great holding power for a moderate input, but as a leading/trailing shoe brake in normal use, having greater stability of output over the working temperature range.

Fig. 7.10   A Perrot brake of leading/trailing (simplex) type when operated by the hydraulic wheel cylinder but acting as a duo-servo brake when operated by the parking system (courtesy of Deutsche Perrot-Bremse GmbH)

To conclude this section on duo-servo brakes, mention should be made of a Lockheed design for the larger medium weight trucks, the parking brake mechanism of which is noteworthy; the exploded view (Fig. 7.11) shows how the anchor, instead of being a solid pin, is formed with a central opening through which a cable can pass to a mechanical expander. This expander locates around the anchor and between the two shoes, being kept in place by a sliding connection to the secondary shoe; the lever into which the cable trunnion fits (it is retained by a spring clip) presses against a pin near the primary shoe tip while the reaction on the frame causes it to press against a similar pin on the secondary shoe. The expander can move a little, according to the direction of drum rotation, so the brake operates as a duo-servo unit for either the hydraulic or the manual mode of operation.

This btake can be self-adjusting, in a similar manner to the design described above, but the adjuster mechanism is then linked to the wheel cylinder by means of the hooked connecting link, instead of to the anchor. Each shoe is fitted with two steady springs to hold it against the backplate; the springs are of different stiffnesses and are painted different colours to distinguish between them, so that they can be fitted in the correct positions.

7.4 Full two leading shoe brakes

Duo-servo brakes are powerful and inexpensive but, as has been noted, lack stability when duty varies widely; attention has therefore

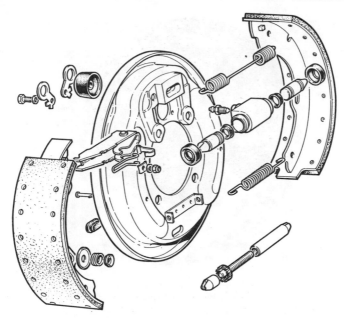

Fig. 7.11 A Lockheed duo-servo brake for medium weight CVs, having manual adjustment (courtesy of Automotive Products PLC)

turned to brakes which function as two-leading-shoe types for either direction of rotation, this type having the alternative name duo-duplex. Some of these types will be considered in Chapter 8, but there are others which it is appropriate to describe here.

The Lockheed design, examined above, which incorporates automatic adjustment within the wheel cylinder can easily be adapted to function as a two leading shoe type for either direction of rotation by equipping the backplate with two double acting wheel cylinders; if required, one of these can incorporate a wedge type expander for parking, as already referred to. When this brake is applied, all four pistons move to lift the shoes towards the drum, any rotation of which then causes the shoes to move with it until they abut at their trailing end; the abutment forces are then supported partly by the pistons and partly by the cylinder bodies. Both shoes will therefore function as leading shoes for either direction of rotation.

Girling have two relevant designs of duo-duplex brake, one of which is the other version of that described at the beginning of this chapter, being a two leading shoe brake with drive ring adjuster; in this alternative configuration (Fig. 7.12), two interconnected single acting wheel cylinders, each with internal automatic adjustment and

Fig. 7.12   A Girling duo-duplex brake, incorporating drive ring type automatic adjustment (courtesy of Lucas Girling Ltd.)

housed in a single casting, and a double acting cylinder are used to operate the brake. The pistons in the double acting cylinder are solid, that for the rear shoe being in two parts; between these two parts is incorporated, as in previously similar cases, an air operated wedge type expander for parking.

The other Girling brake is a unique design of particularly strong construction (Fig. 7.13); two double acting hydraulic wheel cylinders operate the shoes in conventional manner, to achieve two leading-shoe operation for either direction of drum rotation, but the adjustment and parking application is effected by components entirely separate from these cylinders. The forged steel torque plate carries, in addition to the wheel cylinders (which may be fitted with heat shields), an adjuster assembly and a mechanical expander of cone and roller type, as used in the original Girling mechanical brake; these two units lie parallel to the cylinders, only the adjuster tappets being directly in contact with the shoe tips.

The torque plate also has two fixed shoe abutments on which the shoe tips rest adjacent to the mechanical expander; the abutment forces are therefore carried either by these fixed points or by the adjuster assembly, without having to be transmitted through the hydraulic components (Fig. 7.14). Individual adjusting screws are provided for the two shoes and on each of the tappets, beside the shoe web, rests a forged steel shoe carrier which, at its other end, is

Fig. 7.13   A Girling H2LS duo-duplex brake (courtesy of Lucas Girling Ltd.)

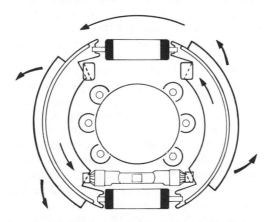

Fig. 7.14   A diagrammatic illustration of the principal design features of the Girling
H2LS brake (courtesy of Lucas Girling Ltd.)

supported by the mechanical expander; the carriers can be seen in Fig. 7.13 but have been omitted from Fig. 7.14 for clarity.

At the centre of the arc of each shoe carrier is a short adjustable strut which contacts the underside of the shoe platform; on assembly this is set so as just to touch the shoe when the brake is released. The shoe carriers are the means by which the mechanical expander applies the shoes to the drum for parking or emergency purposes, independently of the normal actuation. For either direction of drum rotation, each shoe is able to slide over its strut until it abuts at the trailing end; two leading shoe action is therefore still obtained although, as the applied force is not at the shoe tips, at a somewhat reduced brake factor.

A third Girling design of full two leading shoe brake, although sometimes found on vehicles of the medium weight category, and often hydraulically operated, will be described in the next chapter.

7.5 Disc brakes

The year 1956 has already been featured in Chapter 6 as being a significant one in the history of the disc brake, because of the two production cars which, during it, first fitted this type; there was also that year, however, the application of four cylinder Girling calipers to single deck buses belonging to a Midlands company, which later extended the fitment to its motorway coaches. Various other limited production or experimental installations were developed by Girling and by Lockheed during the next few years, but it seems that none of them was wholly satisfactory and most of the vehicles concerned were eventually converted back to drum brakes.

One of the numerous factors involved in this failure of the disc brake to establish itself on commercial vehicles was, undoubtedly, the lack of a really suitable friction material at that time for the application. Having only just developed disc brakes for light and medium weight cars, an attempt was made by the brake manufacturers to jump to medium weight commercial or public service vehicles; the best friction material available for the duty level envisaged was, however, low in friction over part of the working temperature range. To develop the braking torque required, therefore, it was necessary to design calipers with two or four large diameter cylinders, and even to fit two of these large and very heavy calipers per disc.

The weight and cost of such an installation was, therefore, considerable and with twin calipers in use only about half the disc was exposed for cooling, which was, consequently, impaired; the heat flow into the hubs was therefore excessive and bearing problems resulted. There were also the usual development problems to be overcome; the considerable change in scale meant that the engineers concerned were unable to apply the same standards as had only just been established for the limited number of car installations completed. The market for disc brakes for commercial and public service vehicles is, of course, very limited by comparison with that for cars so for many years only low priority was given to projects for the development of such large brakes.

For a number of years in the late 1950s and early 1960s a van, even when based on a car having front disc brakes, retained drum brakes as being thought more appropriate to its sphere of activity; gradually, however, the use of the equivalent disc brake became common on the car derived vans and, eventually, on the larger vans, using the larger size car brakes at the front. There also began to be a fresh approach to the design of disc brakes for the medium weight vehicles, hydraulic units such as those by Deutsche Perrot-Brense (Fig. 7.15) being among those to be tried extensively by UK and European vehicle manufacturers; more suitable friction materials became available and, gradually, experience of design, manufacture and application was gained and confidence built up.

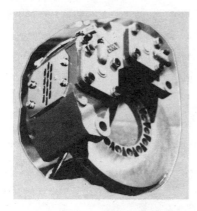

Fig. 7.15   A Deutsche Perrot CV disc brake

In line with the development of car disc brakes, the design of larger calipers has tended towards single sided sliding units with one or two cylinders in the inboard part. A Teves design (Fig. 7.16) introduced some years ago, for use with a ventilated disc, shows the pads to be supported by the mounting plate while the floating fist type caliper slides on pins; the two cylinders are fed from separate hydraulic circuits. The pin sliding principle is also followed by DBA in its PL2 caliper (Fig. 7.17), which is offered with a range of five diameters for the two hydraulic cylinders; this is designed for independent supply to the cylinders and is claimed to be 30% lighter than a drum brake of similar torque capacity and duty capability.

As an alternative to the sliding caliper, Knorr-Bremse GmbH of Munich, in West Germany, developed a pivoted or swinging caliper

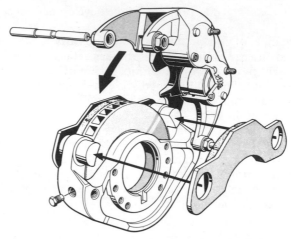

Fig. 7.16   A Teves pin sliding CV disc brake (courtesy of Alfred Teves GmbH)

Fig. 7.17   The DBA type PL2 disc brake for medium weight CVs (courtesy of DBA SA)

(Fig. 7.18), having a similar disposition of the pivot to the Girling car design, but differing in other respects. The caliper incorporates twin hydraulic cylinders which operate the inboard pad directly, one of these cylinders including a mechanical actuator for parking; the pads, which are initially constant thickness, are able to pivot somewhat as they wear so may adopt a radial taper in the intermediate period of their life; as the linings approach the acceptable limit of wear, the pads are constrained by the caliper frame and the piston faces (Fig. 7.19) to wear parallel. More recent designs by Knorr are in line with more conventional practice.

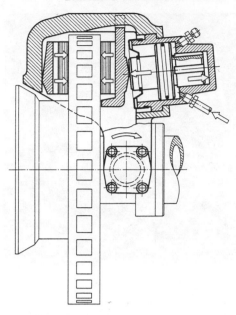

Fig. 7.18   A Knorr design of 'swinging' disc brake for trucks (courtesy of Knorr Bremse GmbH)

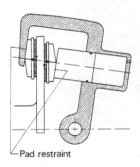

Pad restraint

Fig. 7.19   The Knorr CV caliper seen in Fig. 7.18 with the pads in the fully worn condition (courtesy of Knorr Bremse GmbH)

It is not always easy with a disc brake to develop the required torque within the limited space available inside the wheel specified by the vehicle manufacturer. One approach to this problem is to use a twin disc brake as developed by the Italian subsidiary of Valeo; the caliper (Fig. 7.20) is of cast iron and is, in effect, two fairly conventional calipers made as one, making for a heavy and bulky installation. Dunlop has experimented with a multi-disc caliper, heat dissipation being undoubtedly a potential problem.

Fig. 7.20   The Valeo twin CV caliper (courtesy of Valeo SA)

*Fig. 7.21   The hydrualically operated Girling reaction beam caliper for trucks,
incorporating a mechanical parking mechanism (courtesy of Lucas Girling Ltd.)*

Girling has evolved a disc brake which it designates its Reaction
Beam type (Fig. 7.21), which is aimed at the commercial vehicle
market; it features pads which are largely located and supported by
the mounting plate, which also houses the pins on which the load
applying assembly slides, and are held in position by the two retaining
pins which can be seen. The inboard part of the caliper incorporates

either twin hydraulic cylinders (as in this example), supplied by separate circuits, or two mechanical expanders if the brake is actuated by air; the outboard pads are applied by the movement of the caliper reacting to the direct force on the inboard pads. The pads can readily be inspected through the open gap of the caliper and anti-rattle springs are positioned between the backplates and the retaining pins; pad replacement is a quick and simple procedure once the wheel has been removed. The mechanical actuation incorporated into one cylinder in the illustration is similar to those described for car disc brakes; it is used with rear calipers for parking purposes.

The air operated version of the Reaction Beam caliper, intended for use on the heavier trucks, will be mentioned in the next chapter.

Undoubtedly, hydraulically actuated disc brakes will become increasingly common on medium weight vehicles as experience is accumulated, reliability is demonstrated and confidence in them is gained; the single sided sliding caliper seems likely to predominate for the foreseeable future, but there will certainly be numerous developments and refinements in matters of detail to vary the types at present on the market.

7.6 Brake actuation

Much that has already been written about hydraulic braking systems in Chapter 5 applies equally to the actuation of the brakes described in this chapter; the same principles are involved and many of the components are very similar, but for being on a larger scale and for being more robustly proportioned. There is no limit to the number or the size of the brakes that can be operated by fluid pressure; there is, however, the same constraint as was considered in some detail in connection with stopping the larger cars that, as gross weight increases, so does the fluid displacement required to apply the brakes also increase.

The driver therefore needs assistance when applying the brakes and, although vacuum servos were common on commercial vehicles and buses when petrol engines were still normal, they have largely been superseded on medium weight vehicles with the spread of diesel engines and the general reduction called for in brake pedal efforts. Vacuum servos could still be used on diesel engined vehicles if, as was at one time the case, a vacuum pump (otherwise known as an exhauster) is driven by the engine, but they become unacceptably large when a high boost ratio is required, because of the limit on the maximum pressure difference of which they make use.

The alternatives readily available for this class of vehicles are either

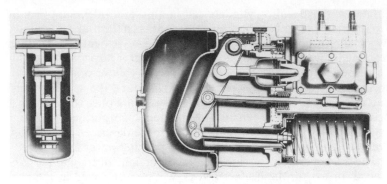

Fig. 7.22   The Clayton Dewandre direct acting vacuum servo for buses and trucks (courtesy of Clayton Dewandre Co. Ltd.)

the use of air pressure servo assistance, air/hydraulic actuation or a stored pressure system, the first two being by far the most common. The most direct way of using a servo is to apply it to the linkage between the brake pedal and the master cylinder, an example of this type by Clayton Dewandre being shown (Fig. 7.22; in this unit, the pull rod operated by the brake pedal is immediately above the servo cylinder. The system of levers employed causes the initial movement of the pull rod to operate the control valve at the top of the unit so that air under pressure is admitted to the servo cylinder; the piston then augments the effort which the pull rod is applying to the master cylinder, which may be of tandem type to serve front and rear brakes separately. The use of this type of unit was restricted by the need for it to be positioned close to the brake pedal.

A more widely used type of servo was that which, like the earlier vacuum servos for cars, was incorporated in the hydraulic system; the Clayton Dewandre ASR unit (Fig. 7.23), based on the American 'Airpak' design is a popular example. Of piston type, it comprises components exactly similar in function to those of the vacuum servos described in Chapter 5, but proportioned to deal with air at a pressure of up to about 6 bar (90 lb/in^2); an obvious visual difference is that the servo cylinder is contained within the air reservoir, the two sharing a common end plate, so that the unit is extremely compact. In service, the pressure generated by the driver in the master cylinder activates the servo control valve, admitting air under pressure to the servo cylinder or exhausting it, so that the output pressure from the slave cylinder is increased in the designed ratio; the compressed air equipment used in connection with this type of servo is described in Chapter 9.

As is the case with cars, this latter type of servo cannot be used with

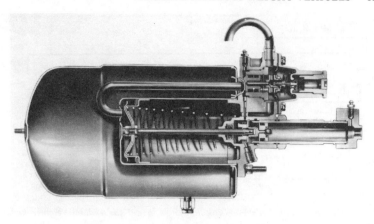

Fig. 7.23 An air/hydraulic servo for medium weight trucks (courtesy of Clayton Dewandre Co. Ltd.)

a tandem master cylinder, so does not enable current requirements, which call for a split hydraulic system, to be met. The direct acting servo described first can be used with a tandem master cylinder, but its use is in some cases limited by other legislation; the EEC, for example, permits the use of the single air system as the source of additional energy provided—if air pressure is lost—a pedal effort of 70 kgf (155 lbf) enables the driver to achieve a deceleration equal to that required from the secondary braking system. This requirement imposes an upper weight limit—which will depend on the braking equipment fitted—on vehicles using this type of servo, so an alternative system may be needed.

Whilst retaining hydraulic brakes, with two separate circuits supplied from a tandem master cylinder, twin circuit air pressure actuation can be used to ensure that a single failure, either in an air or a hydraulic circuit, will still leave braking of secondary degree available. Figure 7.24 shows a system layout, and it will be appreciated that a detailed description of the air compression, storage and control equipment appears in Chapter 9.

A dual concentric brake valve, operated by the brake pedal, allows air stored under pressure in individual reservoirs to be graduated in pressure by separate valves and passed to an air/hydraulic actuator (Fig. 7.25); this contains in one casing two separate air cylinders in tandem which directly apply the tandem master cylinder with its individual fluid reservoirs. A single air system failure thus leaves half the input to the master cylinder still effective; a single hydraulic system failure, on the other hand, leaves the full input to the master

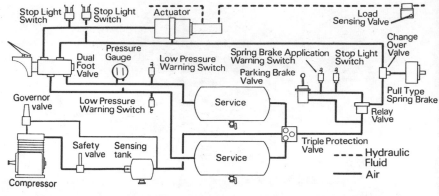

Fig. 7.24   *A dual air/hydraulic braking system layout for medium weight vehicles*

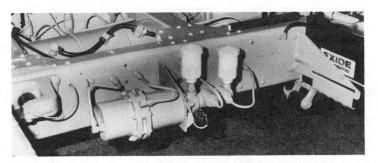

Fig. 7.25   *A dual air/hydraulic brake actuator (courtesy of Clayton Dewandre Co. Ltd.)*

cylinder acting on the remaining circuit (consideration of split braking systems is found in Chapter 11).

7.7 Stored energy

The third way of operating the brakes of medium weight vehicles is by the use of fluid, previously stored under pressure in hydraulic accumulators; Clayton Dewandre have developed such a system, under the name Full-Power, and Fig. 7.27 shows one of the accumulators dismantled. Each of these units consists of a steel pressure vessel containing a flexible bladder which, when the system is in the discharged condition, is held against the walls of the vessel by a charge of nitrogen inside it. The initial pressure of the nitrogen, before fluid is pumped in, is 55–57 bar (800–830 lbf/in^2); as fluid is pumped in,

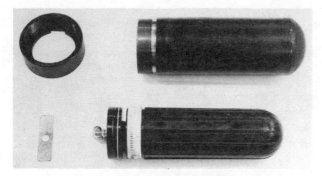

Fig. 7.26   A hydraulic accumulator for storing brake fluid under pressure

between the wall of the vessel and the bladder, the pressure rises to a maximum of 172 bar (2500 lbf/in^2) when fully charged.

The hydraulic accumulators used are of small diameter, because this limits the maximum stresses in the pressure vessel material; this also makes installation easier within a shallow space, such as under the floor of a bus. The required capacity may be obtained either by using an appropriate number of standard length accumulators in each circuit or by using a single unit of increased length. The fluid used in the system may be either mineral oil or conventional brake fluid, as preferred by the customer; whichever fluid is used, the materials used in the system—especially the rubber components—are specified accordingly and only the correct fluid must then be used for replenishment.

A two cylinder, opposed piston pump is shown (Fig. 7.27) dismantled to reveal the principal components; this example is intended for driving directly from the extended shaft of an air compressor. The eccentric near the centre of the picture is splined onto the shaft and drives the two very short connecting rods; these are shown above and below, the latter having the associated small diameter piston assembled to it. The cylinder body on the right contains the inlet and outlet ports; it also houses the unloader valves which relieve the pump of its load when the accumulators are fully charged. The two cylinders in the pump are independent and each supplies a separate group of accumulators, as will be seen when a typical layout is considered; they draw fluid from a common reservoir, but this is divided internally into two compartments, so that the integrity of each circuit is preserved.

The release of fluid from the accumulators at a controlled pressure is by means of either a dual foot valve or a hand parking control and, for simplicity, one of the latter units is illustrated (Fig. 7.28) and

Fig. 7.27   A fluid pump for a stored pressure system with its principal components

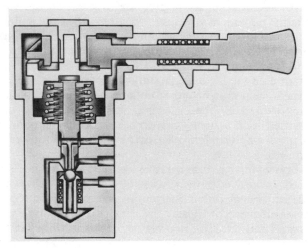

Fig. 7.28   A hand valve for control of parking with a stored pressure system (courtesy of Clayton Dewandre Co. Ltd.)

described; the dual foot valve contains two such units, operated by means of a balance beam to ensure that equal forces are applied to the two plungers, whereas the plunger of the parking control is depressed by rotating a cam plate. In the 'off' position of the control, the plunger is in its uppermost position, so that the central exhaust port in its stem is open, and fluid from the brake actuators can pass through and away to the reservoir through the return pipe; at the same time, fluid at accumulator pressure fills the chamber surrounding the inlet valve and holds it against its seat.

When the plunger is depressed it contacts the ball, closing the exhaust port and isolating the brake actuator supply pipe from the return pipe; further movement of the plunger then moves the ball and inlet valve downwards, so that fluid from the accumulator may pass from below the inlet valve and flow to the brake actuators. At the same time, the pressure in the outlet from the valve acts upwards on the plunger and, by way of the transfer port, upwards on the inlet valve which—since the latter is in contact with the plunger at this stage—augments the upward force on the plunger.

The cam plate in the parking control does not operate the plunger directly, but through the medium of a graduating spring; this is located between the cap—which can slide on the stem of the plunger—and a shoulder on the plunger itself. There is also a return spring which is located between the cap and the valve body, which serves only to return the plunger. The downward force which operates the plunger is, in the parking control, that which is exerted by the graduating spring, which is proportional to the angular movement of the cam plate by a hand lever; in the twin units of the dual foot valve, a similar pressure is experienced as a result of the driver's foot pressure.

When a brake application is made, delivery of fluid under pressure to the brakes continues as long as the downward force on the plunger exceeds the upward forces, the inlet valve being held open; as, however, the fluid pressure rises under the plunger and augments the upward force on the inlet valve (this is constant, subject only to fluctuations in accumulator pressure), the latter is gradually closed so that, with both exhaust port and inlet valve closed, the pressure in the outlet to the brakes remains constant.

Any subsequent change in the downward force on the plunger will now unbalance the valve assembly; an increase in the force will cause the pressure applied to the brakes to be increased, while a decrease in the force will cause a corresponding pressure decrease. When the parking control lever is returned to the 'off' position or the driver's foot is removed from the brake pedal, the plunger returns to its uppermost position and all pressure in the brake pipelines is released. When sufficient of the fluid stored under pressure has been used to lower the accumulator pressure to about 140 bar (2040 lbf/in²), the unloader valve ceases to function and pumping is recommenced to restore the full pressure.

It will be appreciated that the plunger movement is very limited, its range of travel remaining the same whatever pipeline pressure is being developed; however, in the case of the foot valve, the pedal travel is proportional to the pipeline pressure because it corresponds to the

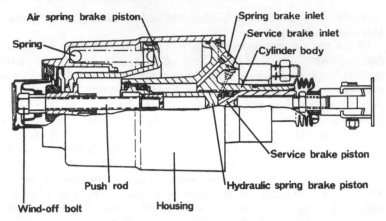

*Fig. 7.29   A sectional drawing of a spring brake unit for a stored pressure system
(courtesy of Clayton Dewandre Co. Ltd.)*

compression of the graduating spring. Because the brake operating
pressures are somewhat higher than those used in non assisted or
servo assisted systems (typically about 132 bar (1925 lbf/in^2) for 60%
braking efficiency), the actuators are correspondingly smaller.

As an example of one of the more complex actuators used, a spring
brake unit is shown (Fig. 7.29); this will be found to have many
similarities with the air operated spring brake units described in
Chapter 8. The cylinder body has a stepped bore, containing two
pistons, the service brake piston and the spring brake piston, each
served by an inlet port; the housing contains a large and powerful coil
spring which, through the medium of the air spring brake piston
(referred to below), the push rod and the two hydraulic pistons in
contact, exerts its force to apply the brake when there is no fluid
pressure acting in the unit. A spring brake unit such as this is used
with an 'inverted' parking control which delivers full pressure when in
the 'off' position; this pressure can then be reduced to zero in a
controlled manner by moving the control to the 'on' position.

In normal operation, when the system is charged up with the
parking control at 'on', the accumulators are fully charged but neither
the foot valve nor the parking control delivers any pressure to the
brakes; the springs in the spring brake units therefore continue to
apply the brakes with which they are associated and the vehicle
remains safely parked. If now the parking control is moved to the 'off'
position, full operating pressure is delivered to the spring brake inlets
and acts on the annular faces of the hydraulic spring brake pistons;
the latter then move to the left, compressing the springs and, by

relieving the force on the service brake pistons, release the brakes so that the vehicle may be driven off.

Operation of the brake pedal causes fluid under pressure to be delivered to the service brake inlets and act on the service brake pistons to apply the brakes; this same fluid pressure also acts on the central area of the hydraulic spring brake pistons and would—if the parking control had not been released—move them to the left and compress the springs. This feature therefore ensures that the brakes cannot each be subjected to the combined output of the spring and the service brake piston, which could cause damage to the brake components.

The air spring piston is for use in workshops, when it is necessary to move the vehicle and it is not convenient or possible to charge up the system so that the spring brake can be released in the usual way; an air supply can be applied to the spring housing, through an inlet not shown, to act upon the air spring brake piston and compress the spring.

Having described the more important of the individual components, consideration may now be given to a typical way in which these are incorporated into a workable system, such as that shown in diagrammatic form (Fig. 7.30), which is intended for a bus. It can be seen that the one pump circuit stores fluid in three accumulators, arranged in parallel, for the front brakes while the other supplies two separate groups of accumulators; the group of three is for the rear brakes while that of two is for parking purposes. The first accumulator in each of the groups of three is supplied directly from the pump, so that pressure fluctuations in the pipeline are smoothed out and meaningful signals are given to the unloader valves in the pump; the other two accumulators in the groups of three, as well as the two for parking, are in each case protected by a non-return valve marked V, a view of such an accumulator installation is shown (Fig. 7.31).

From each group of accumulators, the pipelines continue through a filter (marked F in the diagram) to the controls, as appropriate; those for the foot brake pass to the dual foot valve, from whence the front brake line supplies straightforward actuators, while the rear brake line passes to the service inlets of spring brake units. From the parking control, the pipeline passes to the spring brake inlets of the spring brake units. The air supply pipeline to the spring brake units for use in workshops is also shown, as are connections to low pressure warning switches, pressure test points and the nitrogen charging system for the accumulators. The remaining pipelines to be mentioned are the return pipes from the controls to the reservoir; when fluid which has been passed under pressure to the brake

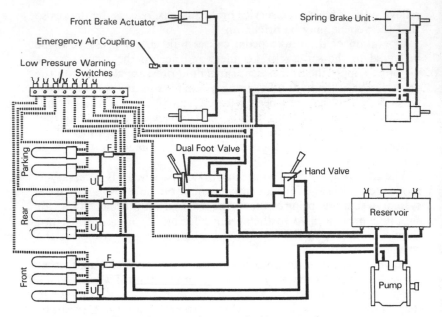

Fig. 7.30   *A stored pressure braking system layout*

actuators is released at the end of a brake application, it is returned at low pressure to the reservoir, from which it is subsequently drawn for recirculation.

7.8 System refinements

Reference has been made in this chapter to the use of divided brake systems, a feature introduced in order to promote safety by preserving the integrity of part of the braking system, should there be a failure in another part; this is in itself a topic needing careful consideration, since it relates to all classes of vehicles and a number of possibilities need to be examined, which will be done in Chapter 11. In the same chapter will be found a section on load sensing, which is of particular importance in connection with the braking of commercial vehicles, and another on systems for preventing wheel locking under conditions when the braking force developed by a wheel exceeds the available adhesion.

The brake actuation, whether it be hydraulic, air or mechanical, is an integral part of the braking installation of the vehicle and is a field within which there will certainly be many developments in the foreseeable future; the aim will be to match braking to adhesion more

Fig. 7.31   Hydraulic accumulators for a stored pressure braking system on a Public Service Vehicle (courtesy of Clayton Dewandre Co. Ltd.)

closely and to minimise the effects of exceeding the available adhesion. Medium weight vehicles form an extremely important and numerous class, including public service vehicles and medium distance delivery vehicles, with many manufacturers competing with each other; it will be interesting to observe the developments of the next decade.

8

Heavy truck brakes

8.1 Introduction

The boundaries between medium weight and heavy trucks are subject to differences of opinion; there will be cases when brakes described in the previous chapter are used on what are undoubredly heavy vehicles, and the reverse will also be found. This chapter is concerned with brakes generally fitted to axles for the maximum permitted loadings, which are used on maximum weight vehicles and which are mostly air operated; it should, however, be noted that while there is— and usually has been—considerable diversity in maximum weights between different countries, there has been rather less diversity—and less change—in permitted axle loadings, so the brakes themselves have not changed drastically. The scope of the chapter includes brakes used on trailers, which form a significant proportion of the commercial vehicle population.

The overall diameter of the brakes considered has in each case been chosen to suit the wheel size of the class of vehicles for which business was being sought and there has often been a constraint on the width of the brake, particularly in the case of front axle installations. In addition to changes in permitted vehicle loadings, the period covered has seen significant increases in the speeds at which heavy vehicles are permitted to travel; this has not so much affected the brake torque requirements, although minimum required decelerations have also increased, but it has forced the vehicle manufacturers to make room for wider brakes because of the greater energy which has to be dissipated. The increased width of brake shoes and drums has generally made it possible to keep duty levels—and hence, working temperatures—within acceptable limits, although there are a number of borderline cases which definitely benefit from the fitting of an auxiliary brake, such as described in Chapter 10.

As already noted, the brakes described in this chapter are mostly air operated, using air which is compressed, stored in reservoirs and used at a controlled pressure, as described in Chapter 9; with this means of actuation, the problem of achieving the required fluid displacement when braking a heavy, multi-wheeled vehicle is minimised, although there is a penalty in terms of system complexity.

8.2 Cam brakes

Undoubtedly the most common type of brake for heavy vehicles, when trailers are included, is the cam brake. This is a leading/trailing or simplex type of brake, with fixed pivot type shoes; it uses mechanical expansion of the shoe tips by means of a cam, attached to a cam shaft passing through the brake torque plate to an exterior actuator. Cam brakes received only a brief mention in Chapter 3, as having been used at one time on cars; they continued in general use on motor cycles until widely displaced by disc brakes but are still to be found, particularly on light weight machines. On heavy vehicles, cam brakes have retained their popularity on account of their simplicity and predictable performance characteristics (provided the linings are accurately made, so as to ensure good contact with the drums straightaway); they are commonly of rugged construction, as seen in the example shown (Fig. 8.1), which is by Kirkstall Forge (now part of GKN, the UK engineering group), and they are relatively inexpensive——an important consideration in the extremely competitive trailer market.

Whereas a single anchor pin is normal for small cam operated brakes, individual pins for the two shoes are now usual for the brakes used on heavy vehicles; the pins are of hardened steel and are locked in place in the torque plate, stainless steel bushings being sometimes

Fig. 8.1   A Kirkstall S cam brake

used to prevent seizure due to corrosion. In addition to holes for the anchor pins, the torque plate has a boss, bored out to carry the camshaft; bronze or other suitable bushes are usually fitted to reduce friction when the camshaft is rotated, but needle roller bearings may be used. Lubrication of the camshaft bearings may be provided on assembly with replenishment only at major overhauls, or grease nipples may be provided for routine attention; sealing of the bearings to retain the lubricant and exclude dirt and water is highly desirable.

Twin web shoes of fabricated or cast construction are usually located over the anchor pins; various forms of retention are then used, or it may be necessary to remove the anchor pins in order to dismantle the shoes from the brake. In other cases, the shoes do not fit over the anchor pins but merely abut against them, their tips having semi-circular cutouts; a cut out giving more than 180° of contact can be used with a D shaped pin, the shoes being swung back to permit removal. The better class brakes may have reinforced bosses lined with anti-friction bushes at the shoe pivots where these encircle the pins; at the other end of the scale, a plain hole or cutaway in the shoe webs is all that is provided in most fabricated shoes. At each shoe tip a roller is usually fitted to reduce the friction when the cam rotates to expand the shoes; in designing the form of the cam, the diameter of the roller has to be taken into account, as the perpendicular distance from the shoe pivot centre to the line of action of the shoe tip force will vary and depends on the form of both components. As an alternative approach, one Girling design of cam brake operates the shoes by way of tappets and struts, enclosed with the cam in a housing (Fig. 8.2); with this design, the line of action of the shoe tip force is always at the same distance from the pivot centre for both shoes. It is important that the cam is so designed that the rollers cannot pass the tips, even with linings worn down to the shoe platform.

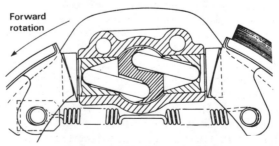

Fig. 8.2   A cross section of the expander of the Girling S cam brake of sliding shoe type (courtesy of Lucas Girling Ltd.)

Fig. 8.3   A Rockwell Q series Cam-Master brake (courtesy of Rockwell International Corporation, Automotive Businesses)

The Rockwell 'Q' series Cam-Master brake (Fig. 8.3) is another popular type of cam brake, which features ease of dismantling for servicing as a strong selling point; with the adjustment taken back to leave the cam at its lowest point, hand pressure on the bottom shoe is enough to deflect it sufficiently to permit the roller to be removed from the shoe tip with the fingers of the other hand, no tools being needed. The upper shoe can then be lifted so that its roller may be removed, this making it possible to unhook the shoe return spring; the lower shoe can then be swung back, away from the cam, through 180°, to relieve the tension in the two retainer springs which can then be uncoupled, leaving both shoes free.

From the operational point of view, one of the most important features is the design of the cam which, as noted above, cannot usually be considered in isolation; a simple, flat cam would have very unsuitable characteristics—the relationship between the amount of lift and the force exerted changing continually as it rotated—so the 'S' form of cam has been adopted. The usual practice currently, is to design the cam so that the shoes are lifted by equal amounts for each increment of camshaft rotation and equal forces are initially applied to the two shoes. In determining the force exerted by the cam, account must be taken of the changing angle between the brake actuator push rod and the camshaft lever as the stroke varies, the aim being to keep the force as nearly constant as possible; the 'S' shape which is commonly seen is the direct outcome of following these aims.

With equal forces initially applied at the shoe tips, the work rates of the two shoes will be unequal, the leading shoe lining therefore wearing faster than the trailing shoe lining; the cam will therefore tend to move towards the leading shoe tip, in seeking to maintain equal forces on the two shoes, until any available clearance in the camshaft bearings is taken up. From this stage onwards, the cam will be restrained by the camshaft bearings (the lubrication of which is all the more important because of the lateral pressure on them) and will exert unequal forces on the two shoes; these forces will stabilise at levels such that the wear rate of the linings on the two shoes is subsequently equal.

Because of the use of fixed pivot shoes, it is not possible to achieve even wear of brake linings which are initially parallel, although in the past this has been attempted by the use of packing pieces at the pivots when linings were part worn; the usual practice therefore, except in the case of the Girling brake mentioned above, which uses sliding shoes, is to use tapered linings (commonly made in two pieces) which are fitted to shoes having a platform curvature such that only when the lining reaches the maximum wear condition is it of constant thickness. The simple approach in these cases is to use a symmetrical lining (or two identical half linings) but, since the resultant pressure on the lining is not usually acting at the centre, this does not give the most effective utilisation of the friction material; linings which are slightly asymmetrical (either in one piece or two) are sometimes used and must be correctly fitted.

Before passing on, one unusual design of cam brake (Fig. 8.4) by Deutsche Perrot-Bremse should be mentioned; this illustrates and endorses the fact that there is a surprisingly large number of ways of applying two shoes to the inside of a brake drum. The brake is very strongly made, with a cast torque plate incorporating local reinforcement at points where the loading is heavy; attached to this is a pressed steel dust shield which completes the enclosure of the brake, the manner of functioning of which is not at first apparent from the picture. In the example shown, drum rotation is anti-clockwise for forward movement.

The right hand shoe is of fixed pivot type, being retained on the pivot pin by the split pin; it is steadied by the coil spring with an integral stem which hooks into the backplate. The left hand shoe is identical in design and is pivoted on the pin which can be seen at the bottom, to the left of the adjuster unit.

The cam which operates the brake does not contact the left hand shoe directly; the component which can be seen touching the cam is a

Fig. 8.4   A Perrot cam brake with interesting features (courtesy of Deutsche Perrot-Bremse GmbH)

balance beam which, at its lower end, rests on the adjuster assembly and which contacts the shoe only at the centre of the web, at a cutaway such as can be seen on the right hand shoe. This balance beam is a casting of channel section with openings for those parts of the shoe web to which the pull off springs are attached.

The adjuster assembly is a sliding fit in the housing bolted to the torque plate; to the left of the toothed adjuster wheel is a forked piece which fits over the web of the shoe and makes contact with the similarly forked end of the balance beam. The forked piece of the adjuster assembly is restrained vertically by the shoe pivot pin and a lug cast on the torque plate. When the brake is operated the cam presses on the balance beam, the centre of which applies the left hand shoe which then acts as a leading shoe; at the same time, the end of the balance beam presses on the adjuster assembly, causing it to slide and apply the right hand shoe which, also, acts as a leading shoe.

This brake therefore differs from those cam brakes described above in that it is a two leading shoe type whereas they are leading/trailing; in reverse this brake reverts to two trailing shoe characteristics.

8.3 Slack adjusters

Brief mention has already been made of the use of a lever on the end of the brake camshaft, this being needed to convert the linear motion of the brake actuator to rotary motion of the camshaft; a simple form of such lever is shown (Fig. 8.5) and it is a general requirement that, for

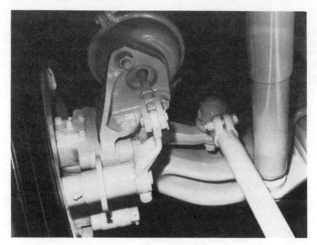

Fig. 8.5   A non-adjustable brake camshaft lever

maximum camshaft torque as the linings are applied to the drum, the angle between the lever and the actuator plunger should be very nearly 90°. Brake lining wear in service would lead to continual variation of this angle so, except in the case of the Girling and Perrot brakes already mentioned which are adjusted internally it is usual for this lever to incorporate a means of adjusting to achieve the required clearance or 'slack'; the resulting component is then usually known as a slack adjuster.

A common form of slack adjuster uses a worm drive, as in the Clayton Dewandre example shown (Fig. 8.6), to vary the angular relationship between the lever and the camshaft as necessary; to prevent the worm from being rotated by vibration when the vehicle is

Fig. 8.6   A manually adjustable brake camshaft lever (slack adjuster) (courtesy of Clayton Dewandre Co. Ltd.)

running, a spring loaded locking sleeve slides partly over the hexagonal worm shaft head. Slack adjusters are produced by a number of manufacturers and are made in a range of capacities and lever lengths; they may be offset to suit the brake chamber position and the number of connecting holes provided will vary. Double arm units are also made, to accommodate a parking brake linkage, such as is often found on a trailer. To give an indication of the state of wear of the brake linings, a small pointer is sometimes attached to the inboard end of the camshaft; the position of this relative to the slack adjuster is readily seen and can be related to the remaining thickness of lining material.

Neglect of brake adjustment will increase the time lag before the brakes become effective and will also increase the air consumption; automatic adjustment is therefore an attractive proposition and the obvious place to provide this is in the slack adjuster, in conjunction with the worm drive mechanism. In order to provide for adjustment as it becomes necessary, there has to be a means of sensing the degree of movement of the camshaft lever during each brake application; alternatives in use are a member anchored to the suspension of the vehicle (and therefore fixed relative to the movements of the lever) and a mechanism responding to the degree of change of the angle between the camshaft lever and the actuator plunger.

An example using the first of these two methods (Fig. 8.7) is by SAB Automotive Co. Ltd., the UK establishment of its Swedish parent company.; this is an extremely neat unit, which will be considered in

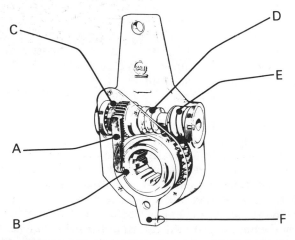

Fig. 8.7   The SAB automatic slack adjuster (courtesy of SAB Automotidve Co. Ltd.)

detail. The external reference point is provided by the control arm F, which is attached to some convenient component; the arm is coupled to the control disc, which has a cut-out B into which is engaged a toe on the rack A. Teeth on A are in engagement with a clutch gear which is freely mounted on the worm shaft but which can drive it in one direction only by means of the one-way clutch C. The worm shaft is assembled against a coil spring E, a thrust bearing behind C serving to minimise frictional resistance when the shaft turns under load.

During the initial part of a brake application, the brake shoes are lifted by an amount corresponding to the desired lining-to-drum clearance; during this stage, the whole unit turns relative to the control disc attached to the control arm F and the toe on the rack moves within the cut-out B, from one extreme to the other.

Any further movement before the linings contact the drums is excess travel, for which the adjustment is needed, and during this the rack is held by the abutment of the toe against the lower face of the cut-out, so that the rack teeth rotate the gear; while this happens the one-way clutch C slips, so that the worm shaft is not turned, and two return springs (not visible in the illustration) are compressed.

All clearance now being taken up, the worm comes under load as pressure starts to build up on the brake lining surfaces; the resistance of the worm wheel to turning causes the worm shaft to move endwise by a small amount, compressing the coil spring E as it does so, and disengaging a small cone clutch which normally couples it to the clutch member C. Also, during the 'elasticity travel', as SAB describe it, the rack continues to turn the gear freely as before until the full application is made.

When brake release takes place, the unit first turns back through an angle corresponding to the elasticity travel; during this movement, the rack return springs keep its toe in contact with the lower face of the cut-out and so it now drives the gear in the opposite direction. In this direction of rotation, the one-way clutch is driven by the gear but, at this stage, the cone clutch is still disengaged as the worm shaft is in the act of returning to its free position; there is therefore no rotation of the worm shaft (which is, in any case, still under load) by the gear.

At the conclusion of the elasticity travel, the worm shaft reaches its free position, engaging the cone clutch, and the worm drive is no longer under load as the linings are just losing contact with the drum. The normal clearance travel follows and during this the rack, having been returned to its original position by its return springs, remains stationary relative to the slack adjuster body while its toe moves back from the lower face to the upper face of the cut-out.

During the final stage of the return of the slack adjuster to the off position, the toe of the rack, being in contact with the upper face of the cut-out, causes the rack to be pulled downwards relative to the gear, which is therefore rotated. The gear, as before, drives the one-way clutch member C but, because the cone clutch is now engaged, this movement also turns the worm shaft; adjustment is therefore brought about during the completion of the return stroke.

The SAB unit is designed to reduce the excessive clearance, if any is present, by a small percentage at each cycle of brake application and release; this provides that whilst a large clearance is initially reduced fairly rapidly, the reduction gets progressively less as the clearance approaches the normal value. The use of small increments minimises the chance of over-adjustment due to short term expansion of drums when brakes are overheated during periods of excessive duty. The unit can be modified by the manufacturer to match the characteristics of different brakes by selecting from a range of control discs having cut-outs of different widths.

When brake relining is necessary, the brake adjustment can be slackened off manually by applying a spanner to a hexagon on the end of the worm shaft; this has to be turned clockwise, which causes the one-way clutch to lock up, so an applied torque of about 18 Nm (13 lbf ft) is needed to cause the cone clutch to slip, so that slackening can take place. The cone clutch surfaces are not smooth, but are serrated to increase resistance to relative motion; slackening of the adjustment is therefore accompanied by a distinct clicking sound.

Other designs of automatic slack adjuster, such as that (Fig. 8.8) designed by the Heavy Vehicle Group of the Bendix Corporation in

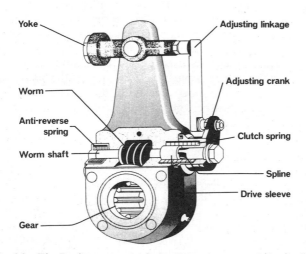

Fig. 8.8 The Bendix automatic slack adjuster (courtesy of Bendix Ltd.)

the USA, which is marked in the UK by the British subsidiary, operate on similar principles to achieve the same result, but with differences in the mechanism by which this is done.

8.4 Two leading shoe brakes

The cam brakes described earlier in this chapter are, with the exception of the Perrot brake, leading and trailing types which achieve simplicity and reliability but which, by their very nature, are somewhat lacking in torque output, because of the characteristics of the trailing shoe; brake manufacturers have, therefore, met the need for higher torque on axles loaded to the legal limit by producing two-leading-shoe brakes. What is more, all the brakes described in this section are designed to give two leading shoe characteristics for both forward and reverse rotation (duo-duplex characteristics), although some variation in this respect will be pointed out.

For many years, Girling has produced a range of brakes making use of a single, double acting expander unit in conjunction with a mechanical linkage in each shoe assembly to achieve full two-leading-shoe effect. In the form with which this section is concerned, the shoes are of twin web type with, at each end, a plain hole through the webs; a pin inserted through each pair of holes carries a small right angle lever, known as a bell crank, and a push rod is located between seatings in the opposed ends of the cranks. The bell cranks and pins are retained in position by spring clips of one kind or another and these may also prevent the push rod from being displaced while the shoes are being fitted; one of the bell cranks will have a lockable adjusting screw so that, as described below, any clearance can be taken up when the shoes have been put in place (Fig. 8.9).

Brakes of this type use a cone and tappet type adjuster, similar in general design to the units used on car brakes but of more robust construction; the tappets have inclined flanks on the head (Fig. (8.10) on which the tips of the shoe webs abut, the central area of the head being in contact with either the tip of the bell crank levers or with the adjusting screw. The expander unit has inclined flanks on the housing, which acts as abutments for the tips of the shoe webs (Fig. 8.11), while the cylindrical tappet is in contact with the bell crank or adjusting screw.

When the brake is operated, the tappet in the expander unit presses on the adjacent bell crank; this transmits the force through the push rod to the second bell crank, which then presses on the adjuster tappet with an equal force. In addition to the equal forces between the two bell cranks and the tappets with which they are in contact, equal forces are also set up between the two pivot pins and their bearings in

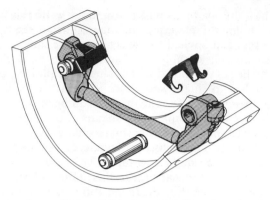

Fig. 8.9   A shoe from a Girling 2LS brake, with bell cranks and push rod assembled
(courtesy of Lucas Girling Ltd.)

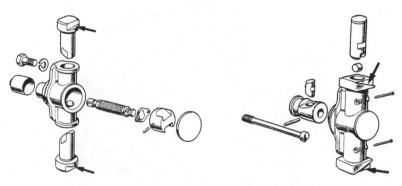

Fig. 8.10   The adjuster from a Girling 2LS brake, showing the inclined abutments for the shoe tips (courtesy of Lucas Girling Ltd.)

Fig. 8.11   The expander for a Girling 2LS brake, showing the inclined abutments for the shoe tips (courtesy of Lucas Girling Ltd.)

the shoe webs; these act to lift the shoe off its abutments at both ends, against the tension in the pull off springs, until the lining contacts the brake drum. Depending, now, on the direction of drum rotation, the shoe moves round a little with the drum until the shoe tips at the forward end contact their abutment either on the expander housing or the adjuster tappet, the bell cranks turning on their pivots as it does so; being free to slide on their abutments, the shoes distribute the force evenly over the lining, which is of constant thickness.

Whichever way the drum rotates, the shoe therefore acts as a leading shoe with the applying force shared equally between the points at which the pivot pins pass through the webs; this is the same, in effect, as a single force equal in magnitude to the sum of the individual forces and applied to the centre of the shoe arc. The shoe factor is therefore considerably less than would be the case if the same force were applied at the shoe tip. The same principle of operation has also been applied to single web shoes for heavy cars and light to medium commercial vehicles, the mechanism being adapted to suit. Correct adjustment of the linkage by means of the adjusting screw is all important; if left slack, expander travel will be excessive and end to end taper wear of the lining may occur while, on twin-web shoes, over adjustment will cause side to side taper.

The latest type of application for this design of shoe is on the Girling air wedge brake (Fig. 8.12); used in conjunction with an air

Fig. 8.12   A Girling 2LS AW brake (courtesy of Lucas Girling Ltd.)

operated spring brake unit, this gives the requisite torque for a fully loaded rear axle under either service brake or parking brake conditions for either direction of motion or inclination of gradient. For use on front axles it is not usual to need full two leading shoe characteristics, since reverse motion is normally at reduced speed and parking is dealt with by the rear axle; front brakes of this type therefore usually have the bell crank and push rod mechanism on the second shoe only so that, for forward motion, both shoes are leading

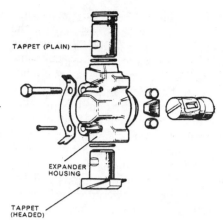

TAPPET (PLAIN)

EXPANDER
HOUSING

TAPPET
(HEADED)

Fig. 8.13   The expander for a Girling 2LS AW front brake, showing the difference between the tappets (courtesy of Lucas Girling Ltd.)

shoes. The first shoe, which is naturally a leading shoe for forward motion, is then in contact with a headed tappet (Fig. 8.13) in the expander unit, the housing of which is modified to accommodate this; the tips of the twin webs are now similarly supported at each end by the inclined surfaces, on which they are free to slide as before. The omission of the mechanism from the one shoe saves weight and cost, the brake being described as 2LS/1, by comparison with the designation 2LS for the rear axle version; the front brake will be operated by a normal air chamber.

Rear air-wedge brakes are also found with puller type air chambers and a mechanical parking brake connection, the brake itself being only different in the detailed design of the expander to allow for the difference in direction of the operating force. Girling 2LS and 2LS/1 brakes have also been very common with hydraulic application by external wheel cylinders; front brakes use pusher type cylinders while rears use a puller type cylinder with mechanical connection for parking. In the UK it is only relatively recently that it has been permissible to use stored energy, such as from a spring in compression, to apply a brake for parking; until this change multi-pull handbrake levers, with quick release, were necessary to obtain the necessary input force for holding a heavy vehicle on a hill by direct mechanical effort.

8.5 Duo-duplex hydraulic brakes

The excellence of the Girling 2LS brake has been demonstrated by its long history of service of some thirty years; the only noticeable change during this period, apart from the introduction of air actuation, has been a slight increase in lining thickness and a considerable increase in shoe width. For a number of years, however, there has been a gradual introduction by all makers of full two leading shoe brakes with dual actuation to achieve the effect, thus avoiding the need for an exposed mechanical linkage and achieving a higher shoe factor.

The Girling and Lockheed hydraulically operated examples of duo-duplex brake have already been considered in the previous chapter; we now consider three examples of air operated brakes of this class for heavy vehicles by Rockwell, Perrot and, again, Girling. In general terms, the Rockwell Stopmaster brake (Fig. 8.14) is representative of the type, with its very strong torque plate, heavy twin webbed shoes and opposed double acting expander units; there are, however, interesting differences between the expanders with their integral automatic adjustment mechanisms and these, together with other points of difference, will be considered.

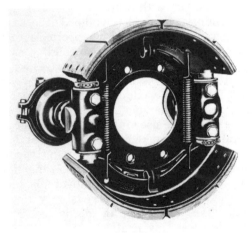

Fig. 8.14   A Rockwell Stopmaster* brake (* A trademark of Rockwell International Corporation) (courtesy of Rockwell International Corporation, Automotive Businesses)

When brakes of this design are operated, the shoes are lifted at each end simultaneously until their linings contact the drum; if this is turning, the shoes move a little with it—the tappets with the wedge assemblies sliding in the expander housings as they do so—until each shoe abuts on the expander housing ahead of it. The force still acting on the tappet at the abutment end now merely serves to reduce the force exerted by the shoe on the housing; the force acting on the tappet

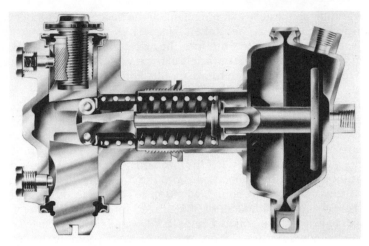

*Fig. 8.15   The expander for a Rockwell Stopmaster brake (courtesy of Rockwell
International Corporation, Automotive Businesses)*

at the leading end now becomes the shoe tip force so that a high shoe
factor is achieved, whichever way the drum is rotating.

The shoes are expanded by a wedge mechanism, illustrated in the
sectional view (Fig. 8.15) which also shows the components of the
automatic adjustment; the wedge is carried on the end of a push rod
and acts on the inclined inner faces of the tappets through the medium
of rollers, guided in a light steel pressing. A choice of wedge angles is
available to the vehicle designer which, in conjunction with the sizes
of air chamber which can be used, enables him to vary the torque
output of the brake as may be required to suit the needs of the vehicle
under consideration.

Of the two tappets, the lower one is solid while the upper one
comprises three parts which form the adjuster assembly. The outer
part, the adjusting plunger, is prevented from rotating by a guide pawl
(this corresponds to the fixed stop pin which holds the lower tappet in
place) which, passing through a slot in its side, leaves it free to slide
when the brake is operated. Inside the plunger is the adjusting
actuator which is threaded inside and has helical teeth on the outside;
the teeth are of saw tooth form and they engage with mating teeth on
the end of the guide pawl, already referred to, which is spring loaded.
Threaded into the adjusting actuator is the adjusting bolt assembly,
which has a toothed wheel for initial manual adjustment, over which
is fitted the shoe locating plate.

When the brake is operated, the actuator moves out with the
adjusting plunger and the adjusting bolt as one unit, the spring loaded

pawl riding up the gently sloping flank of the helical teeth. Only when sufficient lining wear has taken place is the plunger movement sufficient for the pawl to drop into the next tooth; when the brake is then released, due to the steep angle of the reverse face of the tooth, the pawl causes the actuator to rotate slightly and screw out the adjusting bolt.

The components involved in the automatic mechanism are so designed that it operates when lining wear of about 0.018 mm (0.0007 in) has occurred; it then restores the normal clearance of approximately 1.5 mm (0.06 in) at the shoe centre. This clearance is sufficient to ensure that, even if the mechanism has taken up any extra clearance created by drum expansion, the brakes will not rub when the drums contract on cooling. Mention of cooling leads to mention of the fact that the diameter of 381 mm (15 in) chosen for one of the ranges of heavy truck brakes, being slightly smaller than is customary, leaves an increased air space around the drum to promote the flow of cooling air; the consequent small reduction in working radius is offset by the high brake factor achieved.

The small number of parts involved in this automatic adjustment mechanism is an important feature of the design, making for simplicity and reliability; it is, however, imperative that all dirt should be excluded so considerable attention has been given to the sealing of the unit and a number of improvements have been made in this in the light of experience. Brake shoe assembly design has also been refined during the years this brake has been on the market; shoe tips are finished and hardened to reduce friction when the brake is operated, the ends of the shoe platforms are stiffened by forming a tapered rib and the fillet weld between web and platform at the trailing end of each shoe for forward rotation is stopped short of the end to give a measure of flexibility. An interesting development in the linings for these brakes, similar to features adopted by other makers, is the introduction of either a V section groove on the edge or a chamfer at the corners; these are so placed that when a lining is worn either to the apex of the V groove or to the base of the chamfer, it is due for replacing and wear can be checked without the need for drum removal.

Brakes fitted to front axles are generally equipped with two standard air chambers, one screwed directly into each of the two expander units, these being supplied by separate air circuits (as will be explained in Chapter 9) so that if either develops a fault, the brakes are still operated; in such a case, each brake would revert to leading/ trailing characteristics, giving about 60% of normal output. Rear brakes are generally equipped with one standard air chamber and one spring brake unit supplied, as with front brakes, by separate air circuits; the spring brake unit makes use of the energy stored in the spring to apply the brake mechanically, for parking, as a leading/ trailing shoe type.

8.6 Other examples

The Deutsche Perrot-Bremse brake of this class, similarly operated by twin double acting wedge type expanders, may be found with two different automatic adjustment mechanisms, although the difference between them is not great; (Fig. 8.16 shows two views of the original form of this mechanism, one part sectioned and the other fully sectioned, and will serve for a description of both. As with the Rockwell brake, one tappet is solid since, with an expander unit at each end of each shoe, it is not necessary to have an adjuster in both tappets.

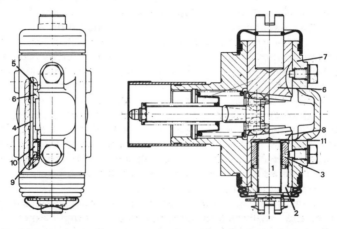

Fig. 8.16   A Perrot design of automatic adjustment for a duo-duplex brake (courtesy of Deutsche Perrot-Bremse GmbH)

The lower tappet in the illustration incorporates the adjustment mechanism, combining both manual and automatic modes of operation. When the brake is assembled, either initially or after relining, the toothed wheel is turned manually to rotate the adjuster and cause it to be screwed out to set the clearance approximately; the clearance can, alternatively, be increased manually to facilitate drum removal.

The automatic adjustment consists of the adjuster 1, screwed into the adjuster nut 2 which rotates inside the forward tappet 8; the inner face of the nut is formed with saw shaped teeth which engage with similar teeth on the face of the adjuster ring 3. The adjuster ring is held in contact with the adjuster nut by the corrugated spring 11, which can permit sufficient axial movement of the ring for the teeth to disengage.

The adjuster ring has a helical groove 10 machined in the outer surface, in which fits a lug 9 which is attached to the slider 4; the other end of the slider has a similar lug 5, which engages a recess in the tappet 6. The slider fits in grooves machined in the two tappets and it lies to one side of the wedge assembly; the lug at the lower end has a pre-determined clearance within the helical groove while the other lug is a close fit in the recess in the upper tappet 6.

When the brake is operated, the tappets 6 and 8 move apart and the slider, having taken up the clearance within the helical groove 10, causes the adjuster ring 3 to rotate slightly; as this happens, the opposing sets of teeth start to slide up each other so that the spring 11 is partly compressed. When lining wear reaches a certain stage, the relative movement of the tappets is such that the adjuster ring is rotated more than one tooth pitch; the ring then slides back axially, engaging the teeth in the next position. During brake release the pull-off springs retract the shoes and the tappets; the slider, by means of lug 9 and the helical groove 10, then turns the adjuster ring and the nut together, screwing out the adjuster 1 by a small amount to reduce the clearance.

The amount of adjustment per tooth pitch movement of the adjuster nut can be varied by design, but is usually about 0.025 mm (0.0001 in), which gives very close control of the working clearance; the working parts of the mechanism are never subject to heavy loading and they are totally enclosed so that reliable operation with a minimum of wear is ensured.

In its later form, the automatic adjustment dispenses with the slider between the two tappets; instead, the locating pin which is screwed into the housing and fits into an axial slot in the tappet to prevent it from turning, whilst permitting sliding, is modified. An inner spring loaded plunger is a clearance fit in the helical groove, which is appropriately repositioned in the tappet body; this brings about the operation of the adjustment in a similar manner to the lug on the slider in the earlier design, but with one particular innovation.

Normally, the return of the tappet containing the adjustment mechanism into the expander housing is during brake release when it is only lightly loaded, but it could happen when the brakes are applied whilst rolling back on a hill; under these conditions, the tappet would be heavily loaded and the adjuster parts could be damaged. The spring loading of the plunger, however, enables it to be pushed back by the axial force developed between the inclined flanks of the helical groove and the V form head of the plunger, so that the other parts are relieved of load. A similar expander unit, but with automatic adjustment of this modified form in both tappets, is to be found in simplex (leading/trailing) brakes.

A third type of duo-duplex air wedge brake is the Girling Twinstop (Fig. 8.17) shown with one standard brake chamber and one spring brake unit, as would be usual on a rear axle so as to provide for

Fig. 8.17   A Girling Twinstop front brake, showing the spring brake unit which provides for parking

parking; this design was first introduced with twin web shoes, but is now made with single web shoes and it is in its later form that it will be described. The particular feature of interest is the adjusting mechanism built into the expander unit, which operates automatically or can be set manually, and which can be understood by reference to the sectional illustration (Fig. 8.18).

As with other brakes of this same general type, one tappet is solid (this is the one which transmits the abutment force to the housing for forward rotation) and the other, called the input tappet, is a sub-assembly of three parts—the body, the adjuster screw (with the integral helical gear) and the roller tappet; the latter component is spigoted into the end of the drive screw, but is prevented from rotating. At right angles to the centre line of the tappets is a spindle on which are assembled several components; the lower end of this spindle is formed with a dog clutch member, used for manual operation,

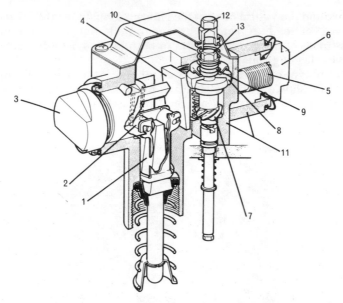

*Fig. 8.18   The Girling Twinstop brake expander unit, showing the automatic adjustment
(courtesy of Lucas Girling Ltd.)*

above which is the adjuster pinion and, above this, an inner cone member. Pressed into contact with this inner cone member is the drive cone, which is acted upon by the overload spring; this spring is retained and held under load by a washer and nut at the upper end of the spindle. The drive cone is tapered both in its bore (where it seats on the inner cone member) and on its outer surface, which seats in a tapered portion of the bore in the housing.

The spindle and drive cone sub-assembly is held in place by a cone spring which is located between a stop plate resting on the drive cone and the pinion cover. Below all these components is the manual adjustment spindle, spring loaded to disengage the dog clutch and with an O ring around it to exclude dirt from the housing.

Between the teeth of the adjuster pinion and those of the helical gear on the adjuster stem, there is sufficient backlash for normal brake operation to occur without the adjustment being disturbed; when, however, brake lining wear has occurred, this clearance is insufficient to allow the full tappet movement and the helical gear engages the adjuster pinion. The latter is held stationary by the engagement of the drive cone in its seat, under the pressure of the cone spring; the effect of the helical teeth is such, however, that the driving force of the helical gear generates an upward component which lifts the drive cone, compressing the cone spring, and allows the pinion to turn a little.

As the brake is released, the drive cone reseats and holds the pinion stationary again; the input tappet continues its inward movement, the backlash between the gears is taken up and then the helical gear is caused to rotate by its contact with the adjuster pinion, so that the adjuster screw reduces the lining to drum clearance. The helical gears are so designed that only a proportion of the excess clearance is taken up at one time; this ensures that over-adjustment is unlikely to occur, even if the drums have expanded because of high operating temperatures.

Should the vehicle roll back while the brakes are applied, the two tappets and the wedge assembly will move in the housing as one unit; the helical gear will not be able to rotate the adjuster pinion, because this will be locked by the engagement of the outer surface of the drive cone in its seating. The lateral movement of the helical gear can, however, displace the adjuster pinion downwards, compressing the overload spring and disengaging the inner cone clutch so that the adjuster pinion can then rotate without being overloaded.

Manual operation of the adjustment, either to facilitate drum removal or to take up excess clearance after relining, is performed by pushing the manual override stem into engagement with the adjuster spindle against the resistance of its return spring; the stem can then be turned in the appropriate direction by means of its hexagon, sufficient force to slip the drive cone being necessary. Some versions of this brake also have an override member protruding from the cover of the housing, spring loaded into the disengaged position, which can be used once the drum has been removed.

8.7 Disc brakes

Although enthusiasts for disc brakes have for many years talked of the prospects for them becoming established on heavy trucks, it has become clear that progress in this field has been slower than in the case of units for medium weight vehicles. Within given sizes of wheel, it has been found possible to modify drum brakes to cope with higher energy dissipation rates by progressively increasing their width; with disc brakes for other than light weight vehicles, although it has become the accepted practice to use a ventilated disc, there is then no further way of increasing their capacity other than that of adopting a multiple disc configuration. The use of low profile tyres would, within an unaltered overall diameter, permit the use of a bigger disc in a larger wheel, but it does seem clear that heat dissipation would continue to be a major problem.

Two principle lines of development have emerged from those which the various manufacturers have considered, the multi-plate type (a Rockwell example for off-the-road vehicles is described in Chapter 10) and the sliding caliper type already favoured for medium weight trucks and lighter vehicles; the problem of heat dissipation and the effect of design complication on cost seem difficult to overcome with the former type, so it seems likely that the sliding caliper will be the configuration to receive most attention in the future.

In the USA, both Rockwell and Eaton have been accumulating operational experience with air operated disc brake installations, an example of the Rockwell Dura-Master being shown (Fig. 8.19); a further illustration (Fig. 8.20) shows a section through the operating mechanism, which is necessary in order to understand how this functions. The caliper slides on two pins located in the torque plate, the length of these pins being such that when their inboard ends are flush with the faces of the bosses in the caliper, the brake pads need replacement; anti-friction bushes are inserted in all four caliper bosses and the pins are lubricated with an anti-seizing compound.

The pad backplates have a dovetail shaped tab on their outer edge; these tabs can be passed through the gap in the caliper bridge at a clearance notch, so that the pads can then be slid sideways into place

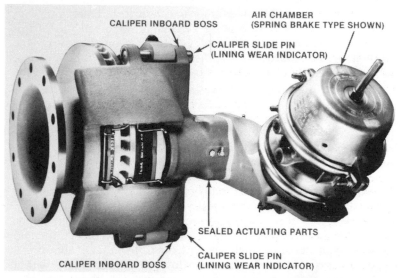

Fig. 8.19   A Rockwell Duramaster* air operated disc brake (* a trademark of Rockwell International Corporation) (courtesy of Rockwell International Corporation, Automotive Businesses)

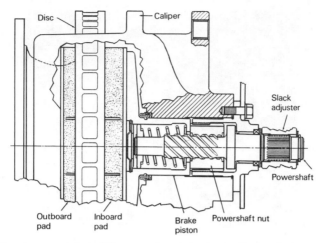

Fig. 8.20   A cross section of the expander of the Rockwell Duramaster disc brake (courtesy of Rockwell International Corporation, Automotive Businesses)

and an anti-rattle clip fitted. The linings on the inboard pads are smaller than those on the outboard pads when a ventilated disc is fitted, otherwise all linings are the same size; the inboard pad locates against the extended flange of the brake piston, which slides in the sealed bore of the inboard part of the caliper.

Assembled to the inboard face of the caliper is the air chamber bracket, on which is mounted either a standard air chamber or a spring brake; the push rod of this unit is coupled to a Rockwell automatic slack adjuster, similar in function to those illustrated earlier in this chapter, which turns the powershaft seen in the line drawing (Fig. 8.20). The powershaft is supported in a bush in the cap assembled to the caliper; the bore of this cap is splined so that the powershaft nut can slide axially in it without rotating. As the powershaft is turned during brake operation, the nut is forced in the outboard direction so that it presses against the inner face of the brake piston; the inboard pad is thus applied directly and the reaction by way of the nut causes the caliper to slide and apply the outboard pad.

As lining wear takes place, the automatic slack adjuster functions just as it would if it were operating a cam brake, to take up the excessive clearance. When a spring brake chamber is used to operate the brake, it is necessary to use the wind off bolt (described in Chapter 9) to compress the spring before the various components can be taken apart; the spring brake is, of course, the means of application for parking and in emergency.

The Girling reaction beam type of disc brake, described in Chapter

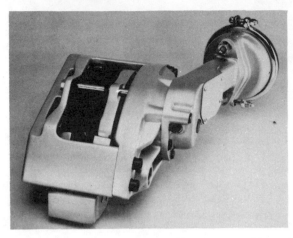

Fig. 8.21   An air operated Girling reaction beam caliper (courtesy of Lucas Girling Ltd.)

7, is also available in air operated form for heavy vehicles (Fig. 8.21); the general form of the caliper is as for hydraulic operation, but with the addition of the air actuator support casting on the inboard side Instead of containing twin hydraulic cylinders and pistons, the inboard beam houses two mechanical expander units; one of these is operated directly by the air chamber and is linked to the other so that the two operate simultaneously to apply the brake. Each expander contains a pair of cylindrical members, the opposing faces of which are each of spiral ramp form, caged balls being assembled between them; one of these members remains stationary in the housing while the other rotates to develop a thrust which is transmitted to a plunger through a needle roller thrust bearing. An automatic adjuster is incorporated in each expander to maintain a constant travel for the air actuator, a spring brake chamber being used if parking is to be provided for.

Other brake manufacturers will undoubtedly continue to develop large disc brakes as they gain experience in other fields but, although the number of heavy vehicles in service which have disc brakes is increasing, there is as yet no clear indication that a definite advantage over a good quality drum installation has been demonstrated; further development of disc designs to minimise distortion at high temperatures and of friction materials is continuing and the brake designs are subject to ongoing refinement, but similar remarks can be applied to drum brakes.

It is not at present possible to foresee the outcome of the attempt to oust the drum brake on heavy vehicles and it will, therefore, be a matter of great interest during the years ahead to observe trends; only experience in the field and comparisons will determine whether the disc brake will further extend its field of application.

9

Air braking systems

9.1 Introduction

In one respect, air and hydraulic braking systems are similar, because in both cases the brakes are operated by a fluid enclosed in a pipeline. Here, however, the similarity ends, because air is a highly compressible gas while brake fluid is a virtually incompressible liquid; the brake pedal of an air system controls the pressure of the air directed to the brakes but does not generate it whereas, with a conventional hydraulic system, the pedal generates at least part of the pressure which operates the brakes.

Air is, of course, a very convenient working fluid to use in a braking system or for many other purposes; it is available free of charge in unlimited quantities on the spot where it is wanted, it is easily cleaned for use and does not deteriorate in storage, it is non-toxic and can be discharged to atmosphere after it has done its job without causing any pollution other than a little noise. It is true that air contains water vapour, and that this can condense and cause problems—especially if the condensate freezes—but it is possible to include components in the system which will virtually eliminate icing.

Pressures in air braking sytems are considerably lower than in hydraulic systems, so the brake actuators have to be large in order to develop the required operating forces; there is, however, no fundamental difficulty in achieving the relatively large displacement of air needed to operate the actuators on a maximum weight multi-wheeled vehicle although, as will be seen, it is necessary to take action to secure a rapid response on a lengthy vehicle. Legislation continues to play a large part in influencing air braking system layouts but, this being a complex and changeable aspect of the subject, only limited reference to its requirements will be made.

It is convenient first to consider the components which are available for constructing air braking systems, these being described in groups, before examining some typical layouts which are representative of recent and current practice. It will quickly be realised that in many cases there are alternatives, which make possible an extremely large number of different circuits, which cannot, therefore, be fully considered.

9.2 Compression and treatment

Air to be stored for use as required is compressed in an engine driven compressor of reciprocating type, which may have either one or two cylinders, depending on the maximum rate of air consumption for the vehicle to which it is to be fitted; in this connection it should be borne in mind that as well as using air for brake operations, a public service vehicle may have an air operated gearbox, doors and windscreen wipers as well as air suspension, so it is important that adequate pumping capacity is provided. The air is commonly drawn into the compressor through the engine air filter so is free from dust, which would cause cylinder wear, but it will contain water vapour which will tend to condense in certain parts of the system and might freeze in cold weather; ways of dealing with this water vapour will be considered later in this section.

A sectional view of a two cylinder Lucas Girling air compressor is shown (Fig. 9.1), and it can be seen that the inlet and exhaust valves are of spring loaded disc type so that they operate by differences in air pressure during the induction and compression strokes; a considerable proportion of the energy input to the compressor is converted to heat and so, although units may be air cooled, this particular one is

Fig. 9.1   A two cylinder air compressor, sectioned to show the principal components; in the foreground is a governor valve (courtesy of Lucas Girling Ltd.)

water cooled. Compressors need to be lubricated and the unit shown takes its oil supply from the engine lubrication system; some oil is inevitably discharged with the air delivered (and has to be removed later, together with condensed moisture) but Girling claim that by careful design they have achieved a notably low rate of oil carry-over.

Compressors deliver air at pressures up to a maximum of about 10 bar (150 lbf/in^2), depending on the requirements of the vehicle builder, and they are usually driven continuously while the engine is running; it is necessary, therefore to provide some means of relief for the compressor so that the reservoirs are not overcharged and energy is not wasted. It is usual to provide a safety valve in the system, either incorporated into the cylinder head of the compressor or fitted between the compressor and the reservoirs; this will be set to release at a pressure in excess of the desired maximum storage pressure, so will prevent overcharge, but it does not relieve the compressor of load.

Either an unloader valve or a governor will be fitted between the compresssor and the reservoirs which, at the upper pressure limit, operates to remove the load from the compressor and prevent the further delivery of air under pressure until the pressure of the stored air falls owing to usage. An unloader valve incorporates a non-return or check valve, which ensures that stored air cannot flow back and escape when the unit operates to prevent charging; it also has a piston or diaphragm operated means whereby, when the maximum charging pressure is reached, an exhaust port is opened so that the air delivered by the compressor is vented to atmosphere without restriction. Since the compressor is not then having to do other than pump air at atmospheric pressure, its load is removed until, when the pressure of the stored air has fallen by about 1 bar (15 lbf/in^2), the unloader closes the exhaust port and charging recommences.

A governor valve operates in conjunction with an unloader piston incorporated in the compressor cylinder head over each inlet valve (Fig. 9.2); whereas the unloader valve passes the full air flow from the compressor, the governor (Fig. 9.3) merely is connected to some point, such as a wet tank provided as a convenient point for condensate to form. A piston or diaphragm, which is under the influence of a graduable spring, responds to the compressor discharge pressure and, at the appropriate level, opens a port to pass some of this air through a pipe to the unloader cylinder(s) in the compressor; the unloader piston then opens the inlet valve disc so that no compression of air can take place. When the storage pressure falls by the requisite amount, the governor valve closes the port which had passed compressed air to the unloader and opens an exhaust port; the inlet valves in the compressor are then able to seat again and recharging commences.

An alternative method of relieving the compressor when the system

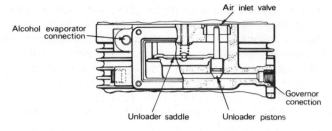

Fig. 9.2 *The cylinder head of a two cylinder air compressor showing the unloader mechanism (courtesy of Bendix Ltd.)*

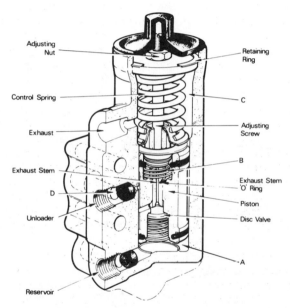

Fig. 9.3 *A section through a governor valve (courtesy of Bendix Ltd.)*

is fully charged has recently been introduced; this is to drive it through a clutch which can be disengaged and re-engaged automatically, in response to pressure signals.

Returning to the matter of dealing with water vapour, there are three principal approaches; it can be allowed to condense and then be ejected, it can be allowed to condense—but with means of preventing freezing—and be ejected or it can be removed from the air. The first of these approaches still suffices in warm countries, but elsewhere the inconveniences caused in winter by frozen condensate are such that the alternatives are commonly adopted.

Condensation commonly occurs when air, heated during compression, cools again; it is a simple matter to provide a small pressure vessel (referred to above as a wet tank) specifically for this purpose and provide it with an automatic drain valve, such as the Clayton Dewandre example shown (Fig. 9.4). This has no external connections, the only working parts being the rubber valve disc and the spring; when at rest, the edge of the rubber disc seals against the annular face formed in the valve body and the central cone shaped portion (into which is moulded a short rod for manual operation) seals the exhaust port in the valve cover.

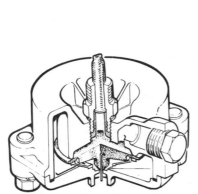

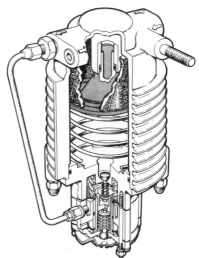

Fig. 9.4   An automatic reservoir drain valve (courtesy of Clayton Dewandre Co. Ltd.)

Fig. 9.5   A moisture condenser with automatic drain valve (courtesy of Clayton Dewandre Co. Ltd.)

During charging of the system, the increasing pressure deflects the edge of the valve disc so that air, together with any condensate which may have formed, flows into the base of the valve, above the cover; when the compressor is unloaded, the valve disc reseats and the pressure is then equal above and below. As soon as sufficient air has been used to lower the stored pressure slightly, the trapped pressure in the lower part of the valve is able to lift the centre of the valve disc, thus opening the exhaust port; the air present then blows out the condensate (which may be a mixture of oil and water) and the exhaust port then closes again.

SAB Automotive Co. Ltd. makes an automatic drain valve which incorporates a solenoid operated plunger which opens and closes two ports to effect the discharge of condensate; the solenoid is normally operated by an electrical connection to the stop light switch but, for winter use, it can be energised continuously (to provide local heating and prevent freezing) except when the brakes are applied. In the first mode of operation the valve discharges when the brakes are applied, in the second it discharges when the brakes are released, the net result being the same.

A more refined alternative to the use of a wet tank is the combined condenser and automatic drain valve (Fig. 9.5), but the more commonly used method of preventing condensate from freezing is to add a small percentage of alcohol vapour to the air drawn into the compressor; this subsequently condenses with any water vapour present and lowers the freezing point of the water which forms.

Alcohol can be added in two principal ways, the simplest being to have it in a container through which the air is drawn; the container is included in the compressor suction line and is left empty in summer. The other way is by the use of a small pump (Fig. 9.6), which is fitted in the air outlet from the compressor and which incorporates a piston which responds to either the fluctuating pressure in an unloader valve controlled system or the pressure signal from a governor valve; each time the pressure cycles, a small quantity of alcohol is injected into the air stream.

As a more fundamental approach to the problems caused by moisture, air driers are available which can remove water vapour from the air discharged by the compressor, so that condensation cannot then occur; two examples will be considered which, apart from differences in their manner of operation, differ in their general form. The Bendix Air Dryer (Fig. 9.7) is a cylindrical unit which is for inclusion in governor controlled systems, is installed vertically and is divided into three compartments; the centre compartment contains a removable cartridge in which is a quantity of a desiccant—a substance in pellet form which has an affinity for moisture.

Air from the compressor enters the unit at one of the points F and flows downwards between the outer and inner casings; it cools and deposits condensate in the sump at the bottom, the liquid consisting of a mixture of oil from the compressor and water. The condensate is retained by the purge valve A, which is closed by a return spring, the air pressure in the unit also acting to keep the purge valve closed; a 60 watt heater, incorporated in the sump at B, prevents the condensate from freezing in winter. Much of the carbon and dirt which

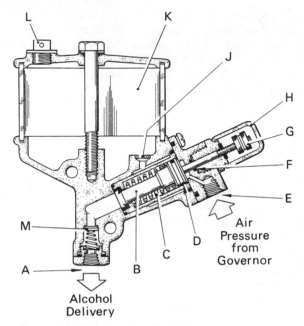

Fig. 9.6   An automatic alcohol pump (courtesy of Clayton Dewandre Co. Ltd.)

may be present in the air is also deposited at this stage and the air then passes upwards through the filter H; this removes any remaining particles of dirt or droplets of oil and water, but the air still contains water vapour.

The air now passes into the second compartment, which forms about 40% of the unit; in this compartment the water vapour is taken up by the desiccant, being held on the surface of the highly porous pellets. From the desiccant chamber, the air passes through a check valve L and into the upper compartment, where purge air is stored, before passing through a further check valve R and out of one of the ports Q to the reservoir.

When the system air pressure reaches the upper control limit the governor operates and, as well as passing an air pressure signal to the unloader piston on the compressor, it also directs one to port C on the dryer. Here the pressure acts on the full area of the purge valve plunger, overcoming the upward force exerted by the spring and by the pressure in the sump acting on the annular under-surface; the purge valve is then opened abruptly and the accumulated condensate is blown out by the sudden expansion of the air in the lower half of the unit.

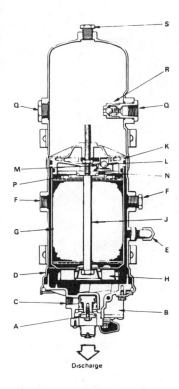

Discharge

Fig. 9.7 The Bendix Air Dryer (courtesy of Bendix Ltd.)

The air which escapes rapidly in this manner also partly clears the assumulated moisture from the desiccant and some of the matter trapped by the filter; this initial stage, which lasts only a fraction of a second, is then followed by a second stage which lasts for several seconds. The air stored in the upper compartment is able to bypass the check valve L by means of a small purge orifice M, through which it can return slowly, expanding back to atmospheric pressure as it passes through the desiccant and the filter. This air has already been effectively dried but, as it expands and cools, it becomes 'superdry' and is, therefore, very efficient in removing the remaining moisture from the dessicant; once purging is completed the unit is ready for the commencement of the next charging cycle.

The second unit to be described is the SAB Twin Drier (Fig. 9.8) which, also, is cylindrical but which is installed horizontally; it is, therefore, particularly suitable for locations, such as under bus or coach floors, where vertical space is strictly limited. The Twin Drier consists of a central body containing valves to direct the air flow, together with filters and separators, a sump and a purge valve; on

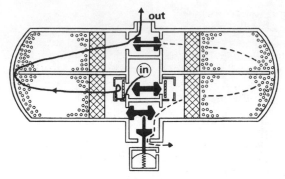

Fig. 9.8   The SAB Twin Drier (courtesy of SAB Automotive Co. Ltd.)

either side are attached identical cartridges containing the desiccant which is used, a lengthwise division creating a U shaped flow path through each cartridge.

This unit has alternative flow paths for charge and purge air controlled by the valves referred to above; these move in response to pressure changes in the system. In a governor controlled system, the pressure signal from the governor is fed to the Twin Drier and its alternation effects the valve change; with an unloader controlled system, it is the alternation of pressure in the compressor discharge line during the charging cycle which achieves this.

In Fig. 9.8, air is entering from the compressor through the central inlet port and is being directed by the inlet valve to the left; it passes first through a filter and centrifugal separator which remove particles and liquid droplets from the air, these draining into the sump where they are retained by the exhaust shuttle. The air flow continues through the left hand cartridge, where it is dried by the desiccant and then it passes through the outlet valve at the top to the reservoirs; the outlet valve, however, contains a drilling which allows a proportion of the dry air to pass through the right hand cartridge, regenerating the desiccant and clearing the contents of the sump out through the passage opened by the exhaust shuttle and through the exhaust port.

When the system reaches its maximum stored pressure, the pneumatic signal to the drier closes the exhaust port and causes the exhaust shuttle to move to the right; the air pressure then becomes equalised throughout the drier. When the stored air pressure falls to the cut-in value, the pneumatic signal to the drier reopens the exhaust port and exchanges the positions of the inlet and outlet valves so that the air flow is now being dried in the right hand cartridge whilst regenerating the left hand one.

9.3 Storage and protection

Compressed air reservoirs are made of steel, convex end pressings being welded to a central shell formed by rolling a plate to make a cylinder with a welded seam; bosses are welded to the ends, for the inlet and outlet connections, and at the bottom of the vessel for a drain valve. Sometimes a single vessel is divided into two equal parts by a central partition, welded in place, to form two separate reservoirs. Both the inner and outer surfaces are suitably finished to give protection against corrosion; reservoirs are usually hydraulically tested to twice the intended maximum storage pressure and an extremely high standard of safety has been established.

The number of reservoirs found on a vehicle depends partly on the type of vehicle and partly on its age (which determines the particular legislation to which it conforms); at one time in the UK a Service reservoir (also indirectly supplying a trailer reservoir, in the case of a tractive vehicle) and a combined Secondary and Parking reservoir were usual; more recently rigid vehicles will be found with three reservoirs—two Service and one combined Secondary and Parking—the Service braking being divided, as will be considered later in this chapter. A tractive vehicle will now often have a fourth reservoir, the trailer reservoir, from which a supply will be taken to the trailer supply coupling; this is in addition to one further reservoir on the trailer (sometimes two on long trailers) and a possible reservoir for air operated auxiliaries.

Reservoirs are usually (but not necessarily) mounted horizontally on trucks, in a fore and aft alignment; their minimum size will be governed by legislation so that a stated number of full brake applications can be made without recharging, before the stored air pressure is reduced significantly. Manufacturers offer reservoirs in a range of diameters and lengths, so that the choice of capacities available meets all needs.

Even when an air drier is fitted in an air braking system, it is still necessary to provide drain valves for the reservoirs. Early systems used drain cocks, but these were later superseded by tilt valves (Fig. 9.9), in which the valve disc 2 is seated by the spring 1 and the pressure in the vessel; lateral movement of the stem 3 unseats the valve and allows some of the stored air to blow out any condensate. Being manually controlled on a once-a-day basis, it was easy for the routine use of these valves to be neglected.

The automatic drain valve, already illustrated (Fig. 9.4) and described, ensures that reservoirs are regularly drained without wasting air and contributes to the satisfactory functioning of the complete system.

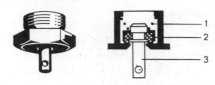

Fig. 9.9 A manually operated drain valve (courtesy of Wabco Automotive Products Group)

At one time, the air supply from the compressor would have been led to each of the individual reservoirs through a check valve; this ensured that, subsequent to charging, a failure upstream of the check valves would not affect the ability of the vehicle to stop. However, while the use of two, three or four reservoirs ensures the integrity of at least part of the entire braking system, should there be a single failure downstream of one of the check valves, such a failure in, say, a reservoir could cause all the air from the compressor to be directed there, instead of recharging those reservoirs which remain functional.

To allow for this possibility, a unit called a system protection valve has been devised which, although it includes the non-return function of a check valve, has an important difference. A check valve incorporates only a light spring, so allowing air to flow into a punctured reservoir and preventing sufficient pressure build-up from occurring to permit recharging of a functioning reservoir; a protection valve has a different characteristic which ensures that air is not lost to a reservoir at atmospheric pressure, provided the undamaged reservoirs retain a minimum stored pressure of about 1 bar (15 lb/in^2). Normally, with a protection valve provided for each of several reservoirs, these are compounded into a single housing, such as in the case of the quadruple Bendix unit shown (Fig. 9.10); in order to explain the manner of operation, it is simpler to refer to a single system unit, such as the Clayton Dewandre unit (Fig. 9.11), drawn part-sectioned.

The Clayton Dewandre system protection valve consists of a disc type non-return valve, the stem of which is guided in the piston above; around this stem is a light spring which assists it in closing. A stronger spring acts on the non-return valve through the medium of the piston, this being set on assembly by means of the adjusting screw shown; there is a tolerance of less than 1 bar (15 lbf/in^2) on the opening value of about 6 bar (90 lbf/in^2) of the valve.

Starting with the system completely empty, the compressor builds up pressure until the disc valve in that protection valve which chances to have the lowest spring setting lifts; as it lifts, its full area is exposed to the air flow and the accumulated air passes through, lowering the

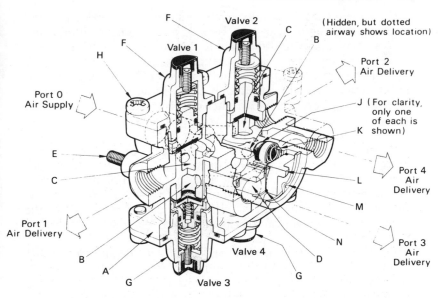

Fig. 9.10   *A quadruple system protection valve (courtesy of Bendix Ltd.)*

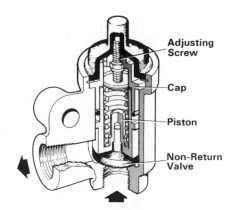

Fig. 9.11   *A single system protection valve (courtesy of Clayton Dewandre Co. Ltd.)*

pressure below the valve, which then closes again. As the compressor again builds up pressure, the same valve may open again or a different one may if its opening pressure has been reached and, gradually, pressure will start to rise in all the reservoirs in turn.

The stored pressure acts on the back of the disc valves in the individual protection valves, helping to keep them closed, but it also acts on the pistons, gradually overcoming the force exerted by the setting springs, until the pistons are held out of contact with the disc valves; charging then continues up to the cut-out point, with the disc valves operating simply as non-return valves.

If all pressure is lost from one of the reservoirs, the setting spring in its protection valve will immediately cause the piston to assist the disc valve to close; the disc valve will then only lift again if the full opening pressure for that unit is reached. The other reservoirs, however, can readily be recharged up to the opening pressure of the protection valve on the failed reservoir because the stored pressure retained in them, lifting their pistons, gives them a favourable operating bias. Only when the system protection valve on the failed circuit opens will air escape to atmosphere while the compressor works continuously; this equipment is intended to facilitate the safe movement of the vehicle to a convenient workshop, but it should not be driven further than necessary in this condition.

Other designs of protection valve differ in detail, some using diaphragms instead of pistons, but they achieve the same result, ensuring that a required braking effort can be maintained for a prolonged period after a failure in one of the charged parts of the system.

Another type of valve sometimes found is a charging valve, of which a Wabco example is illustrated (Fig. 9.12); this can be used, for instance, to ensure that brake reservoirs are charged before that for auxiliaries. The spring 2 is adjusted by the screw 1 to load the diaphragm 4 so that it only opens when the air pressure at 7 reaches the value required; the air then passes through the check valve 8 on its way to the auxiliary reservoir. Other variants allow either a full or partial return flow should the pressure in 7 fall below that in the auxiliary reservoir, the check valve either being repositioned or omitted.

Finally, one or two minor components remain to be mentioned. A safety valve, such as the Wabco unit shown (Fig. 9.13), will be mounted either on a wet tank (mentioned in the previous section) or at some other convenient point; the internal spring is set so that the valve opens at a pressure a little in excess of the normal maximum operating pressure, in case of failure of the governor or unloader. A low pressure warning device (Fig. 9.14) will be mounted on or adjacent to each reservoir and operates an audible warning in the cab if the stored presure is below about 4 bar (60 lbf/in^2), indicating to the driver that he should not proceed; it consists of a spring loaded diaphragm which opens an electrical contact as the pressure rises above the predetermined value. There will also be a connection from

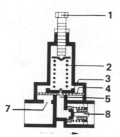
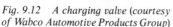
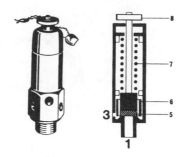

Fig. 9.12 A charging valve (courtesy of Wabco Automotive Products Group)

Fig. 9.13 A safety valve (courtesy of Wabco Automotive Products Group)

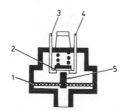

Fig. 9.14 The switch for a low pressure warning indicator (courtesy of Wabco Automotive Products Group)

each reservoir to a pressure gauge mounted in the cab, so that the driver can check the pressure in each part of the storage system.

9.4 Brake actuation

The two previous sections describe how clean, dry air may be compressed and stored in reservoirs at a limited pressure, ready for use as required; before considering how the air is used, by describing the methods of release under the control of the driver, it is helpful first to consider what it is used for, by looking at the means by which the brakes are actuated.

The usual way in which air pressure is applied to generate a force to actuate a brake is by the use of a diaphragm type brake chamber; the illustration (Fig. 9.15) shows a typical example of a unit containing a single diaphragm which transmits a force to the brake by way of a push plate and push rod. The housing consists of two steel pressings which, with the diaphragm located between them, are held together by a clamp ring; the one pressing incorporates alternative inlet ports while the other contains a breather hole and has the mounting studs assembled to it. Units from different makers will vary slightly in their characteristics such as constancy of output throughout their stroke and the maximum stroke available; they are designated by type

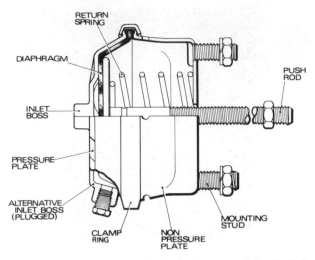

Fig. 9.15   A diaphragm type air chamber (courtesy of Bendix Ltd.)

numbers which indicate the effective diaphragm area in square inches, a range of interchangeable sizes usually being offered which facilitates the adjustment of brake balance between axles.

As an alternative to the use of diaphragms, piston type units are sometimes used (Fig. 9.16); these yield a constant force throughout their stroke, which can be of any suitable length. Piston type units do not readily lend themselves to use for brake actuation with duplicated air systems as do diaphragm type units, because of the inconvenient length of a tandem unit; however, they are commonly used to operate a master cylinder in an air/hydraulic system such as was described in Chapter 7.

Considerations of safety made it desirable in some cases to be able to operate a brake by either one of two alternative air supplies; for this purpose, the double diphragm air chamber (Fig. 9.17) was devised and has been used widely for a number of years, although it is not so often used now. This unit is similar to the single diaphragm type, but for the inclusion of a second diaphragm and the spacer ring, which incorporates the inlet port for the principal or service diaphragm.

In normal braking, with equal pressures fed to the two inlet ports from separate braking circuits, the service diaphragm acts on the push rod and the secondary diaphragm—with equal pressures on both sides—is ineffective; should a failure put the service part of the system out of action, the secondary diaphragm, which has a thickened central portion, presses the service diaphragm against the push plate and the two diaphragms then flex simultaneously. Commonly, the secondary

Fig. 9.16   A piston type air chamber

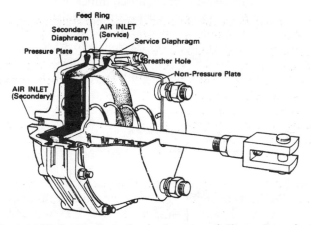

Fig. 9.17   A double diaphragm air chamber (courtesy of Clayton Dewandre Co. Ltd.)

diaphragms have also been used to apply brakes for parking, an external mechanical means being used to hold them on, after which the air was released; the brakes could only then be released by again activating the secondary diaphragms.

Triple diaphragm brake chambers have also been made and applied to trucks with dual air systems, the third diaphragm (of similar design to the secondary diaphragm of a double diaphragm unit) being situated between those for service and secondary use, with an additional spacer ring; the chamber thus created between the secondary and third diaphragms is vented to atmosphere. This type of unit was introduced to give positive separation of the two air systems in the case of a failure of the secondary diaphragm; with the increasingly high quality of diaphragms reducing the number of such failures to very small proportions, the design was not widely adopted.

The accepted method of parking a truck had always been by the use of a mechanical linkage operated by a lever in the cab, multi-pull levers being developed for use on the heavier trucks; the use of power assistance to apply the brakes, the mechanical linkage merely sustaining the application, made parking much easier for drivers. However, acceptance by legislators of the principle of directly sustaining the brake application, without any external mechanical linkage, was a further step which simplified the parking of trucks of the ever increasing gross weights which were coming into service.

Of the two methods introduced in the mid 1960s, the lock actuator has not eventually become firmly established in Europe; it consists essentially of an air operated locking mechanism applied to the push rod of a double or triple diaphragm air chamber (Fig. 9.18). Around the push rod are a number of rollers surrounded by a cone ring; during normal driving, the annular lock piston is activated by air pressure via the lock port and holds the rollers forwards, against the pressure of the roller seating spring. When the vehicle is to be parked, the push rod is operated by the secondary diaphragm then the air

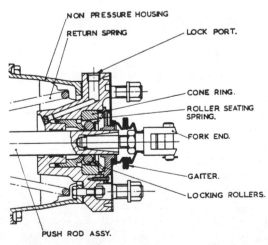

Fig. 9.18   The mechanism of a lock actuator (courtesy of Clayton Dewandre Co. Ltd.)

activating the lock piston is exhausted; this allows the roller seating spring to engage the rollers between the push rod and the cone ring. When, next, the air is exhausted from the secondary diaphragm, the tendency of the push rod to return is resisted by the jamming of the rollers; the brake is released when required by reversing this sequence of events.

Lock actuators could be difficult to release if applied before hot brake drums contracted and the very high contact pressures between the rollers and the other components could cause deformation of the metal; the spring brake unit, which was the alternative device, does not suffer from such problems and has become widely accepted. A typical spring brake unit (Fig. 9.19) shows how a single diaphragm air chamber D is combined with a strongly constructed housing H, containing a powerful spring K, which acts on the piston J and piston rod S.

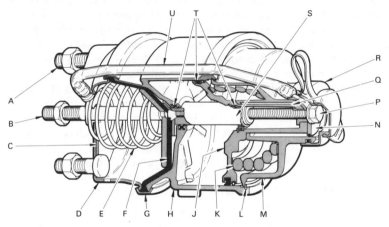

Fig. 9.19   A spring brake unit (courtesy of Bendix Ltd.)

With all stored air pressure discharged, the spring will be extended, applying the brake by causing the piston rod S to operate the push rod B; in this condition, it would be possible when the vehicle must be moved for repair purposes to turn the wind-off bolt P, drawing the piston rod back into the extension of the piston and compressing the spring. Once the air system has been recharged, the controls can be operated to admit air to the spring chamber, so that the piston compresses the spring and releases the brake; however, if the driver had kept his foot on the brake pedal whilst releasing the parking control, air would simultaneously be admitted to the service braking chamber D and would maintain the brake application.

During a spell of normal driving, all the braking is done by the use of the service diaphragm F; only if it is necessary to use the secondary system or to park is the air supply to the piston J affected. For secondary braking, a controlled reduction of the air acting on the piston allows the spring to apply the brake as desired; although it remains a possibility that a system failure between the control and the piston inlet port could permit a sudden, uncontrolled brake application, such failures are virtually unheard of.

A feature of the Bendix unit illustrated is the breather pipe U, which connects the spring chamber to the front portion of the service brake chamber; this provides that when the spring is allowed to expand, the air drawn into its chamber is the relatively clean and dry air which is, at the same time, expelled from the service brake chamber.

The effort exerted by a coil spring reduces as it extends so the torque developed by a brake which is applied by a spring brake unit will depend on the state of adjustment of the brake; this is one of the reasons in favour of the adoption of automatic brake adjustment. Even when the spring is fully extended inside its housing, it still exerts a very considerable force; dismantling should, therefore, only be undertaken with suitable equipment and the disposal of unserviceable units should be undertaken with suitable safeguards.

The mechanical release of a spring brake unit by means of a wind-off bolt is a somewhat laborious matter if the space around the unit is limited, as in the case of buses; Knorr has therefore developed, as an alternative, a quick release mechanism, one type of which is illustrated (Fig. 9.20). By turning the external hexagon head of the device through 45°, the piston and spring are disconnected from the piston rod, so that the spring can abruptly extend completely to remove its effort from the piston rod and release the brake; when the vehicle is to

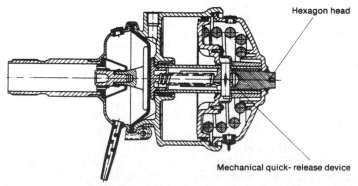

Fig. 9.20   *A spring brake unit of quick release type* (*courtesy of Knorr Bremse GmbH*)

be put back into service and its air system is recharged, the admission of air to the piston chamber recompresses the spring and the piston and piston rod reconnect automatically.

The brake actuators so far described have all been designed for mounting on a bracket in conjunction with a slack adjuster and a cam brake; alternative designs, however, incorporate a tube for direct assembly to wedge type brakes. The illustration (Fig. 9.21) shows a twin wedge, full two leading shoe (duo-duplex) type of brake fitted with tube mounting brake chambers; one of these is a single

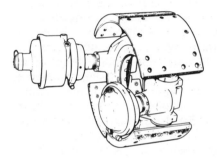

Fig. 9.21   Tube mounting actuators on a twin wedge brake (courtesy of Bendix Ltd.)

diaphragm unit while the other is a spring brake unit so that, for either secondary braking or parking, the brake operates as a leading/trailing (simplex) type.

9.5 Air pressure control and distribution

It is now apparent how, in a braking system, air is stored under pressure for use as required and what it is used for; the next stage is to consider how air is released from the reservoirs at a controlled pressure and guided to the brake actuators. Some of the actuators to which the air is fed are such that operation of the control must yield an increasing pressure, from atmospheric up to the maximum; others (the secondary/parking function of a spring brake unit) are such that operation of the control must bring about a reduction from the maximum operating pressure to a lesser value. The popular names applied to these very different control functions are, respectively, upright and inverted, but it should be noted that these in no way refer to the position in which such valves are mounted.

First, however, it is appropriate to consider the foot valve, which is always of upright type, and the other principal components used to control and distribute the air will be considered in order. Although it was at one time permissible to provide service and secondary braking control by means of a single foot valve and a hand control, foot valves are now normally of dual type, controlling two separate circuits; it is, however, easier to consider how a single valve operates before noting the construction of the more complex dual units.

Figure 9.22 shows in simplified form the principal components of a typical valve assembly; the plunger is acted upon by the treadle and bears on the graduating spring by way of a collar, which can slide on the piston spindle, to which it is not attached. In the 'off' position, the hollow spindle would be clear of the face of the inlet/exhaust valve, allowing air to pass from the brakes to atmosphere through the exhaust breather in the side of the valve body; at the same time, the inlet port would be closed so that no air could pass through from the reservoir.

The valve is, in fact, shown in the 'on' position; the effort applied to the plunger has compressed the graduating spring slightly, closed the exhaust port and moved the inlet/exhaust valve down to open the inlet valve. Air is now passing from the reservoir to the brakes and is also, by way of the small bleed hole, acting on the underside of the piston; as air pressure builds up under the piston it will (acting with the light return spring) eventually lift the piston and close the inlet valve. With equal forces above and below the piston, a constant air

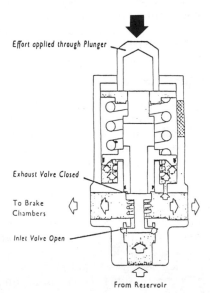

Fig. 9.22   The elements of a single circuit foot valve (courtesy of Clayton Dewandre Co. Ltd.)

pressure, proportional to the effort on the plunger, is then delivered to the brakes, the response time being limited to a small fraction of a second; the driver can feel, acting on the treadle, the reaction force which the air pressure has set up.

Any change in the driver's effort on the treadle will now unbalance the situation. An increase in effort will move the piston downwards and reopen the inlet valve to admit more air to the brakes, until the forces on the piston again balance; a decrease in effort will open the exhaust port and let air out. In either case, the brakes can be held on at some different pressure until a further change of effort is made or they are released; a treadle effort in excess of that which is necessary to cause full opening of the inlet port can achieve nothing extra.

It will be noted that the treadle movement involved in applying the brakes is quite small, being limited to that necessary to compress the graduating spring to create the appropriate force which is balanced by the air pressure. Unlike the brake pedal of a conventional hydraulic system, the travel of which is affected by the number and size of the brake cylinders to be operated, an air valve regulates the delivered pressure precisely with exactly the same travel for any volume of air flow.

Two main types of dual foot valve are found in service, the principal difference being in the configuration rather than in their function; the first of these (Fig. 9.23) consists of two individual control valves of the general type examined above, incorporated into a common housing

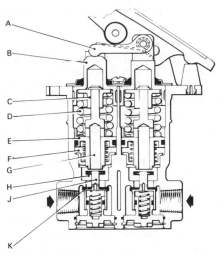

Fig. 9.23   A dual foot valve of tandem type (courtesy of Bendix Ltd.)

Fig. 9.24   A dual concentric foot valve

but entirely separate as regards air flow. Across the two plungers rests a balance beam, in contact at its centre with the foot treadle; the treadle effort is, therefore, shared equally between the two plungers so that, the individual valves being correctly set, they will deliver equal pressures.

The second type of valve is sometimes referred to as dual concentric because the two valves are in line with each other; modern units of this type are very compact (Fig. 9.24) but, to make a description easier, an older model is shown in a sectioned view (Fig. 9.25), because its greater length makes the components easier to identify. Although all of the components are contained in the one casing, the two parts of the complete unit are still entirely separate from each other.

The illustration shows the outlet ports, two to each section of the valve; the inlet ports are at right angles and open respectively into the two chambers marked 'to reservoir', a gauze filter being included in each of these ports as an extra protection against dirt. The principal components in the cylindrical bore of the valve are the graduating spring assembly, upper piston, valve carrier with valve assembly, lower piston and lower valve assembly. The upper piston has a stem which slides in the bore of the valve carrier while the lower piston simply abuts on the lower face of the valve carrier, but has a stem

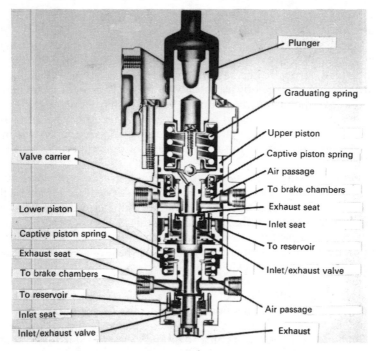

*Fig. 9.25   The components of a dual concentric foot valve; an early design is illustrated
for clarity (courtesy of Clayton Dewandre Co. Ltd.)*

sliding in an auxiliary bore of the valve body; each piston
incorporates an exhaust seat on the end of its stem. Central passages
in the two pistons, together with the bores of the inlet/exhaust valves,
form a continuous path from the upper chamber of the valve, where
the graduating spring is housed, to the exhaust at the bottom when
the plunger is operated; when the plunger is released, the various parts
separate so that air from the two brake circuits can pass to
atmosphere, the inlet valves then being firmly seated.

When the brake treadle operates the valve, the plunger compresses
the graduating spring, forcing the upper piston to move down the
bore until its exhaust seat contacts the rubber face of the inlet/exhaust
valve and closes the exhaust port. Continuing movement of the piston
opens the inlet port, as the inlet/exhaust valve is pushed downwards;
in addition to air then passing into the outlets to one of the two brake
systems, it also acts on the surface of the lower piston, causing it to
move down the bore. This first closes the exhaust port of the lower
inlet/exhaust valve and then opens the inlet port; air is then fed to the

second circuit, this happening virtually simultaneously to the operation of the upper part of the valve.

As the air pressure builds up in the two brake systems, it also reacts on the underside of each piston, passing through the small drilling in the valve carrier in the case of the upper piston and through the drilling in the valve body for the lower piston. The forces set up in this way move the pistons back up the bore, closing the inlet ports and opposing the driver's effort on the treadle as the forces balance; any variation of the treadle effort will then unbalance the system in a corresponding manner to the functioning of the single unit described above.

Before passing to consider hand control valves, it is convenient to describe a component associated with the release of the air fed by the foot valve to the brake actuators on rigid vehicles, when the driver's effort is removed from the brake treadle; this is the quick release valve, which allows pressure to be released from the brake actuators at a point near to them, more rapidly than if all the air had to pass back to the foot valve and be exhausted there.

The quick release valve shown (Fig. 9.26) consists of a flexible diaphragm, sandwiched between two metal castings which form the body of the unit; the inlet port A is connected to one of the outlets of the foot valve, the ports C and G are connected to the left hand and right hand brake actuators on an axle and E is the exhaust port. When a brake application is made, the air entering at A presses the diaphragm against the exhaust seat F, deflects the edges of the diaphragm and passes to the brake chambers as shown; while a constant application is sustained, the diaphragm—while remaining pressed against the exhaust seat—reassumes its flat form and contacts

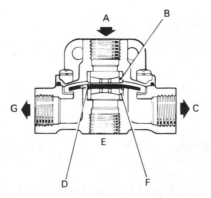

Fig. 9.26   A quick release valve (courtesy of Bendix Ltd.)

the upper body casting at its periphery, so that the inlet port is now isolated from the ports D and G.

As soon as pressure starts to fall at A, because air in the supply line is being exhausted at the foot valve, the pressure below the diaphragm lifts it off the exhaust seat so that the air from the brake actuators is rapidly exhausted to atmosphere, thus releasing the brakes quickly. When atmospheric pressure has been established within the unit, the diaphragm returns to its free form and again contacts the exhaust seat.

9.6 Hand valves

A considerable number of types of hand valve for controlling parts of air braking systems have been designed and manufactured in the period covered by this book; it is not possible or necessary to describe them all, so some have been selected which include the most important features likely to be encountered.

The first example (Fig. 9.27) is an 'upright' valve, such as has been used with double or triple diaphragm brake chambers to provide secondary braking, or to apply trailer brakes independently of the tractor brakes; this example has the operating handle moving in a plane at right angles to the centre line of the valve mechanism, but this need not necessarily be so. A section through this unit (Fig. 9.28) shows that the elements contained in the valve mechanism are as found in a foot valve; the difference is primarily that the effort applied to the piston or graduation spring is derived from the relative movement of the cam and cam follower when the latter is turned by means of the handle.

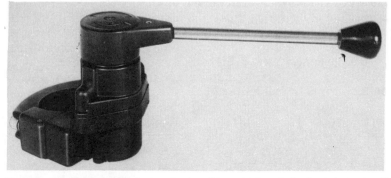

Fig. 9.27   One design of hand control valve; this controls a single circuit (courtesy of Bendix Ltd.)

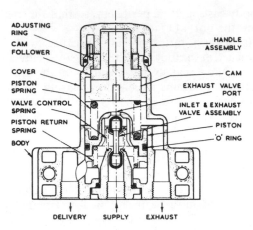

Fig. 9.28   The mechanism of the valve illustrated in Fig. 9.27 (courtesy of Bendix Ltd.)

The construction of an inverted valve, such as is used to control a spring brake unit, is very similar to that of an upright unit; the cam and cam follower are, however, reversed so that when the control handle is in the 'off' position the graduating spring is under full load. Because such a control valve can be used for both secondary braking (controlled partial release of air to partly apply the spring brake) and parking (full release of air for full brake application), there are two stages of movement for the handle and a dash pot may be fitted to ensure that a sudden movement of the handle cannot be made.

Figure 9.29 shows a Knorr unit in diagrammatic form, ports numbers 1, 2 and 3 being for inlet from reservoir, outlet to spring brake and exhaust respectively; with this unit, the first 64° of angular movement of the handle from the 'off' position controls the graduated application of the spring brake and return of the handle to the 'off' position is automatic if it is released. The application of increased effort to the handle to overcome a built-in resistance, enables a further 16° of angular movement to the 'park' position to be achieved, and the handle locks in this position; to release the handle from the 'park' position, an axial pull on the knob is required.

An alternative design of inverted hand valve for the control of spring brakes (Fig. 9.30) features a handle moving in the vertical plane, as referred to earlier; this sectional drawing shows that the plunger A and piston assembly B are operated through the medium of a crank attached to the handle, instead of by a cam, so that there can be a feed-back to the driver as is the case with a foot valve. As the driver moves the handle through the first part of its travel, he feels a

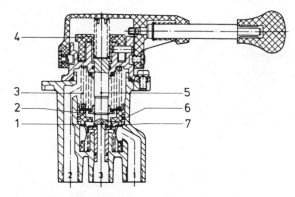

Fig. 9.29   This hand control valve is retained in the 'Park' position by the spring loaded knob. Driving position: 1 = Inlet port, 2 = Graduating piston, 3 = Compression spring, 4 = Cam, 5 = Piston rod, 6 = Outlet port, 7 = Chamber 'a' (courtesy of Knorr Bremse GmbH)

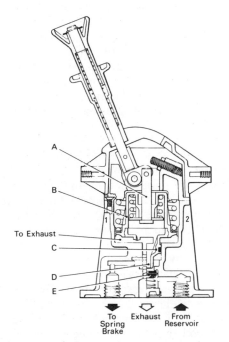

Fig. 9.30   Another design of hand control valve; the pressure graduating mechanism is operated by a lever instead of a rotating cam (courtesy of Bendix Ltd.)

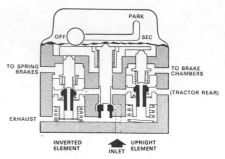

Fig. 9.31   A dual hand control valve for operating an 'upright' and an 'inverted' circuit simultaneously

Fig. 9.32   A simplified illustration of the mechanism of the valve shown in Fig. 9.31 (courtesy of Clayton Dewandre Co. Ltd.)

resistance proportional to the air pressure being delivered; on moving the handle to the 'park' position it locks in place until, when the spring brake is to be released, the sleeve on the handle is lifted.

A more complex valve (Fig. 9.31) contains two graduating elements—one upright and one inverted—which are operated by a single handle; by this means the valve can simultaneously control secondary air chambers and spring brakes on the one vehicle or combination. Figure 9.32 enables the working of this valve to be understood, the handle being in the 'off' position so that the rotary cam plate has released the upright graduating element on the right (so that zero pressure is applied to the brake chambers) and is holding fully open the inverted graduating element on the left (so that the spring brakes are held off).

The common air supply to both graduating elements passes by way of the central, piston rod operated inlet/exhaust valve, the movement of which is controlled by the vertical movement of the operating handle, as it moves into and out of the 'park' position. Each graduating element consists of a plunger, which is operated by the cam, a light return spring, an inlet/exhaust valve (with light return spring), a valve carrier which houses these components and the adjustable graduating spring.

As the cam is turned by movement of the handle towards the 'sec' position shown, the two elements graduate the delivered air pressure in the usual way, supplying pressure to the secondary air chambers and (subject to the particular system design) reducing the pressure to the spring brake chambers. When the handle is moved to the 'park' position the piston rod rises, allowing the associated inlet/exhaust valve to rise and first isolate the air supply from the two graduating elements before opening the exhaust port; when this happens, all air is exhausted from the secondary and spring brake chambers so that the vehicle is parked on the spring brakes alone.

Special versions of hand valves have been designed for the control of lock actuators and for other purposes, but the final example to be considered is one developed for use on town buses which make frequent stops. The handle can be moved clockwise through an agle of some 55° to operate an inverted graduating element, shown on the right in Fig. 9.33, for secondary braking purposes, followed by a

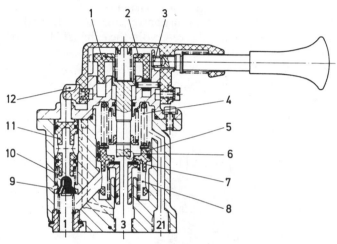

Fig. 9.33   The construction of the Knorr 'bus stop' hand control valve. Position shown: Parking brake, locked. 1 = Cam, 2 = Piston rod, 3 = Lock peg, 4 = Compression spring, 5 = Graduating piston, 6 = Outlet port, 7 = Inlet port, 8 = Chamber 'a', 9 = Inlet port 2, 10 = Outlet port 2, 11 = Piston, 12 = Cam slope (courtesy of Knorr Bremse GmbH)

further 35° of movement to the 'park' position where it locks; on the other hand, anti-clockwise movement through 20° operates the upright valve element on the left in the illustration to apply the service brake chambers on the rear axle. The use of this hand valve reduces driver fatigue; just as when the handle is moved to the 'park' position, it locks automatically when moved to the 'stop' position and must be pulled out to release it. The three ports in the base of the unit are connected as follows: 1 is the air inlet from the reservoir, 3 is the exhaust, 21 is led to the spring brake chambers which control the secondary and parking braking; the outlet port from the upright valve element to the service brake chambers on the rear axle is not shown.

9.7 Relay and anti-compounding valves

Hand control valves are situated in the driver's cab so, if they had to pass the full volume of air concerned in the application of the various actuators, there could be an unacceptable noise level and perhaps, also, an excessive delay in brake operation and release. It is common, therefore, for hand valves to merely supply a control signal to a relay valve situated nearer to the brake actuators; the relay valve draws its air supply directly from the appropriate reservoir and exhausts it direct to atmosphere so is able to ensure that a rapid response is obtained. Sometimes two relay valves in series are used when the brake actuators to be operated are particularly remote.

Figure 9.34 shows a typical relay valve consisting of a body casting with an inlet F for air from the reservoir, the exhaust H, one or more outlets O to brake actuators and the inlet/exhaust valve having a hollow spindle J. The cover A includes the control inlet port D and houses a piston B, to the central spigot of which a valve seat N is attached.

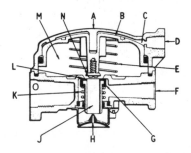

Fig. 9.34   A single relay valve (courtesy of Bendix Ltd.)

When a hand control valve is operated, or a pressure signal comes from another source, air enters the port D and acts on the piston, pressing it down against the resistance of the return spring E and causing the valve seat N to close the exhaust port in the inlet/exhaust valve J. Mounting air pressure above the piston will continue to press it downwards, so that the inlet/exhaust valve is depressed, and air from the inlet F is able to pass through to chamber M and to one of the outlets O; the increasing air pressure in M will also act upwards on the underside of piston B.

As the upwards force on the piston, due to the air pressure below it and the return spring force, becomes equal to the downward force due to the air pressure above, the piston will move up and allow the inlet/exhaust valve to close the inlet port. As long as the incoming signal pressure remains steady, the relay valve will maintain a constant outlet pressure to the brakes; the dimensions of the piston and the stiffness of the return spring are carefully controlled so that the two pressures are equal within very close limits. Any variation of the signal pressure unbalances the piston and causes it to move, either to open the inlet port to admit more air to the brakes, or to open the exhaust valve until the forces are again in balance. When the signal pressure falls to atmospheric, the exhaust valve is opened permanently and the brakes are fully released; it is common for the relay valve to be used in conjunction with a quick release valve (as already described), so that most of the air will be exhausted to atmosphere close to the brakes, the relay valve and the hand control valve each only exhausting a relatively small volume.

Other, more complex, relay valves will be described in the next section, dealing with trailer braking.

Depending on the system arrangement, there are ways in which it is possible for a brake to be affected by two separate controls and special components exist which relate to this possibility. The first of these components is the change-over or double check valve (Fig. 9.35); this is found when a brake actuator may be fed by either a foot or a hand operated control, and it ensures that only the higher of the two pressures can take effect. As can be seen, there are separate inlet ports for the two individual supplies and a shuttle valve which allows only one to pass to the outlet; at any time, the higher pressure will cause the shuttle valve to seal off the inlet at which the lower pressure is acting.

A more complex situation arises when a spring brake unit is

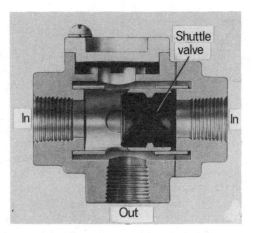

Fig. 9.35   A double check valve (courtesy of Clayton Dewandre Co. Ltd.)

considered, with a service actuator operated by an upright foot control and the spring brake operated by an inverted hand control; if both controls were to be applied fully at the same time, there would be a probability of wheel locking being caused and also of brake components being damaged by the compounding of the two forces. The valve designed to prevent misuse from occurring is called an anti-compounding or differential protection valve; it acts on the secondary/parking system in response to the air pressure in the service system.

In the example shown (Fig. 9.36), the body contains an inlet port from the secondary/parking control, by way of a relay valve, and two

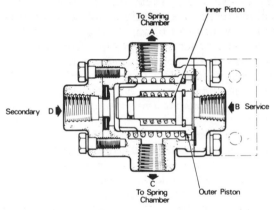

Fig. 9.36   A differential protection valve (courtesy of Bendix Ltd.)

outlet ports to the spring brake chambers; there is also a connection to the service brake system. Inside the body are an outer piston and an inner piston, each acted upon by a spring; there are also two seals, each affected by one of the two pistons. The right hand face of the outer piston is normally seated by its spring on the seal around the port connected to the service system; the left hand end of the inner piston can seal off the inlet port which supplies air to the spring brake units, but is usually held out of contact by its spring.

Under normal driving conditions, full air is admitted from the secondary/parking control to the differential protection valve, and passes through to the spring brake chambers to compress the springs and leave the brakes off; at the same time, the service system is at atmospheric pressure and the pistons in the valve are in the positions illustrated. If the service brake is now applied, the air pressure in that part of the system acts upon both inner and outer pistons but does not displace them against the pressure already acting on their other faces.

Should the driver now also use the secondary/parking control and release the air pressure in the associated system, so that the pressure to the left of the pistons in the differential protection valve starts to fall and becomes less than the pressure in the service system, the dimensions of the pistons and the stiffness of the springs are so chosen that, first, the inner piston moves to the left to close the left hand port and then the outer piston follows it, opening the port from the service system; air from the service system can now pass through the valve to the spring brake chambers to keep the springs compressed. Should the driver subsequently, on halting the vehicle, release the brake treadle whilst leaving the secondary/parking control 'on', the release of pressure in the service line allows the outer piston to re-seat and then the inner piston to re-open the associated port; the air which had been applied to the spring brake chambers to prevent compounding, now exhausts by way of the secondary system (at the relay valve) and the spring brakes operate to park the vehicle.

Had the driver used the brake controls in the reverse sequence, the valve would have operated in a similar manner, responding to the two pressures acting at the opposed ends of the sub-assembly of pistons and springs. The valve operates when the pressure in the service system exceeds that in the secondary system by approximately 2.1 bar $(30 \ \mathrm{lbf/in^2})$; the additional forces created by this overlap are not sufficient to overstress the mechanical parts of the system.

It is convenient here to mention that stop light switches are included in both service and secondary air systems to ensure that a visible indication is given to other drivers; these are commonly of diaphragm type (Fig. 9.37) and operate either with rising pressure (type 1; service braking) or falling pressure (type b; secondary braking by spring brake). A further minor matter is that test points are now required at specified positions in air braking systems so that the correct functioning of components can conveniently be verified by the use of pressure gauges.

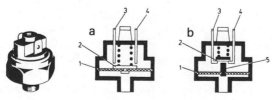

Fig. 9.37   Stop light switches for (a) rising and (b) falling pressure (courtesy of Wabco Automotive Products Group

9.8 Trailer braking

When a draw bar or articulated trailer is to be coupled to a towing vehicle which is fitted with air actuated brakes, it will need an air supply, actuators for the brakes and a means of control and distribution as does the towing vehicle; the brake actuators will be of one of the types already described—nowadays usually spring brake units—and the trailer will carry its own reservoir but the tractor vehicle braking system will include additional components, there will be couplings between the two vehicles and certain system components will be found on the trailer.

Depending on the layout of the system adopted (examples are considered later in this chapter), the control signal to the trailer brakes may need to be taken from one of either two or three sources, the system being required to respond to that signal which would cause the higher value of deceleration to be produced; this is achieved by the use of a special type of relay valve, situated on the tractive vehicle, which automatically prevents compounding of the various signal pressures. The Clayton Dewandre valve shown (Fig. 9.38) is of piston type, having three pistons contained within the upper part of the body and two control ports; the space between the upper and centre pistons is vented into the central exhaust passage, so that any leakage of air from the chambers above or below escapes to atmosphere.

In normal functioning, equal pressures from the two parts of the service braking system are admitted respectively to the space above the upper piston and that between the centre and lower pistons.

The second of these two inputs acts upwards on the centre piston,

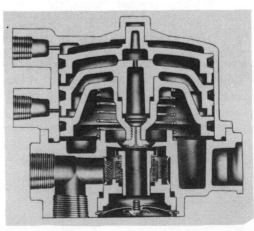

Fig. 9.38   A cross section of a dual relay valve (courtesy of Clayton Dewandre Co. Ltd.)

as well as downwards, and thus balances out the effect of the first input; the net result is then due to the second input acting downwards on the lower piston. In a manner corresponding to the working of the simple relay valve described earlier, the lower piston then moves to close the exhaust port, open the inlet port and admit air into the space below the lower piston until a pressure balance is achieved. Should either of the two inputs be lost because of a failure, that which remains will operate the lower piston as before, either directly or by way of the other two pistons; should the input pressures not be equal, it will effectively be the higher one which acts on the lower piston. The output of this relay valve is the control signal which is passed to the trailer.

The Bendix trailer control relay valve, in the form shown (Fig. 9.39), can accept signals from three sources; it allows only that signal at the highest pressure to act on the relay piston L and isolates any source in which there may be a loss of pressure. On top of the valve cover A is mounted a tee shaped, three way double check valve body E; this is provided with three input ports, of which two are marked D and the third is indicated by an arrow. The body E contains two metal sleeved rubber shuttles F and H, which slide in the shuttle guides G and J; the

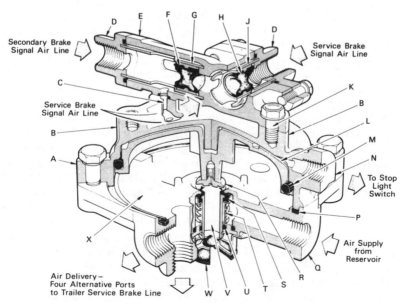

Fig. 9.39   A trailer control valve which accepts signal pressures from any combination of three sources (courtesy of Bendix Ltd.)

guides are slotted, to allow the effective signal to pass to the airway C and into the relay valve chamber.

When the service braking system on the vehicle is operated, equal signal pressures are applied to the two in-line inlet ports while no pressure is applied to the secondary signal inlet port; shuttle H will move to either one end or the other of guide J, sealing off one of the two service signal pressures and allowing the other to pass into the other branch of the tee piece. This pressure then drives shuttle F to the end of guide G, sealing off the secondary signal inlet port, and then passes through the airway C to operate the relay valve in the usual way. The relay valve draws air from the appropriate reservoir on the tractive behicle and its output is the signal passed to a further relay valve on the trailer.

If the secondary braking system on the tractive vehicle is applied when the service brake is released, shuttle F will move to the position illustrated, sealing off the service brake signal inlets; air from the secondary system will then pass through the airway and operate the relay valve. If both systems were to be applied at the same time, the shuttles would ensure that the higher pressure only was effective.

More complex valves are used when it is desired to obtain a signal to operate the trailer brakes from either of the two parts of the upright service brake system or from the inverted secondary brake control used to apply the tractor spring brakes; a number of chambers are formed in the valve so that the supply pressure, the three system pressures referred to and possibly a modulated pressure from a load sensing valve (see Chapter 11) can act on several relay pistons associated with an inlet/exhaust valve. Such valves may also include a predominance spring which acts upon one of the relay pistons, so that the signal pressure delivered to the trailer brakes is increased by a predetermined amount; this feature gives the trailer brakes a slight lead over the tractor brakes and is intended to improve the handling of the tractor/trailer combination, but the effect can be overdone, causing the trailer brakes to be overworked. Setting of the predominance spring is commonly effected by the use of a screwdriver, inserted up the central exhaust port, after removal of the covering rubber flap.

Of a different nature is the supply dump valve, which is designed to give protection to the combination in case of a loss of the signal pressure to the trailer brakes. In the example shown (Fig. 9.40), the sub-assembly of piston E and valve stem D is acted upon by piston spring C so that, when the signal pressures in the service and trailer lines are either equal or zero, the valve stem maintains the inlet/exhaust valve H in the open position; the air supply from the tractor to the trailer reservoir is then maintained. Should the tractor

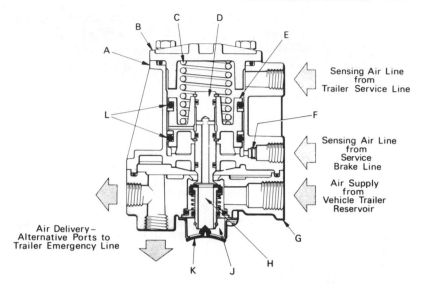

Fig. 9.40   A supply dump valve (courtesy of Bendix Ltd.)

service brakes be applied, so that the associated signal pressure acts below piston E, but no trailer signal pressure be available to act above piston E, the piston and valve stem would be driven upwards; the valve stem would then close the air inlet valve and open the exhaust valve, emptying the trailer supply line and (as will be described in the following section) applying the trailer brakes by using the air already stored in the trailer reservoir.

The supply dump valve may be combined with one of the trailer control valves already described; the close connection of units in this way by the manufacturer reduces the likelihood of installation faults occurring, by reducing the number of external connections.

Another component incorporated for safety reasons is the pressure protection valve (Fig. 9.41); this is fitted on the tractor into the pipeline from the service reservoir to the trailer feed line coupling, downstream of the connection to the service brake control but upstream of the connection to the relay valve which supplies the control signal to the trailer. The function of this valve is to close if trailer breakaway occurs or if, for any other reason, there is a leak in the feed lines; in this way the air supply upstream of the valve is maintained intact.

The valve body contains a seat F for the ball shaped valve D, the stem C of which is guided in the piston B; the piston is loaded by a spring A, which can be adjusted and there is a light return spring on

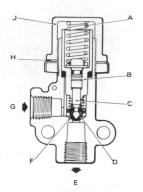

*Fig. 9.41   A pressure protection valve
(courtesy of Bendix Ltd.)*

the valve stem. When the system is exhausted, the valve is closed by spring A, but mounting pressure on piston B by way of the inlet port G eventually causes the spring to be compressed and the valve opened; a sudden loss of pressure at the outlet port E causes the valve to close, protecting the tractor air supply until a repair is effected.

9.9 Trailer-mounted components

Flexible hoses of nylon are commonly used to connect the air actuation systems situated on the tractor and trailer; special connectors are used with these hoses and there are items of control equipment mounted on the trailer, additional to the air reservoir and brake actuators.

There is considerable variation in the number of air lines linking the tractor and trailer; some older continental trailers may still only have one, while two are now increasingly common, many UK vehicles still use three and some have four. Some of these possibilities will be considered in the next section, as well as the problems of matching which can arise when it is desired to use a number of assorted tractors and trailers in different combinations.

In the UK, bayonet type couplings (Fig. 8.42) have been usual for many years but are now being superseded by palm type couplings (Fig. 9.43) of internationally standardised design. Both types of coupling are made in matching pairs which contain automatic shut-off valves which act when lines are disconnected; they are designed and installed in such as way as to prevent incorrect connection of the various lines. Dummy couplings or blanking plugs protect the couplings from damage and prevent dirt from entering the system when the vehicles are uncoupled; these components should be kept as clean as possible when they are handled.

Fig. 9.42   Bayonet type trailer air line couplings

Fig. 9.43   Palm type trailer couplings

For many years in the UK the names 'Service', 'Emergency' and 'Auxiliary' have been popularly used for the two or three air connections most usually found between tractors and trailers, but these are not really indicative of the respective functions; an alternative nomenclature has, therefore, been in use for a time, which will be followed as appropriate in the remainder of this chapter and, where appropriate in Chapter 11. In the same order as above, the lines are called 'Control' (because it passes a controlling signal to the relay valve on the trailer), 'Feed' (because it supplies air to the trailer reservoir) and 'Secondary' (because in the UK three-line system it gives direct secondary operation of the trailer brakes).

It will already be understood that the trailer has its own reservoir, from which air is drawn to apply the brakes for normal purposes, under the control of a signal from the tractor vehicle; this signal is fed

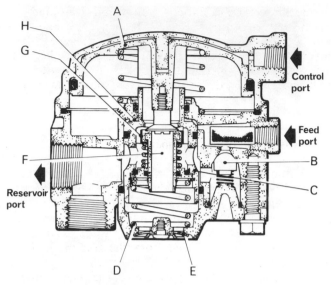

Fig. 9.44   A relay emergency valve (courtesy of Bendix Ltd.)

to a relay valve which regulates the air supply, this valve being of a special nature and being commonly known as a relay emergency valve. In the example shown (Fig. 9.44), it can be seen that the unit is very similar to the relay valve already illustrated (Fig. 9.34) and described; the control signal (which may be modulated by a load sensing valve as described in Chapter 11) acts upon piston A and moves it into contact with the inlet/exhaust valve F, allowing air to be admitted into the chamber under the piston, from which it passes through an outlet (not shown) to the brake chambers.

The differences are first that there is a second piston, marked D, surrounding the inlet/exhaust valve and providing the seat for the inlet valve; also, that there is a check valve B through which air passing from the feed port to the reservoir must flow. The air in the feed port has access to an annular area of piston C (indicated at H in the diagram) so that, as long as pressure is maintained in the feed line, piston C is pressed down, overcoming the force exerted by the spring D; in this position, without the driver making a brake application, the inlet valve is closed and the exhaust valve open, so that the brakes are released and the vehicle free to operate. If the pressure in the feed line is lost, spring D pushes piston C upwards, closing the exhaust port and opening the inlet port, so that the air stored in the reservoir is drawn upon to apply the trailer brakes.

Under normal service conditions, with piston C continuously held down by the pressure acting at H, use of the service braking system on the tractor causes the control signal to act upon the relay piston A in the conventional manner and apply or release the trailer brakes as required. It should be noted that when charging the system after all pressure has been released, piston C is at first in the upward position, as illustrated, so that air passes to both the reservoir and the brake chambers; when the pressure at H reaches 4.1 bars (60 lbf/in^2), spring D is overcome and piston C then opens the exhaust valve, releasing the air already in the brake chambers.

Other components found in trailer air braking systems are, with the exception of those to be described in Chapter 11, of a minor nature. When spring brake units are fitted, there may be a hand control valve; this is used to release the air in the spring chambers, to park the trailer before it is uncoupled from the tractor. A hand operated manoeuvring valve may also be fitted on trailers requiring to be moved by some auxiliary means whilst uncoupled from the tractor; under these conditions, the relay emergency valve would operate, exhaust the air from the spring brake units and park the vehicle. The manouevring valve permits the release of the spring brakes by drawing upon the air supply remaining stored in the trailer reservoir to recompress the springs. Finally, on trailers having brakes operated by standard brake chambers, with mechanical parking by means of a hand lever and cables, there may be a hand operated air release valve to empty the reservoir and release the pressure applied to the air chambers; this is operated after the mechanical parking lever has been applied and the trailer uncoupled.

9.10 System layouts

Over the very many years that air braking equipment has been made, the various manufacturers—acting in conjunction with the considerable number of vehicle builders—have designed an extremely large number of system layouts. Naturally, early layouts were of a simple nature, with only a single supply to all brake chambers and few safeguards but during the intervening years systems have continually increased in complexity in response to demands from users for greater reliability and—in particular—the enactment of legislation requiring the introduction of additional safety features.

The number of variations of the more common basic schemes is so great that it is impracticable to include more than a selected few in this chapter; however, the principal components having been described in some detail, the understanding of typical layouts is made relatively easy. What may not be so easy on any given vehicle is the

Fig. 9.45   The circuits in an air braking system may not always be easy to identify

identification of components, especially if the layout is not systematic (Fig. 9.45). For use in braking system diagrams, there are series of symbols which are nowadays found increasingly in the manufacturers' literature, but as these often bear little visual relationship to the components they represent, they will not be used in the examples which follow.

First, it is convenient to illustrate some of the possible layouts of air supply equipment, including components for dealing by one means or another with moisture contained in the air (Fig. 9.46); many other alternatives may be found but should be easily identifiable from these

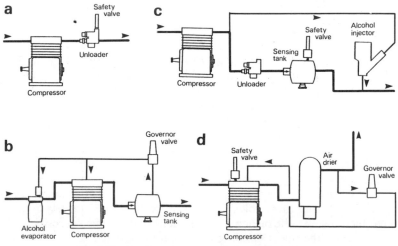

Fig. 9.46   Some arrangements of air supply equipment

examples and the component descriptions given earlier in this chapter. At (a), the compressor is seen with an unloader valve in line, the only refinement being a safety valve coupled to the unloader. At (b), air is drawn through an alcohol evaporator before being discharged to a wet tank with automatic drain valve, from which a line is taken to the governor; from the governor a signal line passes to both the compressor (to unseat the inlet valve) and to the alcohol evaporator (to prevent the use of alcohol while the compressor is running light—a similar arrangement is provided when an unloader valve is used). Example (c) shows the use of an alcohol injector with an unloader valve and a wet tank to which a safety valve is fitted; (d) shows the layout with a governor and an air drier.

The matter of air supply being dealt with in this way, the layout diagrams which follow can be simplified by the omission of this part of the equipment, making them easier to follow; something of the evolution of braking systems can be seen, even in this limited number of examples.

The first example (Fig. 9.47) shows how, in the early 1960s, a British truck might have been fitted with a divided air system, operated from a dual foot valve; the two parts of this system are shown as supplied from a dual reservoir, each compartment being fed through a check valve and having a low pressure indicator switch and a manual drain

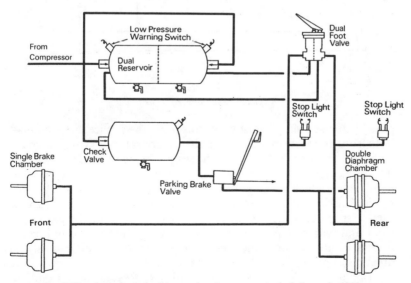

Fig. 9.47   A truck air braking system layout, typical of the early 1960s

tap. The front brake circuit feeds single diaphragm air chambers and the rear circuit is led to the service diaphragm of double diaphragm air chambers; a separate reservoir supplies air to the secondary diaphragm of the rear actuators under control of a handbrake valve to apply the brakes which, for parking, are then sustained by the mechanical linkage, in accordance with the requirements of the period. The air returning from the brake chambers after an application is all exhausted at the appropriate brake valve.

The changes in the UK Construction and Use Regulations in 1966 led to some modification of truck brake systems, the second example (Fig. 9.48) illustrating a typical layout; by making use of spring brake units with a hand secondary/parking valve as was then permitted, it is

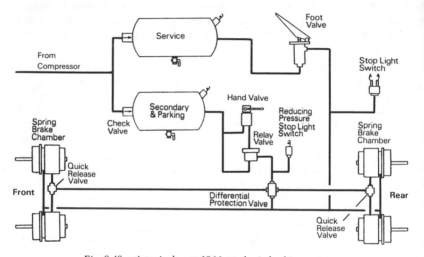

Fig. 9.48   A typical post 1966 truck air braking system

possible to use a simple foot valve to supply the service diaphragm of both front and rear spring brake units. A separate reservoir is used for secondary braking and parking, the supply being utilised to compress the springs to release the brakes; control is by means of the inverted hand valve which gives graduated control of pressure release for service braking and sustained full release for parking, a relay valve is used to speed brake application and quick release valves are fitted for front and rear spring units. To prevent operation of the brakes by means of the service and secondary systems simultaneously, a differential protection valve is incorporated.

Prior to the 1966 Construction and Use Regulations, a code of practice had necessitated the use of three air lines between tractors

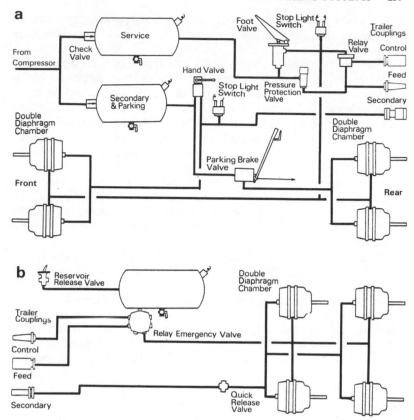

Fig. 9.49   An air braking system layout for a tractor (a) and articulated trailer (b) of the early post 1966 period, with three line trailer connections

and articulated trailers, as against the two previously needed; this was to provide for secondary braking of the trailer by entirely separate means to those used for service braking. The next layout shown (Fig. 9.49) illustrates at (a) how the tractor system had to be modified to allow for controlling the trailer brakes; the system for the tractor itself is still basically simple, with double diaphragm chambers at both axles. Air from the Service reservoir is led to the trailer feed coupling, with a pressure protection valve downstream of the connection to the foot valve; a second output from the foot valve supplies the signal for the trailer service braking, but is taken to the control coupling by way of a relay valve to safeguard the tractor braking in case of a breakaway. Secondary braking is controlled by a hand valve, which feeds the secondary diaphragms of the front axle chambers, this supply being also led to the secondary coupling; parking, by means of the mechanical linkage is (as with the first layout considered) air assisted.

The trailer layout is shown at (b) and it will be seen that double diaphragm brake chambers are used on the twin axles. The supply to the trailer reservoir passes by way of the feed coupling and the relay emergency valve and there is a reservoir release valve; this is to permit the trailer system to be exhausted when the trailer is parked and its manually operated handbrake has been applied. The signal for service braking is led from the control coupling to the relay emergency valve, from which air is led to the service diaphragms of the brake chambers; air to operate the secondary diaphragms, controlled by the hand valve on the tractor, passes from the secondary coupling direct to the brake chambers. Air from the service diaphragms is exhausted at the relay emergency valve; a quick release valve is provided for the secondary diaphragms.

Changes to the Construction and Use Regulations have led to further modifications in systems and a three-line tractor and trailer system of the early 1970s (still very common in the UK) is shown next (Fig. 9.50); the tractor system at (a) shows that a simple foot valve is used to supply the service diaphragm of spring brake units at front and rear, as well as actuating a relay valve to supply a control signal to the trailer control coupling. The dual control valve incorporates an inverted unit to actuate the spring units on the tractor, a differential protection valve preventing compounding, and an upright unit to actuate the secondary diaphragms on the trailer; each of these sections of the system is supplied by way of a relay valve. A variable load valve is incorporated in the supply line to the rear axle service diaphragms; as already noted, such units will be considered in Chapter 11.

The corresponding trailer layout, at (b), is almost identical to the preceding one, but includes a variable load valve.

The entry of the UK into the European Economic Community necessitated acceptance of Community braking regulations and led to further changes; in addition, the increasing adoption of twin wedge (duo duplex) brakes for trucks opened up further possibilities. Considering these changes in stages, we first look at a truck layout for use with spring brake units at front and rear (Fig. 9.51); here we find separate reservoirs for front and rear service braking and for secondary braking or parking, each being guarded by a single circuit protection valve. A dual foot valve controls the two parts of the service system and a hand valve, by way of a relay valve, controls the spring brake units; with service braking split between front and rear, two differential protection valves are needed. Test points are provided

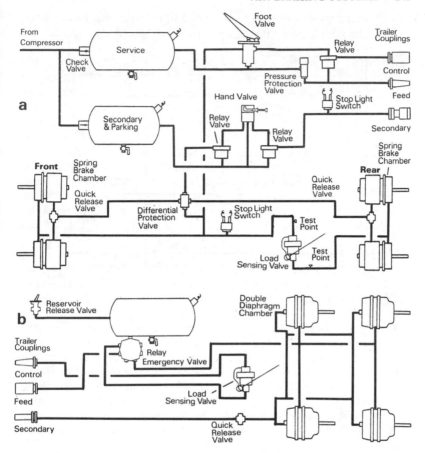

Fig. 9.50   A typical system layout for a tractor (a) and three line articulated trailer (b) of the early 1970s, such as is still very common (with variations) in the UK

immediately before and after the variable load valve, to permit checks on input and output pressures.

When twin wedge brakes are used, there have to be two expander units per brake and the next example (Fig. 9.52) shows spring brake units at one expander of each of the rear brakes with single diaphragm air chambers in all other positions; twin service brake systems are again employed, but these are now arranged so that each feeds one expander at each brake. With this arrangement, which is referred to as a 'horizontal' split (as distinct from the simple front/rear or 'vertical' split of the previous example), all four brake units can still be operated

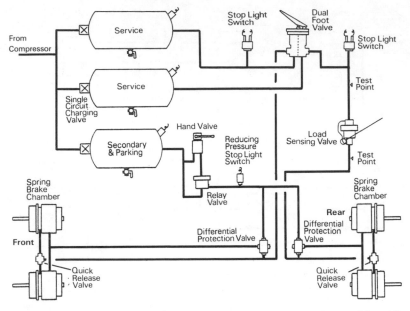

Fig. 9.51 A truck air braking system of the late 1970s, designed to comply with EEC regulations

by one part of the service system, should the other fail; the brake characteristics, however, then revert to leading/trailing (simplex) type. Because the braking of the rear axle is effected by means of independent circuits, each incorporates a load sensing valve.

The twin service reservoirs in this layout are guarded by two of the units of a multiple circuit protection valve; the third is used to supply auxiliaries and the fourth supplies the parking/secondary system which, because it is inverted, needs no reservoir to ensure that a brake application can be made. An interesting feature is the use of 'clean breathing' pipes connected to the back of the spring chambers which receive the air discharged via the quick release valves and through check valves from the spring brake cylinders; this clean, dry air is then conducted to the chambers containing the springs as the pistons move, rather than have moist air drawn in from atmosphere, to the detriment of the springs. The foot valve used in this layout is of the dual concentric type.

One major change in the braking of articulated vehicles in the UK since entry into the EEC has been the reintroduction of two-line connections between tractor and trailer under Community braking regulations. It should be emphasized, however, that the regulations

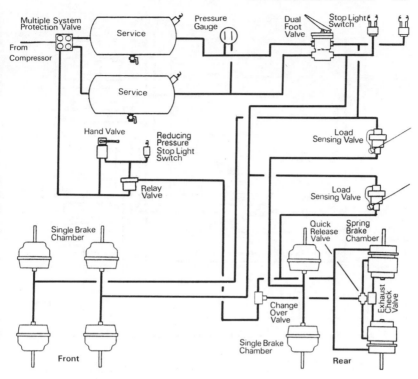

Fig. 9.52   The use of a 'horizontal' split on a system for a truck with twin wedge type brakes, complying with EEC regulations of the late 1970s

do not ban the use of three lines (although it is possible that they may be changed at a future date), but require the use of at least two connections, where one was common usage on the continent. With only two connections, it is not possible to provide secondary braking of the trailer independently of its own air supply and single diaphragm brake chambers.

A typical modern two line tractor and trailer layout is shown next (Fig. 9.53); single spring brake units (with clean breathing pipes) are shown at front and rear of the tractor system (a), there being a vertically split service braking system controlled by a dual concentric foot valve. Separate reservoirs are shown for each part of the service system, for the trailer system and for auxiliaries, all four being guarded by a quadruple circuit protection valve; the pressure in each reservoir is shown on gauges and there are low pressure warning switches, stop light switches and line filters at appropriate positions.

The air supply to the trailer feed coupling passes from the reservoir

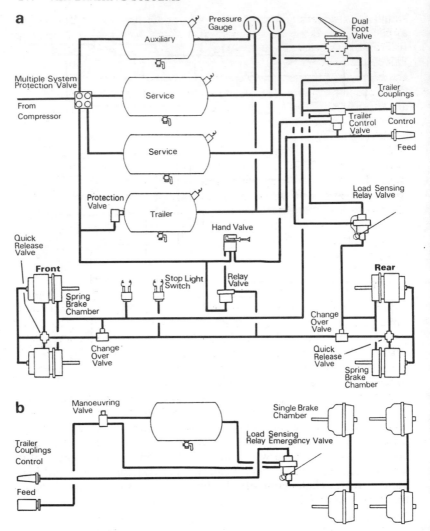

Fig. 9.53   An early 1980s braking system layout design for a tractor (a) and articulated trailer (b) with two line coupling, to EEC standards

by way of the trailer control valve; this valve, in addition, has pipelines connecting it to the two parts of the service system and to the secondary system, the control signal to the trailer being determined by whatever inputs these three pipelines convey to it. The hand valve is an inverted unit which directly controls the spring brake units on the tractor for secondary braking and parking; a separate signal to the trailer control valve causes the trailer brakes to be applied at the same time as secondary braking is initiated on the tractor, but they are released when the tractor is parked. Changeover valves are incorporated at front and rear to prevent compounding of the outputs of the service diaphragms and the spring brake units.

The trailer braking system, shown at (b), is essentially simple. The air supply from the tractor passes from the feed coupling to the emergency part of the relay emergency valve, then to the reservoir; the control signal from the tractor passes to the relay part of this valve, which is also combined with a load sensing valve. From the relay emergency valve, individual pipelines pass to the brake chambers. A manoeuvring valve is provided for use when the trailer has been disconnected from the tractor while the reservoir is still charged; it eliminates the emergency operation of the trailer brakes by reapplying pressure to the supply inlet port of the relay emergency valve, whilst isolating the pipeline from the feed coupling, to permit the trailer to be moved.

9.11 American practice

As an indication of some of the differences between European and American practice, the final example (Fig. 9.54) shows a tractor and trailer system which is in accordance with the requirements of the US authorities, and features at (a) the layout for a typical 6 wheel tractor. A vertical split is used, front and rear axles being served by a dual concentric foot valve, and each part of the service system has its own reservoir; however, the foot valve operates the service braking of the rear axles by way of a relay valve mounted close to them, this also serving as a quick release valve. At the front, a special valve modulates the delivery pressure to the brake chambers at low foot valve delivery pressures. A control valve manifold receives signals from the two service braking circuits and combines these and any signal from the hand operated trailer control valve to provide a control signal for the trailer; this manifold also controls the flow of air to the trailer feed coupling and protects the tractor supply if a breakaway occurs.

The spring brake valve is included in the spring brake delivery circuit; it receives inputs from the unmodulated front axle delivery pressure and the rear axle supply pressure and normally delivers a pre-determined hold-off pressure to the spring brake chambers. If there happens to be a serious drop in the rear axle supply pressure, this valve will reduce the hold-off pressure in proportion to any service pressure supplied to the front brakes; by this means, a high level of secondary braking performance can be achieved from the foot operated system.

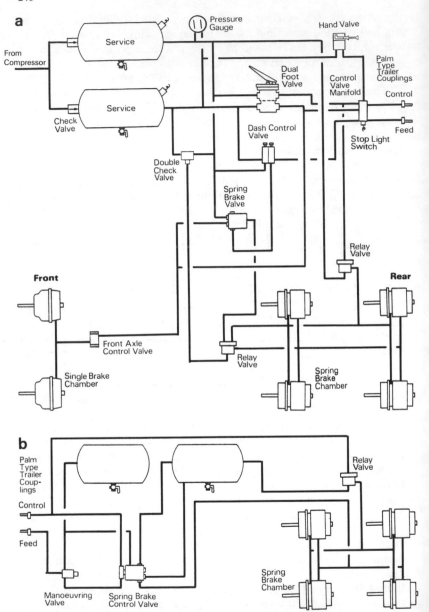

Fig. 9.54   A layout for a tractor (a) and articulated trailer (b) to illustrate some features of American braking system practice

A control valve mounted on the instrument panel is fed from both reservoirs by way of an integral double check valve; it has two push/pull buttons, one red and one yellow. The red trailer supply button must be held depressed when first charging the system until a predetermined pressure is reached; if the stored pressure drops seriously, this button rises automatically to apply the trailer brakes. The yellow parking button controls the spring brakes on the tractor by way of the spring brake valve and the spring brake relay valve, the latter incorporating an anti-compounding valve; use of this button also causes the trailer supply button to rise and initiate trailer brake operation.

The corresponding trailer layout is shown at (b) and it can be seen that there are two reservoirs, supplied from the tractor by way of the feed line and the spring brake control valve; the main reservoir is charged first and the spring brakes remain applied until the stored pressure reaches a certain level. When the service brake on the tractor is applied, the signal to the relay valve causes air from the main reservoir to be fed to the service diaphragm of the spring brake units; this signal pressure is also led to the spring brake control valve to provide anti-compounding protection by operating a single check valve.

Operation of the spring brakes in emergency or for parking is brought about by exhausting the feed line, by means of the instrument panel mounted control valve on the tractor; while the trailer is parked in this way, the manoeuvring valve can be used to release the spring brakes, as long as the air pressure in the spring brake reservoir is sufficient.

American braking system design is under similar development and change as is the case in Europe but, with the guidance of these examples as to how individual components are built into a system, together with the additional information on load sensing and wheel lock prevention in Chapter 11, it should be possible to determine the principal features of newer or more complex systems.

It remains to point out that, with both two-line and three-line systems currently in use for articulated vehicles, there can be problems when mismatched tractors and trailers are brought together; some combinations can safely be coupled but others cannot. Because of the long standing differences in design practice between the UK and mainland Europe, this situation is ongoing and will continue unless harmonisation is achieved.

In general, there is no safety problem involved in drawing a three-line trailer behind a two-line tractor built to EEC standards; the trailer secondary coupling is left unconnected and the trailer service braking system alone is used. However, most three-line tractors built prior to the need to conform to EEC regulations must be modified if they are to draw a two-line trailer safely, otherwise there will be no provision for trailer braking in the case of loss of tractor service braking, because the signal from the secondary braking control on the tractor cannot take effect.

Typically, provision is made on a three-line tractor for connecting the secondary line to a special coupling when a two-line trailer is to be drawn; this coupling on the tractor is connected to an appropriate relay valve, installed between the foot brake valve and the trailer control coupling, so that a signal for the trailer control line can be generated by this alternative means. There are a number of acceptable ways of modifying tractors in this or a similar manner to achieve the desired result, but there are also possibilities which give incomplete protection; in any particular case it is always necessary to seek the recommendation of the manufacturer either of the vehicle or of the braking equipment.

Complicated as tractor and trailer systems are, the principal aim is always simple enough; to provide graduated trailer braking using either of two separate means of control on the tractor and to provide full trailer braking in the event of either a loss of the supply or the signal to the trailer. At the same time, the braking of the tractor must be protected in the event of a system failure on the trailer or a breakaway.

10

Special purpose brakes

10.1 Introduction

Preceding chapters have dealt with some aspects of a wide variety of drum and disc brakes, as found on cars, buses and trucks; there are, however, brakes for other classes of vehicle which have yet to be considered, some of which are of great interest, and there are certain alternative means of braking which come within the scope of this book.

One sizeable application group is the light two-wheel trailer with a caravan body, as widely used by holiday makers. These light trailers are required by law to be fitted with a braking system which commonly comprises mechanical brakes, of leading/trailing shoe (simplex) type, actuated from the connection to the touring vehicle by way of cables; the towing hitch is normally in tension when car and trailer are in motion but provision is made for part of it to telescope slightly when the hitch is put in compression. If the towing vehicle applies its brakes, or descends a hill, the trailer tends to overrun it; the shortening of the hitch then operates a lever pivoted on the trailer chassis, which applies the brakes by way of the cables, the actuating force being approximately proportional to the deceleration of the towing vehicle.

This arrangement is satisfactory for all circumstances except reversing when, despite the generation of a compressive force on the towing hitch, it is necessary for the trailer brake not to be effective; in many cases, this requirement is met by the provision of a physical means of preventing the telescoping of the hitch (Fig. 10.1), but this has to be positioned while the coupled combination is stationary with the hitch extended. Such a method is not altogether convenient because in a difficult manoeuvre, involving alternate forward and reverse movements on a hill, it is not easy to restore the trailer braking for the forward movements nor to cut it out again subsequently; some countries have required forward braking to be restored auto-matically, leaving the braking in reverse to be cut out manually each

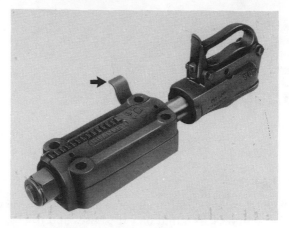

Fig. 10.1   A trailer coupling by Bradley, showing (arrowed) the reversing stop; this company also makes more elaborate types of unit to comply with current legislation (courtesy of H. & K. Bradley (Trailer Equipment) Ltd.)

time. Ideally, a braking system is required which always applies the trailer brakes when the towing hitch is in compression during foward motion, but not in reverse; this requirement is achieved by the Lockheed reversing brake, made by Automotive Products.

10.2 Mechanical reversing brake

In appearance, this brake (Fig. 10.2) is similar to a conventional Lockheed caravan brake with a single acting sliding mechanical expander and a micram adjuster, but with visible differences as regards one of the two brake shoes and the abutment; these

Fig. 10.2   The Lockheed reversing brake for trailers (courtesy of Automotive Products PLC)

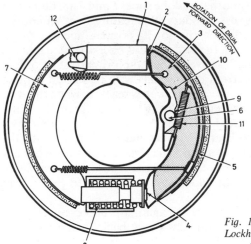

Fig. 10.3   The construction of the
Lockheed reversing brake (courtesy of
Automotive Products PLC)

differences are easily described by referring to Fig. 10.3. The right
hand shoe is a sub-assembly consisting of a carrier 3 (the bold outline),
which at its upper end rests on the specially shaped tappet 2, while the
lower end rests on the abutment spindle 4; the carrier consists of two
plates linked by a pin carrying a roller 6, on which rests the specially
shaped web of the shoe 5. Two springs 11, one on each side of the
carrier, pull the shoe upwards so that its tip rests on the face of the
expander housing, between the forked ends of the tappet; return
springs are fitted between the two shoes, as is usual.

The abutment contains a powerful coil spring 8, which has an
assembled force of about 1330 N (300 lbf), the function of which will
be explained below. The brake is used with a hitch having carefully
controlled travel to operate the brake cables, but no special features
associated with reversing.

In forward motion, when the trailer tends to overrun the towing
vehicle, the brake expander is immediately operated by the usual
cable connection from the hitch; the right hand shoe carrier is then in
turn operated by the tappet 2 and the reaction of the expander
housing causes it to slide and apply the left hand shoe. The roller 6,
which forms part of the shoe carrier, presses on the web of the right
hand shoe 5 and pushes it against the drum; with the drum rotating as
indicated, this shoe abuts on the expander housing, as noted above,
and increases the force acting on the left hand shoe. This brake,
therefore, has a uni-servo characteristic (not duo-servo, since the
effect is uni-directional), by virtue of the transfer of the abutment

reaction from one shoe to another and the shoes 5 and 7 are described respectively as primary and secondary; this feature does, of course, make the brake particularly effective for its normal function.

When the trailer is reversed, the brakes are at once operated and the shoes expanded as before; however, when the primary shoe 5 now contacts the drum, it is carried downwards with its web in contact with the roller 6 until the cutaway in the web is reached, when the shoe tends to drop back from the drum, relieving the pressure on the lining surface. Because of the limited travel of the hitch, referred to above, the expander is unable to keep the shoes hard in contact with the drum and its housing slides to relieve the pressure on the secondary shoe. During reversing, therefore, the linings on both shoes remain in contact with the drum but not under enough pressure to generate an appreciable braking force.

As soon as the trailer moves forward again, the brakes are released and the springs 11 pull the primary shoes back to their normal operating position.

The coil spring 8 in the fixed abutment has two important functions, one applying under emergency stop conditions, when it is desirable to prevent the trailer wheels from locking so that slewing does not occur. At a certain predetermined level of input, the primary shoe carrier abutment force 4 exceeds the force exerted by the spring, which is then compressed slightly so that the brake torque is limited; the spring will also absorb any shocks caused by sudden brake applications.

The second important function of the spring is during the application of the trailer parking brake; the operating lever ratchet is not reached until sufficient force has been developed to compress the spring slightly, the brake operating as a leading/trailing type in the static condition. If the parked trailer tends to move forward, the uni-servo characteristic is developed and the increased torque prevents movement; in reverse, the spring is able to maintain sufficient force on the shoes, even when the primary shoe has moved down to the position at which the pressure is normally relieved.

10.3 Electrical and hydraulic brakes

For general trailer use, electrically operated brakes are sometimes used; of these, the Swedish Linde brake (Fig. 10.4) which is made in a range of sizes and is suitable for use in conjunction with a hydraulically braked towing vehicle, is an interesting example. The brake itself is a cam actuated duo-servo brake of normal configuration, except as regards the means by which the cam is rotated

Fig. 10.4   The Linde electrically actuated trailer brake

between the shoe tips; the cam is, in fact integral with a lever on the end of which is mounted an electro magnet, the connections to which are led out of the brake backplate.

The magnet is so positioned that its poles are close to a ferrous disc, the armature plate, which is mounted inside the drum and rotates with it; when the magnet is energised it is attracted to the armature plate, against which it is designed to rub, so that a friction force is set up which turns the arm and cam, so applying the brake. A cable operated parking brake mechanism is incorporated, a lever pivoted on the secondary shoe being linked to the primary shoe by a strut; manual adjustment is incorporated into the link between primary and secondary shoes.

The source of electrical energy for the electro-magnet is the battery of the towing vehicle, which is connected to the trailer by way of a suitable electrical services coupling; included in the circuit on the towing vehicle is a controller and a variable resistor is situated on the trailer. The controller, which can be matched to suit the braking capabilities of the towing vehicle, is operated hydraulically from part of the brake system (or it may also be operable manually, to brake the trailer independently), and varies the voltage in the circuit in proportion to the driver's pedal effort; the variable resistor on the trailer allows the braking effort developed to be matched to the loading condition of the trailer. Because the brake operating system does not depend on the nature of the forces in the hitch, reversing is no problem; the trailer brake operates equally well in reverse as when going forward, since it is of the duo-servo type.

Fork-lift trucks are a good example of a vehicle with very frequent reversals at frequent intervals and with a need for high torque; often the brakes used are designed and made by the vehicle manufacturer, but they may incorporate proprietary hydraulic components. Brakes for this type of duty have to be of very rugged construction, to suit the duty involved, and it is common to find the drum and backplate mountings dowelled to ensure freedom from relative movement during reversal and to relieve the fastenings from shear stresses. It is necessary that the braking response is the same for either direction of drum rotation, so brakes are usually of either leading/trailing (simplex) or duo-servo type.

Proprietary brakes are sometimes fitted by fork lift and other industrial truck manufacturers and Fig. 10.5 shows the application by Lansing Bagnall of the Perrot duo-servo brake with automatic adjustment, described in Chapter 7 and seen in Fig. 7.9, to one of their vehicles.

Fig. 10.5   A Perrot duo-servo brake on a fork lift truck (courtesy of Lansing Ltd.)

Four-wheel industrial vehicles can be of very many types, besides fork-lift trucks, and have a great variety of functions; they all, however, need to be fitted with brakes and these can sometimes be of unusual design, such as would escape notice altogether if attention were not drawn to them. In this category comes a brake made by the Coventry firm Newage Transmissions Ltd., and incorporated into drive axles—either rigid or steered—which they make; the steered axle (Fig. 10.6) is only different in general appearance from others in

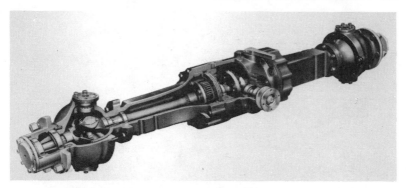

Fig. 10.6 A drive axle with built-in oil immersed disc brakes (courtesy of Newage Transmissions Ltd.)

having no wheel brakes, and in the greater than usual axial length of the central final drive casing.

This casing length is, in fact, partly accounted for by the inclusion of a planetary type reduction gear train on each side of the bevel drive and differential gear; there is also, however, a full disc type brake inboard of each of the planetary gears, working in the oil which lubricates the gear trains. The sectioned view (Fig. 10.7) shows how the friction discs 6, which are lined with sintered metal, are separated by a fixed plate 5 (the number of friction discs and fixed plates can be increased if required), while their outer working faces are mated with the brake spacer plate 4 and the piston A.

The clamping force on the friction pack is generated by applying hydraulic pressure to the piston, which is housed in the cylinder E, by way of a feed port which is not shown; as is usual with hydraulic brake cylinders, a bleed screw 23 is provided for purging air from the system. A section of the cylinder and piston (Fig. 10.8) at right angles to the first view shows two rollers 9 and 10 which may be operated by a fork housed in the central portion of·the casing, to operate the piston mechanically to apply the brake for parking.

10.4 Agricultural and industrial tractor brakes

Another class of vehicle for which a number of special designs of brake have been developed is the tractor, of either agricultural or general industrial type; only one of the designs to be described is of a type not so far featured in this book but there are a number of different features and configurations to be considered. The market for agricultural tractors has always been highly competitive, the working environ-

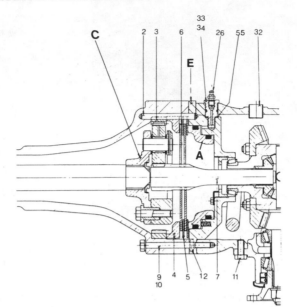

Fig. 10.7 A section through the brake shown in Fig. 10.6 (courtesy of Newage Transmissions Ltd.)

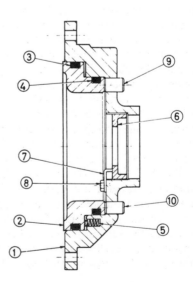

Fig. 10.8 An alternative section through the hydraulic cylinder of the brake seen in Fig. 10.6, showing the rollers 9 and 10 by means of which the brake is applied mechanically (courtesy of Newage Transmissions Ltd.)

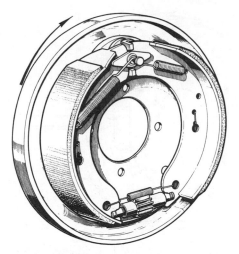

Fig. 10.9   The Girling SAEAC tractor brake (courtesy of Lucas Girling Ltd.)

ment poor and the standards of maintenance often low; brakes for such vehicles have usually, therefore, been of simple and rugged construction whilst having to be sufficiently powerful to cope with heavy loads and steep gradients.

In the UK, Girling have a comprehensive range of tractor brakes, which caters for most needs; first to be considered is a mechanically actuated duo-servo brake (Fig. 10.9), which has a single anchor pin and a simple cam mechanism which applies equal force to the tips of the two shoes; the cam itself and the operating lever are assembled on to the anchor pin assembly, where the cam is held in place by the primary shoe. In operation, as the secondary shoe is forced against the anchor pin, the cam is pushed away; a conventional manual adjuster assembly transmits the reaction force from the primary shoe to the secondary shoe. The pull off springs fitted to the two shoes are of different stiffnesses and so are coloured for identification, black for the primary shoe spring and red for the stronger secondary shoe spring; steady posts to align the shoes are fitted to the backplate, either one or both of these being adjustable for when new shoes are fitted.

The two brakes fitted on an agricultural tractor are sometimes operated by separate pedals, to facilitate compensating for offset loads when using certain implements, but these are latched together when driving on the road. The unequal use which the brakes are liable to get in service in this way will, of course, cause unequal wear; it is important, therefore, to keep the brakes properly adjusted so that both give the same output when the pedals are coupled.

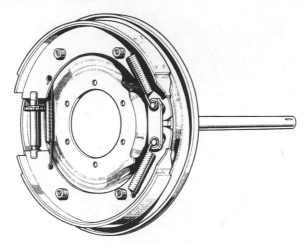

Fig. 10.10   The Girling DAFC tractor brake (courtesy of Lucas Girling Ltd.)

Another type of mechanical duo-servo brake is the double anchor, floating cam design (Fig. 10.10) which, like the type just described, uses identical shoes; the shoes are assembled to the twin anchor pins by means of large holes, which allow a certain freedom of movement, and are retained by means of the anchor plate which, in turn, is held in place by the identical pull off springs. The cam is integral with the camshaft, this component also being retained in position by the anchor plate; a conventional manual adjuster is fitted between the two shoes and two steady springs are used with each shoe to hold it against an adjustable steady post. The camshaft has sufficient lateral float in the backplate to enable the cam to maintain contact with whichever is the primary shoe (according to the direction of rotation) as it moves with the drum, until the secondary shoe is hard up against its anchor pin; there is still, at this stage, ample clearance between the primary shoe and its associated anchor pin which is, therefore, not under load.

Unlike the brake first described, which is of relatively small diameter—254 mm (10 in)—and is designed for fitting on an intermediate shaft in the tractor transmission, this second example is 356 mm (14 in) in diameter and designed for fitting at the rear wheels, where the rotational speed is low but the torque high.

A rather unusual unit, occasionally come across, is a dual brake (Fig. 10.11) which includes entirely independent brakes for service use and for parking; these units are mounted either side of a torque plate, a dust shield being fitted to exclude dirt. The hydraulic service brake is of two leading-shoe type, the shoes having fixed pivots; shoe

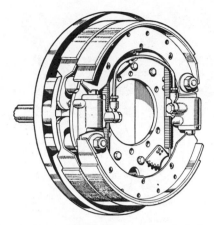

Fig. 10.11   A Girling dual brake for tractors, seen from the hydraulic side (courtesy of Lucas Girling Ltd.)

adjustment for lining wear is by snail cams acting on pins in the shoe webs, the cams being turned by toothed quadrants on long adjuster spindles, the cam spindles having pinions mounted on them. Observed from the other side, with the dust shield removed, the parking brake is seen to be of the mechanical double anchor, floating cam type described above, the cam shaft being cut short in the illustration for convenience; there are small differences of detail, such as the steady springs hooked between the webs of the adjacent shoes and the different type of steady post. An alternative version of this brake uses mechanical units in both positions.

Other drum brakes used on tractors are of conventional type but of appropriate construction and size to match the duty and the torque they are required to develop.

10.5 Tractor disc brakes

Disc brakes have been in use on agricultural and industrial tractors for many years but have merely complemented the range of drum brakes used, without displacing it. In the agricultural category, a popular brake has been of the full disc type illustrated in diagrammatic form as Example (ii) of Fig. 6.3; originated and made in the USA by Auto Specialities Manufacturing Company—now known as Ausco—of Hartford, Michigan and made in Europe by Girling, the brake is particularly suited for application to an intermediate shaft of the transmission and has been made in a limited range of sizes.

The construction of this brake can be understood from Fig. 10.12;

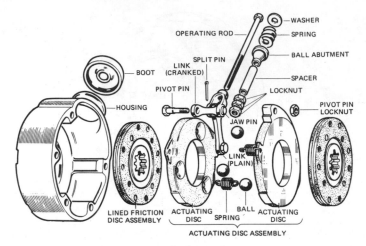

Fig. 10.12   The Girling multi-plate disc brake for tractors (courtesy of Lucas Girling Ltd.)

in this configuration, the inner face of the housing acts as a mating surface, the side of the transmission casing as another and the two actuating discs each have one working surface. Between the actuating discs, which are pulled together by springs, are steel balls which locate in recesses of carefully designed form; the two discs are coupled by links to the operating rod, each disc having a peripheral lug to which a link is pivoted.

When the brake is applied, tension in the operating rod causes the links to turn the two actuating discs slightly, in opposite directions; the shape of the recesses in which the hardened steel balls locate is such that, as the discs move relative to each other, the balls force them apart and apply pressure to the rotating friction discs. The reaction to the brake torque which is then developed causes the actuating disc assembly to rotate slightly, in the same direction as the friction discs, until the peripheral lug on one of the actuating discs contacts a projection inside the housing; there are two of these projections, so placed that whichever way the tractor is moving, the force on the lug which is contacted increases the relative rotational movement of the actuating discs which was initiated by the operating rod. The pressure on the friction discs is increased by this effect and so the brake torque is augmented, the angle of the recesses being critical; a small angle, for instance, gives a high self-servo effect but involves the risk (in conjunction with the friction level of the lining material) that the brake will be too fierce and grab.

At the conclusion of a brake application, the coil springs pull the

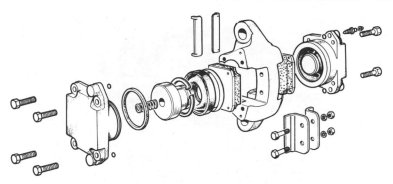

Fig. 10.13   A tractor disc brake based on car brake design practice (courtesy of Lucas Girling Ltd.)

actuating discs back into their original relative positions, the pressure is taken off the friction discs and the brake is released. It should be noted that, although the friction discs used in these brakes resemble automotive clutch driven plates, the linings are more heavily loaded and all holes are of clearance size for the rivet shank; a normal riveting punch must not be used, since this is suitable only for clenching against a metal surface (see Fig. 2.3), so it is necessary to use a special punch (sometimes called a petal snap) which splits the tubular shank of the rivet and turns back the parts.

As described above, this brake operates dry but an oil immersed version is also made, the oil—which is shared with the gearbox—serving to dissipate the heat generated during an application. Sintered bronze facings are commonly used and, to compensate for the lower friction level in oil, the friction disc diameter is increased and the number of friction discs may be increased to three or even four, stationary intermediate plates being then necessary between adjacent pairs of friction discs.

Girling have also used a design of heavy duty opposed piston caliper (Fig. 10.13), originated by Dunlop and acquired when the vehicle brake interest was transferred some years ago; an unusual feature is the inclusion of light springs behind the pistons to maintain sufficient pressure on the lining surfaces between brake applications to prevent the ingress of abrasive particles which, in a hostile working environment, could cause more wear than the actual braking duty.

10.6 Brakes for off-the-road vehicles

Dump trucks and other earth moving equipment for use only on site are unlimited in size and exceptionally large and powerful brakes are

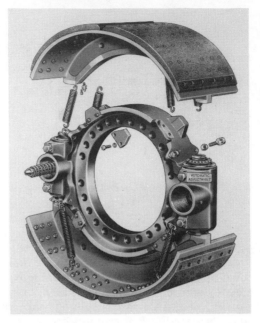

Fig. 10.14   A large Stopmaster brake for off-the-road vehicles (courtesy of Rockwell International Corporation, Automotive Businesses)

made to suit their needs; typical of the ranges which are available is that made by Rockwell, which includes both drum brakes and multi-plate disc brakes. The Rockwell Stopmaster type of duo-duplex brake, considered in its truck form in Chapter 8, is made in sizes up to 1067 mm (42 in) diameter, the example shown (Fig. 10.14) being of 914 mm (36 in) diameter; it can be seen that the torque plate is immensely strong, with a very large number of mounting holes, and that the linings are bolted to the shoes, plugs being inserted to close the holes in the linings. The largest brake, mentioned above, is of three shoe type, with triple actuation, and is suitable for use on axles loaded to 200 tonnes.

Rockwell Dura-Disc wet disc brakes are for use on hub reduction axles so that the torque they develop is multiplied by the final drive gear ratio; they may be cooled either by the oil contained merely within the housing or by forced circulation from an external source. Figure 10.15 shows a section through a typical brake, having three friction discs with a nominal diameter of 432 mm (17 in), but the design of the casing can be varied to accommodate a larger number of friction discs and counterplates if a higher torque capacity is required.

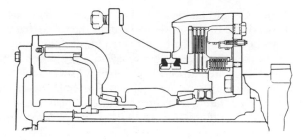

Fig. 10.15   *A section through a Rockwell Dura-Disc oil immersed disc brake (courtesy of Rockwell International Corporation, Automotive Businesses)*

The brake housing is splined internally to match the external teeth on the counterplates, while the friction discs are internally toothed to engage with the splined hub; the housing is closed by a cover, to which is attached the hydraulic cylinder, in which is located the annular piston. In this design, the cylinder has a stepped bore to form the working space, the piston seals both being external; coil springs act on the inner rim of the piston to return it to the off position after an application, to minimise drag. An alternative design has a plain bore to the hydraulic cylinder and the piston return springs are differently disposed.

In brakes such as these, the friction material commonly used is of sintered metal type which, working in oil, gives long life with the ability to withstand continuous heavy duty; the appliances on which such equipment is found are, typically, construction plant which is expected to work on a continuous basis for long periods; initial cost is, therefore, of less importance than reliability and a minimal servicing requirement.

Some off-the-road vehicles have a hydrostatic drive system, fluid under pressure being fed to individual wheel motors; by suitable control means, when braking is required under conditions when these motors are acting as pumps, the return flow of the hydraulic fluid can be restricted so that the desired braking effect is achieved at the expense of some extra heating of the fluid.

10.7 Transmission parking brakes

Earlier chapters have already described in some detail how drum and disc brakes may be operated by mechanical means for parking; in the case of disc brakes it was seen that sometimes the mechanically operated means of parking is either a linkage attached to the hydraulic caliper or a small drum brake housed within the disc.

Certain classic cars and (as described in this chapter) some tractors have fitted two drum brakes, side by side, in the same drum, one for service use and one for parking, but this is not a common arrangement. These brakes, however, were in every case either at the road wheels or, when mounted inboard, directly coupled to them; for very many years, particularly in America, it has sometimes been the practice, on the other hand, to mount a brake in the driveline between the gearbox and the differential, to be used for parking only.

A single brake mounted in this position acts on all driven wheels and the effective torque at the wheels is the actual torque developed by the brake, multiplied by the final drive ratio; the integrity of this means of parking relies, however, on all parts of the transmission beyond it and the adhesion between all wheels and the road. Additionally, the mating member (either drum or disc) rotates at drive shaft speed so must be able to resist the stresses thereby generated; if used dynamically, the thermal capacity of the single brake is so limited that overheating would occur very rapidly.

American practice long favoured band brakes but in the UK transmission brakes—when they are used—are most commonly of leading and trailing or duo-servo drum type; Fig. 10.16 shows a gearbox mounted example of the latter, this position helping to limit unsprung weight, although on trucks a position at the rear of a worm drive differential has sometimes been used. The Lockheed transmission disc brake (Fig. 10.17) is an example of one alternative type of transmission brake and uses a simple linkage to develop the required clamping force.

The use of a separate brake for parking has its attractions, since it is normally always cool and capable (if properly maintained) of giving full torque whenever required; the indiscreet dynamic use of such a brake could, however, be disastrous and the use of transmission brakes has found only limited favour in Europe.

Fig. 10.16   A drum type transmission parking brake

Fig. 10.17   A mechanically operated disc brake for drive line installation (courtesy of Automotive Products PLC)

10.8 Auxiliary braking systems

All of the brakes so far considered have been friction brakes which, in effect, reduce the speed of a vehicle by removing some of its energy of motion (kinetic energy), which is then converted into heat and—either directly or, in the case of oil immersed brakes, indirectly—dissipated to the atmosphere. In the short term the ability of brakes such as these to operate effectively is largely a matter of the thermal capacity of the mating members; if there is a sufficient mass of metal, the average surface temperature of the friction material remains within acceptable limits and the brake torque for a given input force remains reasonably constant, while cooling is relatively unimportant.

If braking is continued for a lengthy period, however, either because of rapid acceleration and brake applications in quick succession or because of a prolonged hill descent, the situation is different; the heat input to the mating members will be very great and their temperature will rise higher so that cooling by convection and radiation will become significant. If braking continues long enough, a stable condition will be reached in which the heat lost during one complete cycle of events will exactly match the heat input during the braking part of the cycle; the temperature of any part of the working surfaces will then be the same at corresponding points in successive cycles. However, there is the possibility, that this temperature might be sufficiently high for an unavoidable loss of braking torque to occur, perhaps with disastrous results, under conditions amounting to misuse or abuse, although it has been found possible to delay the onset of the danger point somewhat by design changes.

It is, however, helpful to consider the general background to the problem. Over a period of many years, axle loads have tended to increase and decelerations which at one time would not have been thought feasible have become required by law; braking torque has, therefore, had to rise correspondingly, but without it always being possible to make this easier by increasing brake diameter. More significantly, the permitted maximum speed of trucks has risen dramatically (in the UK, the limit for what were then heavy goods vehicles was 20 mile/h in the late 1950s and is now 60 mile/h on motorways) in the last 25 years, so that the maximum kinetic energy of a vehicle of a given weight has increased many times over.

It may not have been possible to increase brake diameters very much in recent decades but it has been possible to increase drum brake widths considerably; greater lining area and drum mass have made it possible just about to cope with the higher energy loadings. The increases in maximum permitted gross vehicle weights are not directly relevant to this problem, of course, except where axle loadings have increased.

There is no doubt, however, that conventional friction brakes for trucks and public service vehicles often run hotter than is desirable in terms of rate of lining wear, heat crazing and wear of drums, reserve of braking power for emergencies, wheel rim temperatures (as affecting the strength of tyre sidewalls), etc; with a limit on the ability of conventional brakes of practicable sizes to dissipate heat, there has, therefore, been scope for the use of auxiliary means of braking heavy vehicles which can readily dissipate energy for long periods without any adverse effects. This problem is of much less significance with cars, because the braking equipment generally has a sufficient thermal capacity and ability to dissipate heat to limit the working temperatures to acceptable limits under most conditions, with no other help than engine braking; auxiliary braking systems for cars have, therefore, received little consideration.

It is convenient to classify auxiliary braking systems in two ways, those which are applied to the engine and those which are applied to the transmission, the former being considered first.

10.9 Engine and exhaust brakes

As has been briefly mentioned above, the effect of conventional friction brakes is frequently augmented by engine braking; with the throttle closed (and little or no fuel being supplied to diesel engines or to petrol engines with fuel injection) power can be absorbed by the engine as it is driven by the transmission and converted to heat, which is then dissipated by the engine cooling system. On level roads the transmission is usually left in direct drive for a moderate braking effect which, as it will not lock the driving wheels, is of particular benefit on slippery surfaces; when a greater effect is needed, as on steep descents, and the speed is low, an indirect ratio will be engaged.

Useful as normal engine braking is, it is insufficient to make a significant contribution to the braking of heavy vehicles such as trucks and buses; there are, however, two ways in which the engine can be made to absorb an increased amount of energy when driven by the vehicle on a down gradient. The first of these is the exhaust brake, which has been common in the more mountainous parts of Europe for decades, although much less common in the UK; this consists essentially of a means of restricting the exhaust flow from the engine so that power is absorbed during each exhaust stroke. Either a butterfly (Fig. 10.18) or slide type valve may be used, an air cylinder being commonly employed to operate it when desired; the degree of restriction achieved is chosen so as to ensure that the exhaust valves are not held off their seats at the end of the exhaust stroke. The exhaust brake operation can easily be integrated with the service braking system, so that it is applied by the first movement of the brake pedal; the cost of installation is relatively low. It should be noted that, because the operating member of the slide type valve is fully retracted when not in use, it is not then subject to the effects of the gas stream and it is self cleaning of carbon deposits.

A more refined way of enhancing diesel engine braking, although at greater cost, is the American 'Jake Brake' which is a product of The Jacobs Manufacturing Company; this is an engine conversion which causes the exhaust valves to be opened briefly at the end of the

Fig. 10.18   An exhaust brake installation

compression stroke, so that the energy used to compress the charge of air is lost, instead of being recovered during the succeeding stroke. With each cylinder exhausted at the commencement of the downward stroke this, also, absorbs energy; pairs of cylinders can be activated individually (the fuel supply being cut off automatically) so that the braking effect can be varied in stages.

The Jake Brake makes use of additional components above the rocker gear and is only suitable for use on engines with rocker operated fuel injectors; when the device is in operation the rising end of the injector rocker lifts a piston which, hydraulically, causes an associated piston to open the exhaust valves for that cylinder independently of their rocker. It is claimed that by means of this equipment the engine can absorb virtually its full rated horsepower; in use it maintains the engine at an even temperature and the discharge of air into the exhaust system is said to blow out accumulated carbon.

10.10 Retarders

The second class of auxiliary braking system, that applied to the transmission of the vehicle, is generally known as retarders and these are of several types; probably the electric retarder is the best known type, but there are also hydrodynamic and friction types on the market. There are several manufacturers of electric retarders, the French Telma being a good example of the principles involved; several models are made, of which two types have their own centre shaft and are for mounting at the mid bearing position in the drive line, but the lightweight Focal type (Fig. 10.19) is designed for gearbox or axle mounting with only a minimum reduction in propeller shaft length. Telma retarders are fitted to trucks and buses and are available for vehicles having gross weights up to 50 t; they can also be incorporated into trailer axles and, with their rapid response, can be integrated into electronic anti-locking systems.

The electric retarder consists of a stator assembly and a rotor, the stator of a Focal unit being mounted on the casing of either the axle or the gearbox; the rotor is assembled to the gearbox output flange or the axle drive flange as the case may be. On each side of the stator frame are mounted eight electro magnetic coils, connected together in pairs on either side of the stator in a symmetrical manner so that they can be energised in groups of four, according to the position of a control switch operated by the driver. Rotating in close proximity to the pole pieces of these coils are ferrous discs in which, as they rotate, the magnetic field set up by those coils which are energised creates

Fig. 10.19   An installation of a Telma Focal type electric retarder on a bus

eddy currents; the eddy currents set up a magnetic drag in the discs which resists rotation and thus provides a braking force, the magnitude of which is, therefore, in four stages.

As the retarder operates, the energy absorbed appears in the form of heat in the ferrous discs which are, therefore, backed by light alloy bladed rotors which dissipate this heat to atmosphere. An electric retarder is effective down to low rotational speeds and its torque is little affected by operating temperature; its weight is, however, considerable and the operating current may be as high as 200 A at 24 V, while it is necessary to reroute the wiring and brake pipelines to avoid the high ambient temperatures which are generated. With the appropriate one of the four stages selected for the gradient concerned, a long descent can be negotiated with the minimum of effort on the part of the driver, who need only use the wheel brakes for fine adjustment of speed or if it is necessary to stop completely; brake lining and drum life are considerably extended under these circumstances, the retarder itself having no wearing parts.

The second type of retarder is hydrodynamic in principle and the units made in Germany by Voith (Fig. 10.20) are a good illustration of how a liquid can be used as a braking medium. Voith makes a 'bolt on' retarder, the VHBK 130, which is most often directly mounted on the rear of the vehicle gearbox, but the company also obtains a similar continuous braking effect from the torque converter which is an integral part of its DIWA transmission. The construction of the

Fig. 10.20   A retarder of hydrodynamic type, for inclusion in a vehicle drive line (courtesy of Voith Engineering Ltd.)

VHBK 130 unit is similar to that of a hydrodynamic coupling (fluid flywheel), except that the shaft which drives the impeller passes straight through the unit and the turbine is anchored to the casing, so that it is more properly referred to as the stator; when not in use, the casing is drained of fluid, this returning to a sump at the bottom of the unit. When the retarder is brought into operation, the casing is partially filled with fluid, the amount admitted determining the degree of the braking effect which is generated; the impeller accelerates the fluid, flinging it at high velocity into the stator where it is decelerated, losing energy which is converted into heat in the process. The energy imparted to the fluid by the impeller is at the expense of the power transmitted by the drive shaft, so a smooth braking effect is the result.

The retarder casing is generously finned, particularly around the sump through which the oil is circulated, to assist cooling, or the waste heat can be utilised for interior heating of the vehicle; the unit is compact and light in weight and may be fitted on buses and trucks up to 38 ft gross. The oil capacity of the Voith retarder is sufficient to ensure that, in conjunction with the cooling provided for, working temperatures are no higher than those of a normal gearbox and no special problems are created; the unit can operate continuously without loss of performance, has good torque/speed characteristics, makes only a small demand on the electrical and air systems of the vehicle to which it is fitted and needs virtually no adjustments or replacement parts.

The torque converter in the Voith DIWA transmission is so incorporated that, by application of a multi-plate clutch, it can be caused to act as a retarder; in this mode, the converter turbine rotates in the opposite direction, against the locked impeller, to that for the drive condition and circulates the fluid which is always present in the casing. The other two elements of the converter, which are stationary, redirect the fluid and, in so doing, absorb energy from it so that a braking effect is generated which is dependent upon output shaft speed, three different levels being obtained by varying the retarder circuit pressure.

The third type of retarder utilises friction and so, unlike the other types, has wearing surfaces; however, the friction elements are usually bronze-faced discs working in oil so that wear is at a very low rate and replacement should seldom be necessary. In addition to the hydro-dynamic retarder which it makes, Voith also produces a friction unit which is built into one of its automotive transmissions so that certain components can be shared.

Friction retarders are also made of 'bolt on' type, either for original equipment or after market fitting, and the unit developed by Ferodo and since acquired by Self Changing Gears is a good example of this kind, utilising the Ferodo expertise with sintered bronze friction materials to achieve the desired friction and wear characteristics; the heart of the design is a multi-plate assembly of friction discs, able to slide axially on a spider mounted on the rotating shaft and interleaved with cast iron stator plates. The clamping load needed to generate a friction force is applied to the working surfaces by means of hydraulic pressure acting in a stainless steel bellows; the pump which creates this pressure also circulates the main flow of oil through a filter and a heat exchanger before it is directed into the rotating parts to cool them.

This unit is housed in a casing which may be designed to suit mounting either at the rear of the gearbox, in the drive line (Fig. 10.21) or on the driven axle; although in most applications the main shaft passes right through the casing, in some cases the retarder is single ended (the casing being modified accordingly), the shaft merely applying the braking torque to an appropriate point in a transfer box or final drive. Depending on the control equipment fitted, the retarding torque can be variable or developed in two stages; usually control is integrated with the service braking so that the retarder operates first so as to perform the greater part of all normal requirements, leaving the foundation brakes relatively cool and ready for additional braking when needed.

Fig. 10.21   An installation of the Self Changing Gears friction type retarder (originated by Ferodo Ltd.) on a double deck bus

The capacity of this unit can be varied at the design stage by choosing the number of plates to be used and it has so far found its widest field of application on public service vehicles of both single and double deck types; as with the hydrodynamic type, it is compact, light in weight, undemanding on electrical and air supplies and has only a moderate external temperature which raises no installation problems. The heat removed from the unit by the oil flow is transferred to the engine cooling system by the heat exchanger, for maintenance of engine temperature or dissipation to atmosphere. Other friction retarders use a similar multi-plate friction pack integrated into the gearbox.

Retarders have been mandatory in some countries for many years and it may be expected that their use will increase; they offer an increase in the safety of heavy vehicles under arduous conditions of operation, provided they are integrated with the foundation brakes in such a way that brake balance is not disturbed and, although they are an expensive item, they offer considerable savings on the maintenance costs of the foundation brakes. There have been attempts to promote legislation requiring the fitting of retarders of a particular type to certain classes of vehicle, especially to touring coaches; it can, however, be seen that there are three distinct types of unit (others may be developed), each having its good points, so it would be a retrograde step to specify the exact means by which the desired auxiliary braking effect is to be achieved.

The one further possibility which should be mentioned is that of regenerative braking, for use either on an occasional or—for electric vehicles—on a continuous basis. There have, from time to time, been experiments in which the kinetic energy of a vehicle to be decelerated is used to accelerate a flywheel; this flywheel is subsequently coupled to the transmission to assist in starting the vehicle from rest, thus conserving energy. Electrically driven vehicles can also give a saving of energy if, with suitable control equipment, they can convert kinetic energy to electrical energy for storage and subsequent re-use. It is certain that development work in this field will continue but it is not yet apparent that an economically viable outcome will be achieved.

11

Braking system refinements

11.1 Introduction

Although a considerable amount of information about braking systems has been given in earlier chapters, certain important aspects have received no more than a brief mention; these refinements are largely modifications to the basic systems, made with the aim of either directly or indirectly making them safer.

In a simple hydraulic braking system failure of a component which is subject to pressure when a brake application is made may cause a total loss of braking force, the brake pedal going to the floor. If the component failure is only partial, causing an external leak instead of complete loss of pressure, braking may not be totally lost instantaneously, but safety is affected proportionately to the scale of the leak. The safety record of simple hydraulic systems is extremely good, despite the neglect which has more often than not taken place, although any improvement which can be made without incurring an excessive cost penalty is greatly to be desired.

The way in which the risk mentioned above may most easily be reduced, and the one which is now very widely adopted, is to divide the hydraulic system into two parts; a single failure of the type considered, then causes a loss of pressure in only one part of the system. Because the system is designed so that the other part remains effective, this can be used to brake the vehicle, although the maximum braking efficiency which can be achieved will then be reduced. In order to generate pressure in a hydraulic system divided into two parts in this way, a tandem master cylinder is normally used, although two single master cylinders operated through the medium of a balance bar have been used on production cars and still are (the balance bar then usually being adjustable) on racing cars.

11.2 Tandem master cylinders

As with single master cylinders, tandem units are made in many shapes and sizes; a description of two Girling units will, however,

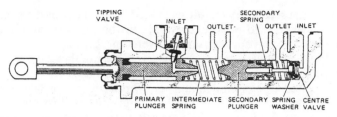

Fig. 11.1   Tandem master cylinder with one tipping valve and one centre valve (courtesy of Lucas Girling Ltd.)

cover all of the important features which need to be noted. The first of these units (Fig. 11.1) shows how, within a long cylinder bore, two plungers are used to form two independent chambers, each with its own fluid inlet and outlet; each plunger is fitted with a pressure seal and there are two return springs which restore the plungers to their 'off' positions when the brake pedal is released. Two different types of valve are fitted in this unit; the tipping valve, associated with the primary circuit, which controls the admission of fluid from the reservoir to this circuit, and the centre valve, associated with the secondary circuit, which fulfils the same function for the secondary circuit, but in a different way.

In operation, the primary plunger is moved first and allows the tipping valve to seat, so that pressure can then start to increase in the primary circuit; this pressure, together with the force exerted by the intermediate spring as it is compressed, then acts on the secondary plunger to overcome the rather stiffer secondary spring and initiate movement which closes the centre valve. Pressure can now start to rise in the secondary circuit as is already happening in the primary circuit.

The practice with tandem cylinders has generally been to connect the primary circuit to the front brakes in a front/rear split system (described in the next section) so that, in accordance with the generally accepted views on brake balance, they tend to be applied first and to receive a slightly higher pressure; front brakes, often being of disc type in contrast to those at the rear, may need a greater volume of fluid to operate them, a requirement which can more easily be met by using the primary circuit. It will be noticed from the illustration that there is a slight step in the bore of this unit; this is to facilitate assembly.

In service, if there should be a loss of pressure in the primary circuit, the primary plunger will move forward until it contacts the secondary plunger when the brake pedal is operated; the two plungers will then move together so that pressure can be generated in the secondary circuit. If the secondary circuit has failed, movement of the primary plunger will start to build up pressure in the primary circuit until, when the secondary spring has been overcome, the secondary plunger moves to the end of its travel; further pressure can then be built up in the primary circuit to operate the associated brakes.

The second type of tandem master cylinder to be considered (Fig. 11.2) is shown complete with the fluid reservoir, to illustrate how an internal baffle divides this into two parts so that, even if there is a loss of fluid from one of the two circuits, the supply for the other is maintained. Fluid reservoirs often now include a float unit which operates a low level warning should the level fall beyond a certain limit, because of either neglect or loss by way of a leak.

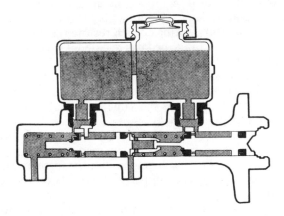

Fig. 11.2   Tandem master cylinder of 'American Standard' type, designed to give simultaneous cut-off of the two circuits (courtesy of Lucas Girling Ltd.)

The fluid admission control in this unit is of AS type (as described in Chapter 5) for both circuits, the two plungers are linked and there is a stop pin to limit the return movement of the secondary plunger; the special feature of this design is that the pressure rise in the two circuits is initiated simultaneously, so that it is particularly suitable for the diagonally split type of system, to be described in the next section. Each plunger is fitted with two seals, a recuperation seal and a plunger seal; in the 'off' position, as illustrated, the lip of each recuperation seal is just level with a small diameter cut-off port. A second, larger diameter port (that for the primary circuit is not visible in the illustration) behind the recuperation seal keeps the annular space around the plunger filled with fluid, this space being closed by the plunger seal; it will be noticed that the two plunger seals face in opposite directions, because of the differing pressure conditions under which they operate.

In the unit shown in Fig. 11.1 and certain others, the secondary spring is stronger than the primary spring, which is why the primary circuit is pressurised first; to achieve simultaneous cut-off in the unit now being considered, this arrangement is reversed and the primary spring is made the stronger, so that the two plungers at first move together. It is, however, necessary to ensure that the primary spring does not move the secondary plunger while the brake pedal is released; the two plungers are, therefore, linked in the manner shown and described next.

In the 'off' position, the secondary plunger returns to its stop pin and the primary plunger to the limit allowed by the sliding link; this link consists of a retaining bolt, screwed into the end of the primary plunger, and a spring retainer which is in contact with, but not attached to, the secondary plunger. The two pistons can, therefore, move closer together, compressing the primary spring, but cannot normally move any further apart; no retaining component is, therefore, needed at the mouth of the cylinder bore.

When the brake pedal is applied and both plungers have moved to cover the cut-off ports, pressure can be built up in both circuits simultaneously, as fluid is displaced into the brake pipelines; the stiffness of each of the two springs and their initial settings are chosen so as to ensure that pressure rises evenly. To obviate any tendency for the recuperation seals to extrude into the drillings through the flanges of their respective plungers when under pressure, they are supported at the back by special washers.

As with the single AS type master cylinder, the brake circuits are kept full of fluid even if the brake pedal is released rapidly, so the plungers are returned by their springs faster than the fluid can be returned into the cylinder. Failure of either circuit will, as before, leave the remaining one operative once the plunger associated with the failed circuit has taken up the available movement.

Because of the partial braking still available to the driver of a vehicle with a divided braking system should one circuit fail, it is possible that the failure might go unnoticed or that its significance might not be understood; it is, therefore, now increasingly commonly required that the driver is given a visible indication of loss of pressure in one circuit. Figure 11.3 shows a Girling Pressure Differential Warning Actuator (PDWA), which consists of a cylinder containing a piston and having a chamber at each end which is in communication with one of the two circuits; as long as the pressures in the two circuits remain substantially equal, the piston is undisturbed, but an excessive difference will cause it to be displaced. Movement of the piston

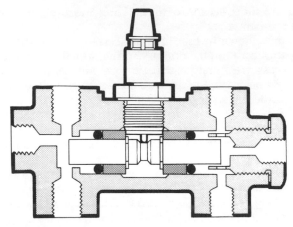

Fig. 11.3   A pressure differential warning actuator (PDWA), for use with divided or duplicated hydraulic circuits (courtesy of Lucas Girling Ltd.)

operates the central switch to activate a warning light and alert the driver to the fault; whilst the car may then still be driven, extreme care is required and it should only be driven as far as is necessary to have the system repaired.

With early units of this kind, the piston had either to be reset manually, with a tool applied through an aperture in the body, or by careful control of pressures during bleeding of the system; the unit shown is, however, self centring once normal operation of the system has been restored. Each end of the piston is housed in a sleeve, an O ring being fitted as a pressure seal; under the influence of the normal pressure in each circuit, the sleeves are pressed against spring rings fitted at either end of the centre portion of the piston and against a spigot formed at the base of the switch. When the piston is displaced, it pushes one sleeve and O ring with it to the stop provided; when the system fault has been corrected and pressure is again generated in the affected circuit, the pressure acting on the combined area of sleeve and piston pushes both back to the central position.

This type of unit is commonly made integral with the master cylinder, so as to reduce the number of external connections, each of which is a potential point of failure; it may also be further combined with one of the pressure modifying valves described in a later section.

11.3 Divided braking systems

The most obvious way to divide a braking system into two parts—and the one which has been most widely used—is to separate the supply to front and rear brakes (the vertical split) and to operate the two circuits thus formed by means of a tandem master cylinder; a system of this type is shown in diagram form (Fig. 11.4) and similar schemes have already been considered in Chapter 9, which dealt with air braking equipment.

This arrangement meets the basic requirement that, if there is a failure at any one point in the system, the brakes at two wheels can still be applied to slow the vehicle; however, the maximum braking force which can be developed at any wheel is limited by the adhesion at that wheel. For example; ignoring the effects of weight transfer, assuming a percentage weight distribution between the two axles of 65:35 (with the braking ratio to match) and assuming a coefficient of adhesion of 0.8, the rear wheels alone cannot achieve more than 28% braking efficiency while the fronts alone can achieve 52%. It will be seen that there is thus a very different response from the two parts of the braking system and it will be realised that, in the event of a failure, an increase in pedal effort above that which yields either one or other of the two values of braking efficiency indicated, will merely cause locking of the wheels still being braked.

At this point, it may be noted that locked wheels lose their ability to control the direction of motion of a vehicle; a vehicle with locked rear wheels will, even if the front wheels are rolling freely, invariably spin whereas a vehicle with locked front wheels will follow a straight path, whatever direction those wheels point in. The locked rear wheel condition, resulting in the vehicle spinning, is held to be the more hazardous and so it is usually required as noted above, that at the maximum attainable braking efficiency, it will be the front wheels which will tend to lock first.

Another way of dividing a braking system, sometimes called the L split, requires the use of specially designed front disc brakes; these may be either of fixed four cylinder opposed piston type or sliding two cylinder single sided type. In either case, the adjacent culinders are not linked but are fed by separate circuits. The L split layout (Fig. 11.5) connects one circuit in each of the front brakes with a single rear brake, so that the two parts of the system will each develop the same braking force; with weight ratio and other conditions as in the previous example, either circuit working alone will enable the vehicle to achieve 40% braking efficiency.

With this scheme, when only one circuit is operational, the front wheels will be underbraked; however, no increase in pedal effort can be made beyond that which would lock the one rear wheel still being braked (unless the rear pipelines incorporate pressure limiting valves, as described later), so no increase in deceleration can be achieved under the conditions described. Although the braking of only one rear

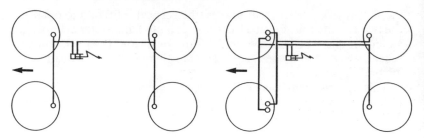

*Fig. 11.4   A front:rear (vertical) split
of a hydraulic braking system*

Fig. 11.5   The 'L' type system split

wheel in conjunction with both front wheels introduces slight asymmetry into the forces acting on the vehicle, this is insignificant. The L split is not widely used.

A further alternative—again not common—is known as the IH split and this, also, uses twin circuit front calipers, but with differing cylinder sizes (Fig. 11.6); the large cylinders in the front calipers are fed by one part of the tandem master cylinder, while the small cylinders in the front brakes and both rear brakes are fed by the other. By an appropriate choice of cylinder diameters, the designer can provide for the achievement of an equal response from the two parts of the system, but at the expense of an increased effort when the fronts only circuit is left operational. A greater pedal effort than that which gives maximum braking when both circuits function cannot be used if the 'fronts only' circuit fails, without locking the rear wheels, unless a pressure limiting valve (as referred to above) is fitted; if the 'fronts only' circuit is the one that does not fail, increased effort can be applied to make full use of the adhesion at the front wheels.

The final possibility, and one which is gradually increasing in popularity is the X or diagonal split (Fig. 11.7), which links one front wheel and the diagonally opposite rear wheel in each of the two circuits. Half of the adhesion of the vehicle can now be utilised for braking (permitting 40% braking efficiency under the stated conditions) if either circuit fails, no difference in the pedal effort being involved, and the unbraked wheels will promote directional stability even if some locking of the braked wheels were to occur. There is, with this system, a greater asymmetry of the forces acting on the car when only a single circuit is effective, but the magnitude of the turning moment about a vertical axis is still small in relation to the available directional control; there is, however, a potentially more dangerous effect to be considered.

If a line is projected downwards through the centres of the swivel joints which enable a front wheel to be steered, it meets the ground at

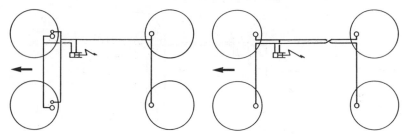

Fig. 11.6   The 'IH' arrangement of a
split system

Fig. 11.7   The widely used 'X' or
diagonal split of a braking system

a point which may coincide with the centre of the contact area of the tyre or which may be offset towards or away from the centre line of the vehicle. The degree of offset (if any) is decided by the vehicle designer, usually as a compromise between conflicting requirements relating to the braking and handling of the vehicle, and provided both front brakes develop the same force, the amount of offset is immaterial as regards brake performance. When, as in a diagonally split braking system with a failure, one front brake develops much more force than the other, the amount of offset is critical; the absence of the balancing force on one side will cause a reaction on the steering which will depend on the amount and direction of the offset, tending to turn the steered wheels either one way or the other. The diagonal split system is, therefore, only suitable for use on vehicles with a small offset.

In connection with steering offset and unbalanced braking (or the unexpected drag caused by a burst tyre), it should be further noted that, if the offset is away from the centre of the car (positive offset), the reaction on the steering and the turning moment on the car induced by the asymmetry of the braking forces are cumulative in their effect, increasing the likelihood of loss of control. If the offset is caused to be towards the centre of the car (negative offset), the two induced tendencies are in opposition and the net effect is greatly reduced.

With the diagonal split, premature rear wheel locking can be ruled out by use of the normal criteria for determining front to rear braking ratios; it requires a greater length of piping than a simple front:rear split but it obviates any need for complication of the brakes themselves.

11.4 System duplication

The four divided systems just described all enhance safety by preserving a proportion of the braking normally available in the case of a single system failure; however, the failure is probably most likely

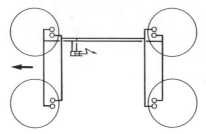

Fig. 11.8   A duplicated braking system

to occur when, in a sudden emergency, a particularly hard pedal application is made and there is an urgent need to utilise fully the adhesion at all wheels. No simple division of the brake system can fulfil the needs of this situation, but a duplicated system (Fig. 11.8) is much better able to. As the diagram indicates, each circuit operates all four brakes, thus generating half of the total braking force; in the event of a single fault with such a system, all four wheels are still braked and an appropriate increase in the pedal effort applied can enable the braking efficiency to be restored to the level achievable when both circuits are effective.

A duplicated system of this type (otherwise known as a horizontally split system) is more expensive than the splits described above but, as has been shown in Chapter 9, is now common on trucks, although it is still rare on cars. Disc braked cars can readily be provided with a duplicated system by fitting twin circuit calipers at front and rear (one car maker uses two separate single circuit calipers at each front wheel), but only limited progress has been made with suitable drum brakes for cars and light vehicles. Girling have, for example, developed a hydraulic cylinder (Fig. 11.9) for use with leading/trailing shoe brakes operated by a duplicated system; this enables a brake to be operated by either or both of the two circuits.

As can be seen from the drawing, the fixed cylinder body A incorporates the feed and bleed ports for one circuit, the ports for the other circuit being incorporated into the annular piston B; C is a solid piston, having an integral flange, so that between B and C two fluid spaces are formed which are equipped with pressure seals so that each acts as a cylinder. Under normal circumstances the forces developed by the two cylinders, which are of the same cross sectional area, are equal and act in parallel to push B and C apart and apply the brake shoes; if a single failure occurs, the circuit remaining effective will still operate the associated cylinder. Increased effort can be applied, in order to generate the same force from the one cylinder as was formerly generated by the two.

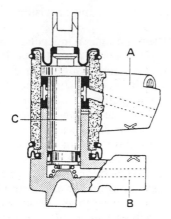

Fig. 11.9   A double acting hydraulic wheel cylinder for operation by duplicated braking systems (courtesy of Lucas Girling Ltd.)

Even though a duplicated system enables all four (or more) wheels of a vehicle to make full use of the available adhesion after a single hydraulic system failure has occurred, there is still an important factor to be reckoned with. Using a conventional tandem master cylinder, there will be a sudden and dramatic increase in pedal travel as the failure occurs; this happens just as the driver's mind is most likely occupied with interpreting a hazardous situation, which has necessitated an emergency brake application. There is, however, at least one design of tandem master cylinder which does a great deal to eliminate this second shock to the driver; when used with a duplicated system it also removed the driver's need to react to the situation and increase the applied pedal effort.

The Teves 'Twintax' design, seen (Fig. 11.10) in diagrammatic form, differs most obviously from conventional designs in having a stepped bore such that (in the most usual case) the cross sectional area of the large part is twice that of the small part; there is also a sleeve (black in the illustration) assembled between the two pistons. Ports I and II are

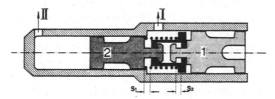

Fig. 11.10   A diagrammatic representation of the Twintax tandem master cylinder for duplicated circuits (courtesy of Alfred Teves GmbH)

for delivery to the two circuits, but the feed ports and provisions for recuperation etc, are not shown.

With both circuits intact, the two pistons can move independently and the sleeve is suitably dimensioned so as to permit this; the pressures in the two circuits will then be equal and (assuming the fluid displacement requirements of the two circuits are the same) the movement of piston 1 will be equal to that of piston 2. Unlike the state of affairs with a conventional master cylinder, the primary piston does not move closer to the secondary one when it displaces fluid except when, as is sometimes the case, there is a difference in the requirements of the two circuits; the relative movement of the pistons must not then be such as to eliminate either of the two clearances S_1 and S_2.

If circuit I fails, piston 1 pushes the sleeve into contact with piston 2, eliminating the clearance S_1; this movement is relatively small. The force originally applied to piston 1, which generated a certain pressure in circuit I, is now applied to piston 2; this being (usually) of half the area of piston 1, the pressure now generated in circuit II is twice what it was before, thus automatically causing the brakes to develop the same output as before. If circuit II fails, piston 2 moves freely down its bore, taking with it the sleeve until clearance S_2 is eliminated; pistons 1 and 2 are now coupled rigidly, which affects the pressure in circuit I. Because of the coupling of the pistons, the pressure in circuit I is calculated by dividing the input force by the effective area of piston 1, which is the annular outer portion corresponding to the step in the cylinder bore, and which is equal to half the total area; the hydraulic pressure now achieved is, therefore, twice the initial value, as was the case with failure of circuit I, and with the same correcting effect on brake output.

11.5 Braking ratio control

The braking systems described in some of the preceding chapters are mostly such that the pressures applied to front and rear brakes of a rigid vehicle are always equal; the ratio of the magnitudes of the braking forces developed by the front and rear brakes is always, therefore, the same. However, the final section of Chapter 1 noted that the value of the adhesion at front and rear of any vehicle is subject to (1) dynamic change, due to weight transfer during braking (particularly in the case of short wheelbase vehicles with a high centre of gravity) and (2) occasional static change, due to changes in loading (particularly in the case of trucks). It is, therefore, now necessary to consider ways of varying the braking ratio, in order to take some account of these two sources of change in the adhesion available; for convenience, the dynamic effect will be considered first.

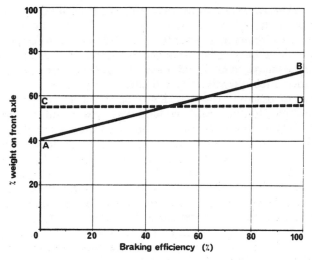

Fig. 11.11   The relationship between the ideal braking ratio line AB and the usual fixed ratio line CD

In order to understand better the dynamic effects of weight transfer, it is helpful to consider Fig. 11.11 which, like the related Fig. 11.15 which appears later, is drawn rather for clarity of the braking characteristics illustrated than to bear any exact relationship to an actual vehicle; the imaginary case which is illustrated is that of a two axle vehicle, but it is possible to couple two or more such diagrams so as to consider multi-axle vehicles.

The vertical scale in the diagram is for the percentage of gross weight on the front axle of the vehicle (the balance of the total therefore being on the rear) and the horizontal scale is of braking efficiency achieved by the vehicle; a line AB is so drawn on the diagram that, at every value of braking efficiency from zero to 100%, it indicates the front axle loading as a percentage of the total, taking into account the effect of weight transfer due to deceleration. At zero braking efficiency, there is no weight transfer, so point A corresponds to the static value of the front axle loading, assumed in this case to be 40% of the total; at 100% braking efficiency, it is assumed that the load value for the front axle is 70% so point B is drawn at this value. Intermediate values of axle loading are directly proportional to the braking efficiency (equivalent to *a* in Equation 1.6 in Chapter 1), so a straight line may be drawn between A and B.

In fact, for the axle loading ratio to vary from 40:60 to 70:30 as braking efficiency increases from zero to 100%, the value of the ratio of height of centre of gravity to wheelbase (h/l in Equation 1.6, referred to above) would have to be 7/4, which is extremely unlikely; however this extreme variation gives the desired vertical separation of the lines to be added subsequently to this diagram.

A braking system of the type described so far has, as just noted, a fixed front:rear braking ratio, which takes no account of changes in axle loading due to weight transfer, and so matches a single value of front axle loading for all values of braking efficiency; this can, therefore, be represented by a horizontal line, such as CD, drawn on the diagram. If the line CD were to lie below point A or above point B, this would imply that the braking ratio was wrong for all values of braking efficiency; the vehicle concerned could then never achieve the maximum deceleration theoretically possible on any practical surface because either the front or the rear wheels would lock prematurely.

Line CD is actually drawn to cross line AB at the 50% value of braking efficiency, which can be seen to correspond to a front axle loading of 55% of the total, equivalent to a braking ratio of 55:45; on a surface which yields a tyre/road coefficient of adhesion of 0.5, making 50% braking efficiency theoretically possible, this fixed value of braking ratio (i.e. 55:45) will just enable that maximum theoretical value of braking efficiency to be achieved. On a surface yielding a lower coefficient of adhesion, so that only values of braking efficiency less than 50% are theoretically possible (to the left of the intersection point in the diagram, so that the horizontal line is above the inclined one), the fixed braking ratio is too high to match the adhesion at the front, and the front wheels will lock prematurely; on a superior surface, the fixed braking ratio is too low to match the adhesion at the front and, therefore, too high to match the adhesion at the rear, so the rear wheels will lock prematurely.

In either case of premature wheel locking, the braking efficiency will be less than would be theoretically possible; the choosing of the value of braking efficiency at which line AB (the required braking ratio) and line CD (the actual, constant braking ratio) intersect is, therefore, a matter of compromise. If it were possible with currently available technology (which it is not) to make line CD coincide with line AB, then it would be possible to make full utilisation of the available adhesion for any condition of tyre/road adhesion; as it is, manufacturers of hydraulic braking systems offer several different items of equipment which seek to provide a better compromise than the single intersection point, at which the braking ratio is correct, illustrated in Fig. 11.11.

11.6 Pressure limiting valves

The simplest approach to the matter of modifying the braking ratio characteristic is the inclusion of a pressure limiting valve in the pipeline to the rear brakes; this may be one of a number of possible types, of which three are illustrated and described. The first of these (Fig. 11.12) is a simple device containing a spring loaded plunger, on which is assembled a rubber seal; the valve is connected into the pipeline to the rear brakes so that the pressure delivered by the master cylinder acts on the plunger, on an area equal to that of the extension against which the spring acts. During a brake application, the pressure in the valve body moves the plunger until the force exerted on it by the fluid is just equal to that exerted by the spring in compression. At a predetermined pressure the compression of the spring is just sufficient to allow the plunger seal to seat itself, and so isolate the fluid outlets to the rear brakes.

Any further increase in pipeline pressure will now only act on the front brakes so that, beyond the cut-off point, the front:rear braking ratio will vary in a manner whose effect will be considered below; as soon as the pressure in the system is released, the spring will return the plunger to its initial position. Because this valve is operated by pressure and the setting cannot be varied in service, its usefulness is limited; it cannot take account of such factors as a change of braking lining friction level (such as when relining) or a change of loading, both of which affect the relationship between pipeline pressure and deceleration, and hence have a bearing on weight transfer during braking and the possibility of rear wheel locking.

Another type of pressure limiting valve (Fig. 11.13) responds not to the pressure itself, but to the deceleration achieved; it, therefore, automatically takes account of the factors mentioned above and may be expected to give a more uniform response in repetition in service. The valve body is inclined to the horizontal and contains a ball which, at rest, holds open an inlet valve; fluid from the master cylinder can then flow freely through the valve and out to the rear brakes. At a predetermined deceleration, the inertia force acting on the ball causes it to roll up the cylindrical valve body and permit the valve to close, isolating the rear brakes; even with this type of valve there is the disadvantage that during prolonged hard braking, when rear drums might become hot and expand, it is not possible to maintain the desired pressure at the rear brakes because of their isolation.

The inertia sensitive valve must be mounted in a true longitudinal position and the angle of inclination must be carefully controlled at a value, the tangent of which is equal to the required braking efficiency

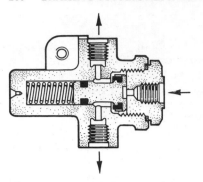

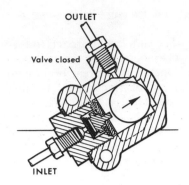

Fig. 11.12   A hydraulic pressure limiting valve (courtesy of Automotive
Products PLC)

Fig. 11.13   A deceleration actuated
pressure limiting valve (courtesy of
Automotive Products PLC)

at which cut-off occurs, expressed as a decimal. Any gradient on
which the car happens to be situated when braking affects the
functioning of the valve, but in a favourable manner; on a falling
gradient, the valve will act sooner, but this matches the forward
weight transfer caused by the gradient, and the reverse situation
occurs on a rising gradient, enabling the rear brakes to contribute
more.

The third type of valve (Fig. 11.14) is similar to that shown in Fig.
11.12 but, instead of the plunger being loaded by a preset spring, it is
loaded by a member responding to rear axle loading; the cut-off point
does not, therefore, occur either at a predetermined pressure or

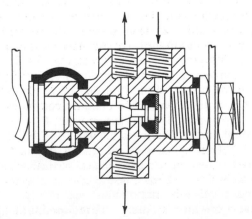

Fig. 11.14   A load sensitive pressure limiting valve (courtesy of DBA SA)

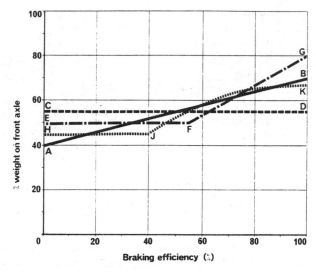

Fig. 11.15 The diagram of Fig. 11.11 with additional lines to show the effect of a pressure limiting valve EFG and a pressure reducing valve HJK on the braking ratio

deceleration but at a condition determined by the condition of loading. With this type of valve, correct operation depends on the consistent setting of the component coupling it to the rear axle, and on the suspension load/deflection characteristics being maintained over a long period. Components such as this are not without their problems in service.

Whatever the valve of this simple type which is fitted to the vehicle, the cut-off point is determined during any particular journey and may be shown on a diagram (Fig. 11.15), which repeats lines AB and CD from Fig. 11.11 and adds two new lines, EFG being used to indicate the effect of a pressure limiting valve. As drawn (for convenience, as explained above), the portion EF corresponds to a fixed braking ratio of 50:50 which applies up to a braking efficiency of 56%; at point F, the pressure cut-off occurs so, beyond that point, the braking ratio changes steadily as the front brake pressure continues to increase while the rear brake pressure remains constant.

As can be seen, line EFG crosses the ideal line AB at two points, equivalent to 35% and 72% braking efficiency and is relatively close to it for a large part of the range; the braking ratio is, therefore, correct at two values of adhesion and more nearly correct at a range of other values than was previously the case.

Further developments in the design of pressure limiting valves have taken place and one further Lockheed design (Fig. 11.16) shows how it

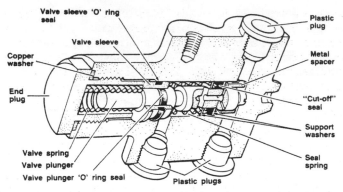

Fig. 11.16 A compensating pressure limiting valve (courtesy of Automotive Products PLC)

is possible to maintain the rear brake pressure, even if drum expansion does occur. The spring loaded plunger now passes through a cut-off seal, drillings in the plunger allowing fluid to pass freely when there is only low pressure in the system; as pressure increases during a brake application it acts on the end face of the plunger only, to the right of the cut-off seal, and moves it to the left, compressing the spring. At the limiting value of the pressure, the spring is compressed sufficiently for the bypass drilling to be drawn within the cut-off seal, so that the rear brakes are isolated from the master cylinder; this valve then has a similar characteristic to the others described, any increase in front brake pressure not being transmitted to the rear brakes, because it does not act in such a way as to move the plunger.

Should the pressure in the rear brake pipeline fall during a sustained brake application, the spring will cause the plunger to move to the right a little and allow more fluid to pass through the bypass drillings; this will restore the rear brake pressure and return the plunger to the cut-off position. At the conclusion of the brake application, pressure is released in the annular chamber around the plunger, to the left of the cut-off seal, but is still trapped beyond the seal; this pressure then moves the seal to the left, compressing the light seal spring and uncovering the bypass drilling so that the trapped pressure can be released.

11.7 Pressure modulating valves

This matter of braking ratio correction is of great importance if the maximum use is to be made of the available adhesion in an emergency, so a great deal of work has been done—and is continuing—on more complex valves. Most of these are what are known as pressure modulating valves which, beyond an activation point, do not isolate the rear brakes but transmit only a proportion of any increase directed to the front brakes; the magnitude of this proportion can be determined by the designer and the unit can respond to either pressure or deceleration but, before examples are considered, the effect of this type of valve will be examined with reference to Fig. 11.15, where its operation is represented by line HJK.

In the fictitious case illustrated, the straight line HJ is at a level corresponding to a fixed front:rear ratio of 45:55 and the activation point J is at a braking efficiency of 40%; beyond the activation point, the ratio of the output and input pressures is constantly changing, according to the selected characteristics, so the line JK is a curve which, rising steeply at first, gradually falls away. By appropriate design, the line HJK can be made to cross the ideal line AB at three places, as shown, and to lie generally closer to AB than was possible in the case of a limiting valve, as represented by line EFG. It must, however, be realised that, as with line EFG, the likelihood of premature wheel locking occurring at either front or rear will alternate each time the actual braking ratio line crosses the ideal line; the slight chance of premature rear wheel locking under certain of these conditions might not be in accordance with the requirements of legislation, so it might be necessary to design the system so that, under most conditions, line HJK lay above line AB.

Turning to the valves themselves, an early Girling design (Fig. 11.17) combined an inertia type limiting valve with a pressure proportioning device; in this unit, the ball rolls towards the seal during braking and has to seat precisely against it in order to activate the valve, so it is important that the centre of the ball is exactly on the seal centre line when the unit is assembled. Up to the point at which the ball seats, the rising pressure at both ends of the reducing device sets up opposing forces proportional to the piston areas; the larger primary piston, therefore, pushes back the differential piston, compressing the main spring in the process. After the ball has seated, with the pressure from the master cylinder still rising, the increased force on the differential piston, acting with the main spring, starts to push back the main piston, increasing the pressure of the fluid isolated in the rear brake pipelines. This increase in the rear brake pressure is less than that delivered by the master cylinder, because of the difference in the piston areas.

A more recent design (Fig. 11.18) produces the same effect from a greatly simplified layout, with the ball and a compound piston in line with each other. Until the ball seats, fluid can flow freely through the axial port (the central pin was at first incorporated to facilitate

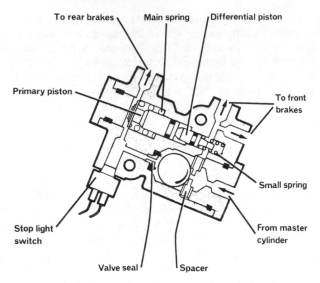

Fig. 11.17   *A deceleration conscious pressure reducing valve (courtesy of Lucas Girling Ltd.)*

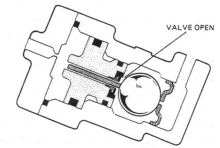

Fig. 11.18   *A further design of deceleration conscious pressure reducing valve (courtesy of Lucas Girling Ltd.)*

bleeding, by unseating the ball when the piston reached full stroke) and away to the rear brakes; the greater force developed by the larger piston as pressure rises, merely presses the piston against a shoulder in the bore of the valve chamber. After the ball seats, the fluid pipeline to the rear brakes is isolated from the master cylinder; however, the force generated by the rising pressure on the smaller piston, eventually overcomes the constant force exerted by the larger piston so additional pressurisation of the isolated fluid occurs, at a rate determined by the ratio of the piston areas.

Other designs of pressure modulating valve are entirely pressure

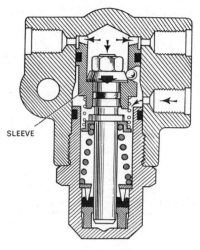

Fig. 11.19   A pressure reducing valve (courtesy of Lucas Girling Ltd.)

activated, a Girling example being illustrated in Fig. 11.19; this consists essentially of a housing containing a spring loaded spindle fitted with a tapered plunger, a sleeve (also spring loaded) and a ball. In the 'off' position, the ball is unseated by the tapered plunger, so that fluid can flow freely through the port in the wall of the sleeve to the rear brake outlets; rising pressure throughout the unit then drives the spindle downwards (the lower end is not subject to fluid pressure), compressing its spring, and allows the ball to seat, so that the outlet chamber is isolated.

Increasing pressure in the inlet chamber of the valve can act only on the narrow annular face of the spindle, just below the seal, but will eventually be able to lift the spindle in conjunction with the force exerted by the main spring, and unseat the ball; additional fluid will now pass into the upper chamber, where it will increase the pressure, this acting on the end of the spindle as before. If, during a sustained brake application, the rear brake pressure should tend to fall because of drum expansion, the valve will operate to maintain this pressure at a constant level. Depending on the relative areas of the relevant faces of the spindle, only a proportion of the extra pressure applied to the valve inlet will be passed through, before the forces again balance and the ball is reseated, thus achieving the required characteristics. When the brake pedal is released, the pressure in the upper chamber forces the sleeve down, compressing its light return spring and unseating the ball.

A valve of this type may be modified to take account of axle

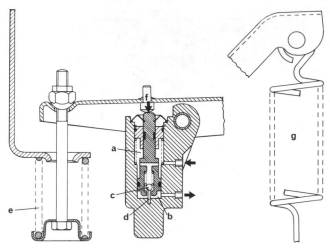

Fig. 11.20   A load sensitive pressure reducing valve installation (courtesy of Automotive Products PLC)

loading, by arranging for an external force, proportional to the load, to act on the exposed end of the plunger (Fig. 11.20); this suitably modifies the pressure at which the valve is activated when correctly set. In this Lockheed example, the fluid passage and ball valve are central in the plunger, the ball being moved by a pin set in the end of the cylinder bore; operation of the unit is, apart from the load bias, similar to that of the previous example, the pressures in the two chambers of the valve body acting on different areas of the plunger to operate it.

As an example of how components can be combined, enabling the number of external connections to be reduced, the Girling combination valve (Fig. 11.21) is noteworthy; this not only incorporates a pressure differential warning actuator and a pressure conscious reducing valve in the one body, but also adds an extra feature. One possible criticism of the use of a pressure limiting or reducing valve in the rear brake pipeline of a front:rear split system is that, in the event of front brake system failure, the valve would interfere with the operation of the rear brakes; this unit, therefore, provides for this condition. The pressure differential actuator piston is, at the rear brake circuit end, assembled into the bore of an insert; through this is a passage to the rear brake outlet, in parallel with the path through the pressure conscious reducing valve. Should the front brake circuit fail, the pressure in the rear brake circuit will drive the piston to the left, so that it withdraws from the insert; this opens up the direct

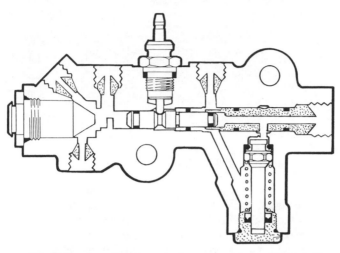

Fig. 11.21   A combination valve (courtesy of Lucas Girling Ltd.)

passage for fluid to pass to the rear brakes without pressure modulation until, after the system has been repaired, the piston is automatically centred.

When a diagonally split system is used, and pressure limiting or modulating valves are to be incorporated, it is necessary to use one unit in each of the two circuits; however, for convenience, Girling offer a twin version of their GP valve (shown in Fig. 11.18) having the two separate units within a single housing. An alternative approach to those already described has been announced by DBA, although full details are not yet released; this places each valve within the double acting wheel cylinder of the rear drum brake operated by the circuit with which it is associated. This combination of functions within a single unit again minimises the number of external connections and reduces the chance of a leakage of fluid.

11.8 Load sensing with air brakes

The components just described are all for use in hydraulic brake systems, but air braked vehicles have the same need to have their braking ratio as nearly correct as possible, so as to be able to make full utilisation of the available adhesion under differing conditions. In general, however, with those vehicles which have air braking systems, weight transfer during braking is not an important effect by comparison with changes in static weight distribution, such as take place when the pay load is varied; the equipment to be considered,

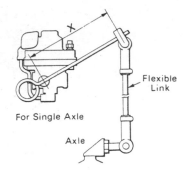

Flexible
Link

For Single Axle

Fig. 11.22   The installation of an air brake
load sensing valve (courtesy of Bendix Ltd.)

Axle

therefore, responds only to load and modifies the air pressure delivered to the brakes concerned accordingly.

The most common way of sensing the load on an axle and using the resulting indication to control a pressure modifying valve, is to mount the valve on the frame of the vehicle and couple a pivoted control arm to the axle (Fig. 11.22); as the load on the axle varies, the suspension springs will deflect accordingly and the control arm will be rotated. The radius X at which the link is connected to the control arm is determined to suit the vehicle concerned and the valve being installed. A single valve can also be used with twin axles, by connecting the link to a balance beam between the two. The setting of the valve when correctly installed is such that at full load, the pressure at the outlet is the same as that at the inlet port; as the load on the axle reduces and the deflection of the suspension springs decreases, the valve operates to reduce the pressure delivered to the outlet so that the change in braking ratio approximates to the change in the static loading.

A sectional view of a Clayton Dewandre automatic load sensing valve (Fig. 11.23), enables the working of this unit to be understood; the major components contained in the valve body are the valve plunger 11 and the piston 8, to which is connected the annular diaphragm 15. The control lever 12 (which is adjustable for length) is carried on a shaft which passes through the bearings in the valve body; internally, this shaft carries the ball pivot which, as load increases and the control lever rotates anti-clockwise, moves the valve plunger 11 upwards. Piston 8 incorporates the disc valve 7, which is spring loaded, which in its closed position isolates chamber (a) from chamber (b).

Air enters the load sensing valve at port 1 and passes into chamber (a), where it acts downwards on piston 8; it also passes through connecting pipe 17 to act on the underside of piston 14, which supports ball pivot 13, to eliminate approximately the reaction force

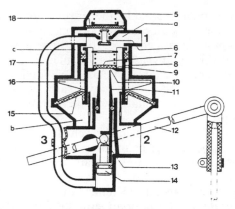

Fig. 11.23   A cross-section of a load sensing valve (courtesy of Clayton Dewandre Co. Ltd.)

on 13 which would otherwise apply a torque to the control lever shaft, and—at first—also passes through valve 6 and channel (c) to act downwards on the diaphragm 15. Piston 8 has a number of vanes 16 formed on its exterior, onto which the diaphragm rolls as the piston moves down; the air pressure acting below the diaphragm therefore only affects the piston by means of that part of the diaphragm which is in contact with the vanes. Since, as will be seen, the movement of the piston when the valve is operating depends on the position of the valve plunger 11, which in turn depends on the load carried by the axle concerned, the upward force on the piston for any given air pressure in chamber (b) depends principally on this load; it is this feature which therefore enables the valve to relate the output pressure at port 2 to the load.

As air pressure builds up in chamber (a) and piston 8 moves down, disc valve 7 contacts the annular face of the valve plunger 11, which is the exhaust valve and closes it, isolating chamber (b) from the exhaust port 3; further movement of the piston opens the inlet valve 9, allowing air to pass through into chamber (b) where it acts on the underside of the diaphragm, as well as passing to the outlet port 2. The upward force on the diaphragm will tend to push piston 8 back, closing the inlet valve, so that a balance is reached, the major forces then being the downward one on the piston due to the air pressure in (a), the upward one on the annular area of the piston around the valve plunger 11 due to the air pressure in (b) plus the upward force on the diaphragm due to the same pressure and the upward force on piston 14 due to the air pressure in (a).

At low inlet pressures, there is also an additional downward force, that on the diaphragm exerted by the air pressure in channel (c); this ensures that at these low air pressures piston 8 is always moved down sufficiently to pass air into chamber (b) without modulation, despite the position of valve plunger 11. As the inlet air pressure rises to a predetermined value, disc valve 6 is closed by the effect of this pressure on diaphragm 18, limiting the downward pressure applied to diaphragm 15, so that modulation of the output air pressure starts from that point.

It should be noted that when the vehicle is in motion with the brakes released, the absence of any air pressure either above piston 8 or beneath piston 14 removes any restraint from the ball pivot 13; this may therefore move up and down freely as the suspension deflection varies during the passage of the vehicle over a bumpy road.

In an earlier design of Clayton Dewandre load sensing valve, the balancing of forces took place between two pistons—both compound assemblies—at right angles; these were coupled by a linkage having a roller at its central pin joint, this roller resting on an inclined ramp. The ramp was incorporated into the spindle of the control lever, so that its inclination was changed as the axle load varied; this variable inclination of the ramp caused a corresponding variation in the relationship between the two opposing sets of forces which, in turn, was the means of achieving a variable relationship between the input and output air pressures.

A current design of Bendix unit is similar to that shown in Fig. 11.23, as regards having a piston with vanes and diaphragm and a valve plunger with a lower piston adding to the upward force on the ball pivot; it differs, however, in the construction and layout of the means by which pressure modulation is eliminated at low inlet pressures. Bendix use a patented feature which they name the Inshot Valve (Fig. 11.24), which is contained in a cylindrical body formed on one side of the unit; this cylinder communicates with the upper chamber of the unit by means of the passage S, with the chamber above the diaphragm by means of passage Ee, with the balance pipe Dd by means of passage Cc (shown by the broken lines) and has an exhaust port Bb at one end.

The Inshot Valve body is divided into two chambers T and Y by the internal wall which carries the valve seat X; normally in contact with X is the inlet/exhaust valve U, under the influence of valve spring W, and within U is the secondary piston V. Chamber Y contains primary piston Z, acted upon by the Inshot spring Aa. With all air pressure exhausted, the primary piston is in contact with secondary piston V (so that no air can then pass to the exhaust port) and has moved this and the inlet/exhaust valve U away from the valve seat X.

When air at only a moderate pressure is admitted to the unit, it acts

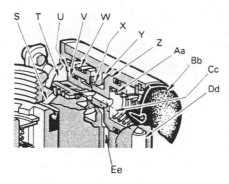

Fig. 11.24   An 'Inshot' valve incorporated into a load sensing valve (courtesy of Bendix Ltd.)

directly on the control piston P and also passes through port S into chamber T; from chamber T, this air has direct access by way of passage Cc to balance pipe Dd (the function of this balance pipe being as for the valve previously described) and also can pass through the open inlet valve and into the passage Ee leading to the chamber Ef, where it acts upon the free part of the diaphragm A. Under these circumstances, even with a lightly laden vehicle, the downward forces on the diaphragm and the control piston will be sufficient to ensure that unmodulated air is passed from the inlet port to the outlet port of the unit.

If the inlet pressure is caused to rise, the pressure in chamber Y will rise and, acting upon the primary piston, will compress the Inshot spring until the primary piston moves sufficiently to allow the inlet/exhaust valve U to seat, isolating chamber Y from chamber T and preventing any further increase in pressure from reaching chamber Ff above the diaphragm; the extra pressure at the inlet port always acts, of course, on control piston C and, by way of Cc and Dd on the balance piston underneath the ball pivot.

Any further pressure increase at the inlet enters chamber T and, although it cannot act directly on the primary piston in chamber Y, it acts on secondary piston V which is in contact with it; the Inshot spring is therefore further compressed, so that the hollow stem of the primary piston moves clear of the inlet/exhaust valve. The face of the secondary piston, which is in contact with the primary piston, is slotted so that air in chamber Y and air from chamber Ff can pass through the slot to the exhaust passage through the hollow stem of the primary piston.

As the pressure in chamber Y falls, the Inshot spring is able to reseat the primary piston against the inlet/exhaust valve U, so that the

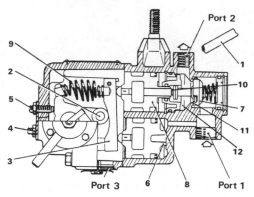

Fig. 11.25   A variable fulcrum lever type load sensing valve (courtesy of Paul Dahl SA)

pressure remaining in chamber Ff is retained, to continue to act above the diaphragm. In this way, the transition from no modulation of the pressure of the transmitted air to normal modulation, according to loading, is achieved smoothly.

A third type of load sensing valve (Fig. 11.25) is by the French company, Paul Dahl, of Saint Cloud. In this a control piston 6 is always acted upon by the inlet pressure and applies a bias to the graduating piston 8 by way of the balancing lever 3; this lever pivots on the roller 2, the position of which varies with the angle of the adjusting lever, which is connected to the axle concerned. The loading of the axle therefore directly varies the ratio of the balancing lever and thus affects the bias on the graduating piston, achieving in this way the required modulation of the output pressure of the unit.

Paul Dahl also markets, amongst other components, a load sensing valve for use on vehicles with air suspension; in this case the air pressures in the suspension units are proportional to the loading, so that a constant ride height is achieved, and these pressures can therefore be used directly to apply the required bias to the graduating piston in the unit concerned. These load sensing valves have no external moving parts.

Although load sensing valves have not been without their problems—partly caused by variability in suspension stiffness—since their introduction, it may be expected that development of them will continue and the installed performance improve. Despite interest in anti-locking systems, which are described in the following sections, it is clearly desirable that within the limitations of adhesion, the braking ratio should be as closely matched as is practicable to the axle loadings.

11.9 Wheel-lock prevention

Reference has already been made a number of times to the desirability of avoiding wheel locking by matching braking effort to axle loading as closely as possible; in an emergency on a poor surface, however, there remains the possibility that the driver may press the brake pedal too hard and cause the locking of those wheels (usually, by design, the front wheels of a car but more likely to be the rear wheels of a truck) which make the greatest use of the available adhesion for braking. Alternatively, apprehension that wheels may be locked and directional control lost may deter the driver from braking sufficiently hard to achieve the maximum possible deceleration.

The first modification of a braking system to prevent wheels from being locked under conditions of excessive braking was the original Dunlop Maxaret system, which was applied to aircraft brakes in the early 1950s; the difficulty of controlling a skidding aircraft on, for example, a wet runway when wheel brakes were the only effective means of reducing speed, justified the cost and complication. Even under dry runway conditions, the elimination of flat spots on tyres (and with multi-wheel undercarriages the locking of a single wheel could easily go undetected) with the attendant risk of an eventual burst was highly desirable. This Maxaret system, however, was used in conjunction with a different type of hydraulic actuation to that commonly found on motor vehicles; its use could not, therefore, be extended at that time, but suitably designed and developed systems will be referred to below.

Before proceeding to consider the various ways in which wheel locking may be prevented, it is necessary to recognize what any viable system has to do and, fundamental to this matter, is the relationship between the rotation of a wheel and its linear velocity; in particular, the case of an automotive wheel and pneumatic tyre will be taken. A wheel only moves without slip when it is transmitting no force in the horizontal plane; that is to say, when the vehicle is rolling freely in a straight line. As soon as the driver either accelerates, steers or brakes the vehicle, the generation of the necessary horizontal force at the road/tyre interface is accompanied by the initiation of slip between the tyre contact patch and the road surface; for the present purpose, only the conditions during braking will be examined, but similar considerations apply during acceleration and cornering.

The amount of slip between tyre and road is directly proportional to the force transmitted—and therefore to the deceleration—over the greater part of the range of braking efficiencies; this is illustrated by Fig. 11.26, which is typical of the relationship which exists. The exact shape of an actual curve depends, of course, on all of the relevant

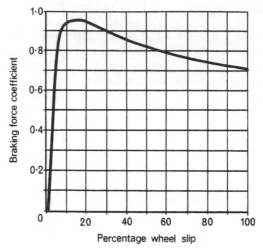

Fig. 11.26   The relationship between wheel slip and braking force (courtesy of Lucas Girling Ltd.)

factors, including the tyre and road surface materials. It will be seen from the diagram that as the braking force approaches its maximum value, the percentage of slip starts to increase rapidly; beyond about 15% slip in the case illustrated, the braking force declines considerably.

The significance of this in connection with the prevention of wheel locking is that, up to the point at which the maximum braking force is being developed, the angular deceleration of a wheel will not exceed a certain value which (allowing for possible variations in conditions) can be calculated; as the limits of the available adhesion are exceeded and slip increases rapidly, with the wheel tending to lock, its angular deceleration will become greater than the value referred to above.

The first requirement, then, for a wheel lock prevention system is to detect excessive deceleration of the wheel or wheels concerned so that, as a second requirement, action can be initiated to reduce the braking force; once the braking force is within the capability of the available adhesion to sustain, the tyre will again grip the road, the wheel will accelerate and directional control will be restored. It is, however, not enough to obviate wheel locking by simply reducing the braking force either to zero or to some low value; this would leave the vehicle still in danger because of its inability to stop. The further general requirement, therefore, is for braking to be restored on an appropriate cyclic basis so that the deceleration approximates as closely as possible to the maximum theoretically available.

11.10 Methods of control

In designing and developing wheel lock prevention—popularly referred to as anti-lock or ABS systems—component manufacturers have to provide for the use of both hydraulic fluid and air and they have made use of two ways of detecting excessive wheel deceleration. The original Dunlop Maxaret system incorporated an inertia device—a method which has at least one current exponent—but most present day systems use electrical detection with electronic processing of the data obtained to initiate control signals.

Although there have been viable anti-lock systems on the market for some years, development and refinement are proceeding rapidly and it is too early to say whether both the mechanically and electronically controlled systems will continue in parallel, although in appropriate applications, or whether the one will dominate; certain it is that where recent years have seen the introduction of individual electronic control into selected areas of road vehicle management, the future is bound to see the emergence of integrated electronic control of most dynamic systems on vehicles. Anti-lock systems, being markedly safety related, are therefore certain to be much more common in the not-too-far-distant future and may well be taking account of adhesion, as assessed by the degree of wheel slip during acceleration, and the likelihood of ice on the road, as assessed by one of the devices already in existence. This section will therefore review some past and present systems as an indication of the directions in which development is proceeding, but it will be understood that, unlike most other braking equipment considered, there is not yet the same firm base of established practice.

As has been noted above, most anti-lock systems currently in use feature electrical detection and there is a general unanimity of approach to this one matter, if not in other parts of the subject. Use is made of a slotted or toothed exciter disc, mounted on the rotating member concerned; it may be mounted in a brake drum (Fig. 11.27) or on the drive flange of an axle (Fig. 11.28) and an inductive sensor is mounted close to it. During the rotation of the exciter disc, an electrical impulse is generated in the sensor as each tooth and gap pass it; the frequency of these signals and the rate of change of that frequency are therefore measures, respectively, of the angular velocity and acceleration or deceleration of the rotating member.

Individual sensing of wheels is the ideal, but is expensive; wheels coupled on a drive axle may therefore be sensed as a pair, as in Fig. 11.28, or only the wheels on the side of trailers nearest the edge of the road may be sensed, on the assumption that most puddles and mud are likely to be that side. Cost again usually dictates that while drive

Fig. 11.27　A drum mounted sensing disc for detecting wheel locking (courtesy of Lucas Girling Ltd.)

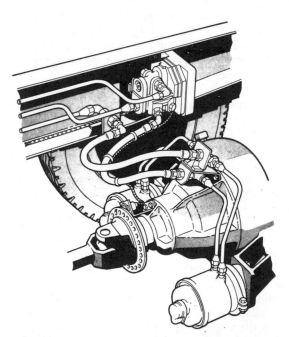

Fig. 11.28　A sensing disc for anti-lock operation mounted at an axle drive flange (courtesy of Bendix Ltd.)

axles of tractors and rigid vehicles and trailer axles may be controlled,. front axles of trucks seldom are; most car systems, however, sense all four wheels. The control system may respond to the wheel which locks first (low selection) or that which locks last (high-selection) and the whole matter of the control philosophy being evolved is very much subject to accumulating experience and the external pressure of regulatory legislation.

The design, construction and manner of operation of electronic circuitry is beyond the scope of this book, but some of the features which are of importance to the designers of anti-lock systems are as follows: the ability to process data extremely rapidly and to repeat the processing at extremely short time intervals, the low electrical power requirement and the high degree of reliability. Electronic systems are designed to be self checking on a continuous basis and are currently well protected from exterior electrical interference, although this was not always the case; should any part of the control circuitry develop a fault, all modulation of brake fluid pressure is prevented and the driver is warned that, with the equipment out of action, he should use extra caution when braking because wheel locking will no longer be prevented.

During the late 1960s and early 1970s a number of working anti-lock systems for trucks were developed and explored various of the possible ways of achieving the principal requirements; by the mid 1970s two notable systems which were on the market in the UK were the Girling Skidchek (based on components designed by Kelsey-Hayes in the USA) and the Dunlop Maxaret III. Skidchek employed a simple solenoid controlled valve, inserted in the supply line to the brakes on the axle concerned, which when it operated, isolated those brakes from the foot valve and then released sufficient air to enable the wheels involved to regain their grip; air would then be readmitted and the valve would operate—if necessary—on a cyclic basis until either the brakes were released or the vehicle came to a halt. Maxaret III operated independently of the existing brake system, apart from isolating the brakes concerned during its operation, by applying air direct from a reservoir to the reverse side of the service diaphragms in the brake chambers, to oppose the normal applying force; this was claimed to give quick response and a sensitivity control incorporated into the valve was designed to smooth the operation of the system.

11.11 Later designs

Whilst the early anti-lock systems achieved most of the aims set at the time, they tended to make a heavy demand on the air supply and the pattern of relief of the input force to the brakes controlled did not achieve a very high level of utilisation of the adhesion available; by the late 1970s, however, Bendix at Bristol in the UK (then in being as Bendix-Westinghouse) introduced what they claimed as the first of the second generation systems, concentrating most of their attention on tractor drive axles and using propeller shaft sensing as already illustrated (Fig. 11.28).

Before describing the modulator which controls the air pressure applied to the brakes on the axle concerned, the basis on which control is effected will be considered, with reference to Fig. 11.29. Figure 11.29(a) shows, by means of the line AB how the speed of a vehicle may be supposed to fall steadily during braking to a standstill, from the moment A when the brakes are applied; line CD represents a reference, updated at frequent intervals during the stop to allow for variations in AB, which the electronic control panel establishes automatically.

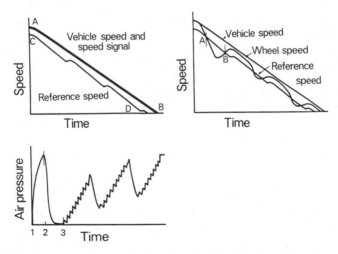

Fig. 11.29   Diagrams to illustrate the control of wheel locking with an air braking system (courtesy of Bendix Ltd.)

Figure 11.29(b) superimposes on the two lines of the first diagram a 'wheel speed'line as sensed from the propeller shaft (allowance being made, of course, for the final drive ratio); this does not coincide with the vehicle speed line, because of the slip necessarily occurring between tyres and road, but in fact is drawn so as to indicate the initiation of wheel locking almost as soon as the brakes are applied.

As soon as the controller detects that the wheel speed line has crossed the reference line (point A), it actuates the modulating valve to reduce the brake air pressure; it is therefore seen that the wheel speed line, after dipping below the reference line, rises again and crosses it at B.

The controller limits the rate of rise of air pressure so as to avoid immediate relocking of the wheels, by readmitting air in successive small stages (Fig. 11.29(c) is of air pressure, to the same time scale); braking therefore approaches the maximum progressively, the wheel speed curve slowly falling away from the vehicle speed curve as slip increases, until locking is again initiated. The response of the controller is now modified by the 'learning process' associated with the first cycle of control and less air is released, with a quicker recovery of grip and the wheel speed curve is subsequently kept under close control until the vehicle stops, with high utilisation of the available adhesion and a limited air consumption.

A simplified representation of the complete system (Fig. 11.30) shows that the modulator valve, to which the electronic controller is attached, is in two sections; the lower part is based on a standard relay valve while the upper part houses the solenoid valve which effects the control. When braking is within the limits of adhesion, the solenoid will be in the position shown and air in the control pressure line from the foot valve will pass directly to the relay valve pistons; as it does so, it will close the quick release valve.

When the controller actuates the modulator, the solenoid moves to the right, isolating the control pressure line and opening the exhaust

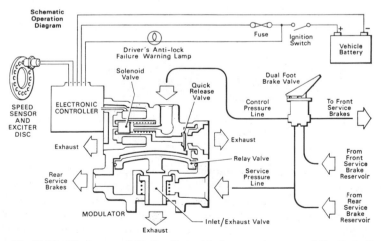

Fig. 11.30   The layout of the Bendix anti-lock system (courtesy of Bendix Ltd.)

valve to its left; with the rapid fall of pressure in the solenoid chamber, the quick release valve will open and release pressure from the relay valve. Reversal of the solenoid position will reconnect the control pressure line and reapply pressure to the relay valve, the air supply for the brakes coming, of course, direct from the service reservoir. During the operation of the modulator, as indicated by Fig. 11.29(c), the solenoid operates in such a manner, the movements of the quick release valve and relay piston matching it, that the air pressure is varying extremely quickly to achieve the sensitive degree of antilock control which the system demonstrates.

The Maxaret name is now the property of Anti-Skid Controls Ltd. of Coventry and Dublin and updated systems are currently offered for both tractor drive axles and semi-trailers. For tractors, propeller shaft sensing is used, the signals being processed by an electronic control unit which then actuates the solenoid valve in the Maxaret CR valve (Fig. 11.31). In the normal condition as shown, the air supply passes through to the brake actuators without interruption; operation of the solenoid valve, however, allows air to be diverted to the back of the upper diaphragm, closing the supply valve and opening the exhaust valve. Suitable control of these two valves allows appropriate modulation of the brake air pressure to be achieved.

For multi-wheel trailers, the Maxaret MDR system has been developed, the valve assembly shown (Fig. 11.32) being marked up as for use on a tri-axle trailer. Sensing is of the individual wheels on that axle which, by design, is the first to lock, and 'hold' valves are incorporated between the main valve and the air supply lines to, in this case, axles one and two and axle three. The hold valves have the function of preventing a further increase in pressure being applied to the axles concerned if a tendency to wheel locking is sensed, but

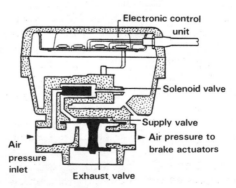

Fig. 11.31   The Maxaret CR valve (courtesy of Anti-Skid Controls Ltd.)

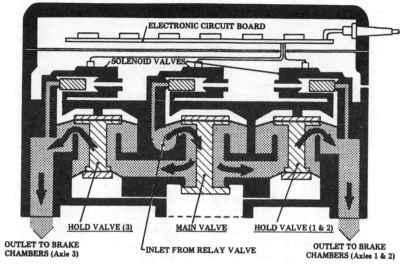

Fig. 11.32   The Maxaret MDR valve (courtesy of Anti-Skid Controls Ltd.)

without releasing any air; only if wheel locking is confirmed does the main valve operate to modulate the pressure, the hold valves then opening to allow some air to be released from the brake chambers.

11.12 Pneumatic memory

The latest form of the Girling system, called Skidchek GX, is suitable for use on any axle of a vehicle or combination (although there is a preferred order for its application) and individual sensing of wheels is used; the principal development from the earlier system relates to the modulating valve, which is called the MCR (Memory Controlled Relay) valve, and which may control the brakes on one or more axles, depending on which they are. In effect, this valve in part achieves by pneumatic/mechanical means a similar degree of pressure modulation to that which other systems achieve entirely by means of an electronic controller. A diagram of the valve (Fig. 11.33) in the normal condition (no locking occurring), reveals that it contains a relay piston which works in conjunction with a modulation tube valve, a solenoid operated popppet valve, a memory chamber and a latch valve.

With an air signal pressure from the foot valve, the relay piston is shown to have depressed the modulation tube to allow air from the reservoir to be passed to the brakes, balancing pressures in the normal

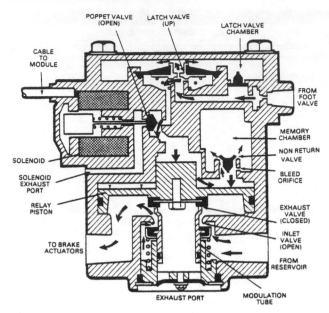

Fig. 11.33   The MCR valve of the Skidchek 'GX' system (courtesy of Lucas Girling Ltd.)

manner of a relay valve; on the conclusion of the brake application, the relay piston rises and air from the brake chambers exhausts through the centre of the modulation tube valve. During each normal brake application, air at the signal pressure not only acts on the relay piston, it also charges the memory chamber and the chamber above the latch valve; these pressures have no significance, however, in the absence of wheel locking and when the brakes are released they each discharge—that above the latch valve opening the valve to the right and falling quickly while that in the memory chamber escapes slowly through the calibrated orifice provided.

When locking of a wheel is sensed, the solenoid is energised and the poppet valve moves to isolate the signal pressure from the relay valve; it also opens the exhaust port to release air from above the relay piston. The pressure built up in the memory chamber is retained by the inlet valve but is able to fall slowly, as noted above, through the bleed orifice; the pressure above and below the latch valve remains constant.

As the wheels concerned regain their grip and accelerate, the solenoid is de-energised and the poppet valve reverts to its original position; this causes the pressure below the latch valve to fall momentarily so that this valve is then closed by the pressure remaining above it and it then restricts the passage of air from the foot valve to the relay piston slightly. The volume of air required at this stage to operate the relay piston is small and so a rapid initial response is achieved.

When the pressure above the relay piston matches that still present at that moment in the memory chamber, the inlet valve to that chamber opens and this considerably increases the volume which must be filled; the rate of pressure rise is thus reduced so that it is less likely to rise much above that which causes locking. During a stop with the system functioning to prevent locking, its characteristics will maintain braking at a high proportion of the theoretically possible efficiency, the control cycle being repeated as necessary down to a road speed of 8 km/h (5 mile/h).

Lastly, in this review of some of the anti-lock systems which have been developed for use with air braking equipment, that by Wabco not only uses individual wheel sensing but also has individual wheel control as a standard feature; Wabco-ABS, as it is called, is suitable for application to both tractors (or rigid vehicles) and trailers. The solenoid operated control valve (Fig. 11.34) is again the component of particular interest and this diagrammatic drawing shows that two solenoids are incorporated; port 1 is the inlet and 2 the outlet to the brakes, 3 being the exhaust port. With the valve in the normal condition as shown, air entering chamber (a) can lift the diaphragm (c), pass into chamber (b) and go out through port 2; it also passes through passage (d) into chamber (g) to hold the diaphragm (f) in the upward position. At the completion of a normal brake application, the pressure in (g) having fallen, the pressure in B deflects diaphragm (f) so that the air from the brake chambers escapes into (e), which communicates with the exhaust port 3.

Under the control of the electronic unit, either solenoid I alone or both solenoids may be energised. In the first case, the movement of the solenoid valve (i) seals the exhaust passage at its lower end and allows air from A to pass through the communicating passage to chamber (a) where it acts on diaphragm (b) to close the inlet (c); the pressure in (b) is then held and no increase in that at A will be transmitted. If both solenoids are energised, the additional effect to that described above will be that solenoid valve (h) will seal the inlet from chamber A and open the passage to the exhaust port; the pressure in (g) will then be released and that in B will be able to deflect the diaphragm (f) so that air from the brakes passes through (e) to the exhaust port. The ability of the solenoid operated control valve to either limit or reduce the pressure of the air being passed to the brake chambers, should wheel

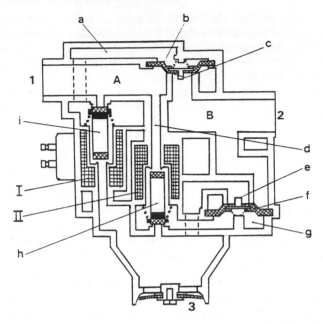

Fig. 11.34   The control valve of the Wabco ABS system (courtesy of Wabco Automotive Products Group)

locking tend to occur, enables the system to achieve the desired aim, the pressure being cycled as necessary.

From the descriptions given, it will be apparent that great ingenuity has already gone into the control valves used to limit or reduce the working air pressure and also, although this part of these systems has here received so little attention, into the electronic equipment which responds so rapidly and accurately to the signals received. Undoubtedly the future will bring continuing refinement of these systems and others not mentioned so that, with the benefit of accumulated experience and further innovation, even greater effectiveness and reliability may be achieved.

11.13 Anti-lock for cars

Sensing of incipient locking of car wheels can be effected in a very similar way to that described for trucks and other heavy vehicles, the toothed wheel which determines the frequency of the electrical pulses generated being suitably accommodated in or around a brake disc or brake drum; these pulses are then processed electronically so as to provide a signal to initiate brake release, the electronic controller being programmed to achieve, as for the larger vehicles, the desired high utilisation of the available adhesion during the cycles of brake pressure modulation. Because, however, the working fluid in the braking system is not air, but a liquid, there have to be significant differences in the means by which the input forces applied to the friction elements are varied.

As has been understood in the case of air braking systems, air under pressure can be released at any convenient point in the system by exhausting to atmosphere; the subsequent reinstatement of pressure being then achieved by drawing on the air stored under pressure on the vehicle (with the Dunlop Maxaret III counter-pressure system, the usage of air was in the reverse sequence). Because the anti-lock system is called upon to operate relatively infrequently (an investigation on a truck, carried out by Bendix Ltd., showed that the system operated once every 160 km (100 miles) on average), and because care is taken to minimise the air consumption during operation, the extra demand on the air compression and storage equipment is small.

With a hydraulic braking system, by contrast, fluid cannot be discharged from the system and there is usually no reserve stored under pressure; the modulation of pressure is therefore usually achieved by causing a momentary slight increase in the volume of the system to occur so as to achieve a reduction (the master cylinder being then isolated), followed by the application of energy from an external source to reduce the volume by a corresponding amount, and thus restore the pressure. Use has been made of vacuum servo units as an energy source, although the response of these was found to be too slow, and also of engine driven or electric pumps whilst, as will be described below, Girling use a road wheel driven pump. There is also, however, an increasing interest in stored pressure systems as being particularly suitable for use with an anti-lock device; Teves, for example, have shown their very compact hydraulic unit which combines pump, accumulator, brake control valve, booster and anti-lock equipment and is little larger than a comparable vacuum servo and master cylinder assembly (Fig. 11.35).

Although a number of car anti-lock systems have been developed and offered and some have been put into limited production, the extra cost involved has limited their application to cars in the upper part of the price range and the number of installations has not been large. The experience gained in service has, however, served to guide the further development work so as to improve the characteristics achieved and reduce costs; at the same time, the mounting interest in the anti-lock concept ensures that there will be a worthwhile market for the first system shown to meet the needs of the medium price sector of the car range. It may yet be some time, however, before prices of

Fig. 11.35   A combined stored pressure car hydraulic brake unit with anti-lock incorporated, compared with a conventional vacuum serve and tandem master cylinder (courtesy of Alfred Teves GmbH)

even simplified systems fall low enough for significant penetration of the high volume small car market to be achieved.

Little detailed information has been made generally available regarding the hydraulic components used in anti-lock systems such as are most commonly on the market at present; undoubtedly there will be still further development work on them before sufficiently stable designs are evolved for their manufacturers to make their principal features and characteristics public. By contrast, the Lucas Girling SCS (Stop Control System) has now been described in sufficient detail by the manufacturer for a good understanding to be formed of this entirely mechanical system.

The Girling system has been conceived for application particularly to light/medium weight front wheel drive cars, having the diagonally split hydraulic system which was described earlier in this chapter; this is a very popular category of car, but one which is very sensitive to component costs so simplicity and ease of manufacture and installation have been important considerations. By applying one SCS unit to each of the two parts of the hydraulic system of this class of car, with pressure apportioning valves of appropriate design in the rear brake pipelines to ensure that the rear wheels cannot lock prematurely, Girling claims to have achieved the major characteristics of complex four wheel systems at a substantially lower cost.

The basis of this system is a modulator unit, one of which is driven

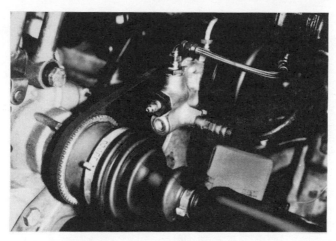

Fig. 11.36   A belt driven anti-lock unit for a mechanical system applied to a car hydraulic brake installation (courtesy of Lucas Girling Ltd.)

by a belt from each of the front wheel drive shafts of the vehicle (Fig. 11.36); the use of a toothed belt and pulleys ensures that no slip occurs in the drive. Each modulator comprises two principal sections, shown in schematic form in Fig. 11.37; the belt driven shaft 1 which carries the flywheel 2 and the operating mechanism for the dump valve 7 and which are enclosed by the black metal cover seen in the installation picture form one part, while the hydraulic pressure modulating components are housed in the light alloy casting which also is visible.

During normal braking, fluid from the master cylinder passes through the cut-off valve 13 without restriction, and on to both the front and the rear brake supplied by the circuit concerned; the flywheel, meanwhile, rotates at the speed of the shaft 1 (to which it is not directly attached), being driven by a ball and ramp mechanism 4, through the medium of a clutch 5. At the same time, the pump piston 11, which would otherwise be oscillated by the cam 10, is held out of engagement by the spring 12; the pressure below the de-boost piston 15 pressurises the fluid above it (only minimal movement of the piston occurring) and this fluid with the dump valve 7 and the pump outlet valve 18 both closed, exerts a net downward force on the pump piston to balance the upward force due to the pressure below it.

If one of the wheels concerned tends to lock, its deceleration then exceeding the predetermined value, the modulator drive shaft 1 is decelerated correspondingly; the flywheel, however, being suitably massive, is caused by its inertia to overrun the shaft. This relative movement between the flywheel and the shaft causes the ball and

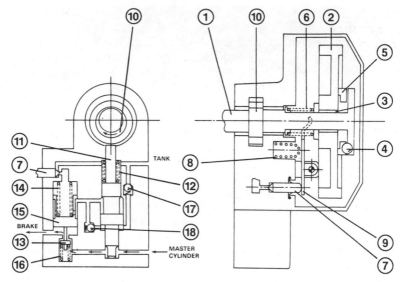

Fig. 11.37   The construction of the braking modulator unit seen in Fig. 11.36 (courtesy of Lucas Girling Ltd.)

ramp mechanism to operate and push on the clutch, moving the flywheel axially on its journal bearing and actuating the dump valve lever 9; this lever, in turn, allows the dump valve 7 to rise, initiating the pressure modulation sequence.

With the dump valve open, the pressure above the de-boost piston 15 is released and this piston rises, the fluid displaced passing away to the reservoir; simultaneously, the rising of the de-boost piston allows the cut-off valve 13 to close, isolating the master cylinder from the brakes supplied by that circuit. The rising of the de-boost piston also relieves the hydraulic pressure in the brake circuit, so that wheel lock is prevented, and the rotating flywheel is decelerated at a controlled rate by the slip occurring within the clutch. Finally, at this stage of the sequence of events, the master cylinder pressure still acting below the pump piston, being no longer opposed by a downward pressure, lifts the piston into contact with the cam; because, however, the dump valve is still open, no fluid is yet displaced by the pump.

The reduction in brake pressure not only prevents wheel locking, it allows the wheel to pick up speed again, so that it accelerates towards the angular velocity corresponding to the road speed of the vehicle at that moment; as the front wheel does this, its angular velocity reaches a value matching that of the decelerating flywheel, so that the ball and ramp mechanism reverts to its initial condition, the flywheel slides back under the influence of its spring 6 and the dump valve spring 8 moves the lever to allow the dump valve to close.

At once, the pump starts to draw in fluid from the reservoir, through its inlet valve 17, and discharge it through the outlet valve 18, to restore the pressure in the volume above the de-boost piston; at the same time, the road wheel continues to accelerate, the modulator shaft accelerating the flywheel through the medium of the clutch. During this process, the brake pressure is increased progressively with each revolution of the cam until either the maximum possible deceleration is achieved again, and the pressure reduction sequence is repeated, or the master cylinder pressure is restored without further wheel lock occurring. In the latter case, the cut-off valve opens again, the pump piston is disengaged from the cam and normal un-modulated braking is restored.

Among other aims that, it is claimed, have been achieved, is that of developing a system which—in its entirety—is as readily serviced as other hydraulic system components by a competent mechanic. Combination of the SCS with the diagonal split ensures that wheel locking is prevented and directional control maintained under conditions such as combined cornering (causing lateral weight transfer) and braking or when there are adhesion differences between left and right hand wheels.

Anti-lock systems enhance road safety, but it is considered that their use should not be supposed to eliminate the need to balance braking correctly to match dynamic weight distribution as closely as possible; they assist in the achievement of the best attainable stopping distances on poor surfaces without the need for skill on the part of the driver and their frequency of pressure modulation far exceeds that attainable in cadence braking by experienced drivers.

The further possibility, when the integration of vehicle electronic control systems already envisaged becomes a reality, is that on major routes at least, signals from roadside installations relating to visibility and road layout, in conjunction with warnings of vehicles ahead from on-board radar, speed signals and assessments of tyre/road adhesion might be used to provide an overriding control of speed so that, hopefully, a driver could not proceed in such a manner as not to have a safe stopping distance available.

Space precludes a description of the Citroën stored pressure hydraulic braking system, which is a notable feature of most of that company's cars. The pumping and storage components, whilst of distinctive design, function in a similar way to those described in Chapter 7 (they usually also serve the suspension and power steering); the dual brake valve, however, operates on a novel principle to graduate the pressures delivered.

12

Braking equipment in service

12.1 Introduction

Earlier chapters have considered the purpose of braking systems and the ways in which this purpose is achieved by the design, construction and combination of various items of equipment; the expectation is then that any given new vehicle, equipped according to a correctly prepared specification, will be capable of stopping in a satisfactory manner under the conditions of the moment. After an extended period in service, however, it will be necessary for the owner or operator of the vehicle to take certain action with regard to the braking equipment if its expected performance is to be maintained, just as other major systems or components will require attention. Apart from any repairs which may become necessary because of accidental damage, routine attention will be necessary to make good the effects of natural wear and tear and maintain all parts in the 'as new' condition, so that they function as intended.

There may, alternatively, be some malfunctioning of the braking equipment which may develop in service, requiring that a fault or combination of faults be diagnosed and corrected in order that normal braking can be restored; the number of possibilities is almost endless, but a systematic approach, coupled with a knowledge of the function and construction of the various parts of the system, is likely to succeed in isolating the cause of the trouble. In any problem with a braking system there are four areas which should always be considered before an opinion is formed as to what is in the wrong: the brakes, the brake linings, the brake actuation and the mating surfaces; each of these areas will be examined in turn in this chapter with regard to the routine attention likely to be needed and the possibilities for faults to develop.

12.2 Brakes

Disc brake calipers are usually well protected against corrosion by electroplating and, being self adjusting, require no routine attention

318

on a short term basis; when brake pads are replaced, it is advisable to clean the caliper thoroughly, using only ethyl alcohol (methylated spirits) if a solvent is needed, and checking that rubber dust covers fitted to pistons are intact. If the dust covers are damaged, they should be replaced with new ones, applying a proprietary rubber lubricant (as specified by the brake manufacturer) to the inside; these rubber lubricants are the only ones which may be used in or adjacent to components of hydraulic brake systems and it is vital that no unsuitable substance is used.

Some disc brake calipers are not fitted with rubber dust covers to the pistons but have, instead, a scraper seal in the cylinder bores (see Fig. 6.27) to protect the pressure seals; although the scraper seals can be expected to deal with a moderate amount of build up on the piston surfaces when the pistons are pressed in during relining, major accumulations of dirt should first be removed, using ethyl alcohol as a solvent.

After a stated mileage or period in service, calipers may require replacement of pressure seals, rubber dust covers, lubricants on sliding surfaces, etc, and the brake or vehicle manufacturer will specify the work which will be required; the removal of conventional caliper pistons is not difficult if the instructions given are followed carefully, but their replacement is less easy if the new seals are not to be damaged and absolute cleanliness is essential. If opposed piston calipers are divided into their two parts, to renew the pressure seal around the fluid port at the joint face, new bolts must be used and tightened correctly. Unless properly trained personnel, having the correct equipment, are available to carry out such jobs as these, it is advisable to use reconditioned units.

Some disc brake calipers incorporate handbrake mechanisms with automatic adjustment; these may require special tools or techniques when retracting the pistons and the manufacturers instructions should be followed.

If caliper pistons become jammed or if a sliding caliper jams, the pads will most likely drag on the disc; this will cause excessively rapid wear on one or more of the pads and the heat generated is likely to damage rubber components—dust covers and pressure seals—even if it does not lead to brake fluid vaporisation. Jammed pistons are uncommon, the most likely cause being the trapping of a particle of dirt between the piston and its bore, but sliding calipers with exposed slides are very prone to sticking because of contamination and corrosion; regular attention may be required to keep them free.

If calipers are dismounted for any reason, it is necessary to ensure that they seat correctly when remounted and that the mounting bolts are tightened correctly; any variation in the rigidity of such components which is introduced in service is likely to alter the vibration characteristics and may then be a cause of noise.

Drum brakes are very often automatically adjusted, so that—like disc brakes—they need little attention; however, the little maintenance which they do need is vital to the development of the expected brake torque without noise or judder. In particular, the metal-to-metal contact points between brake shoes and other parts of the brake assembly need to be adequately lubricated with a proprietary brake grease; this should be used in sufficient quantity to ensure its effectiveness over a long period, but must not reach either the lining surfaces or the hydraulic cylinder bores. Typical places where such greases should be used in this way (Fig. 12.1) are on shoe pivot or anchor pins, on the tips of the webs of sliding shoes, at the points on the edge of the shoe platform which rest on the backplate, at the contact face of shoe steady posts and at steady spring contact points. The same greases are suitable for use on adjuster spindles of the threaded type (snail cam or similar adjuster spindles must not be lubricated), in cone and tappet type adjusters and on the mechanical parts of handbrake mechanisms, including the threads (but not the pawls or ratchets) of any automatic adjuster incorporated.

Both hydraulic cylinders and air operated expander units are usually fitted with rubber dust covers; these should be checked to ensure that they are intact and correctly fitted, so that water, dirt, oil, etc, are excluded from either the hydraulic components or the mechanical expander. The clearances in both hydraulic and mechanical units are very small, so particles of dirt can easily cause jamming or damage, apart from the risk of contamination of brake fluid in the former cases. Dust covers should be lubricated internally with rubber lubricant, but where they leave the centre of a piston or tappet exposed as a contact point for a shoe tip, brake grease should be used in that area.

12.3 Brake relining

Brake shoes need to be relined when the thinnest lining is worn (1) to any indicator mark machined on the edge or (2) almost to the rivet heads or (3) if the linings are bonded to the shoes, to a minimum thickness of $1\frac{1}{2}$ mm (0.06 in) for cars and 2 mm (0.08 in) for larger vehicles; sometimes inspection openings (which may be closed with rubber plugs) are provided in the brake backplates, and cam brakes for trucks may have a wear indicator mounted on the cam shaft. The replacement procedure will depend on the brake design, and the vehicle workshop manual should be consulted for detailed

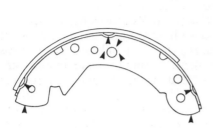

Fig. 12.1   Points on a typical brake shoe which should be lubricated with brake grease

Fig. 12.2   The use of the Girling Shoe Horn makes it easier to lift shoes from their abutments against the tension of the pull off springs (courtesy of Lucas Girling Ltd.)

instructions, but certain basic operations will usually have to be carried out. First, however, it is advisable to ensure that an illustration of the brake is available or, if not, to make a sketch; this should show all relevant features such as positions of springs and short or long linings and it must be kept in mind that drum brakes on either end of an axle are mirror images of each other.

The first stage of relining is to slacken off the brake adjustment to facilitate drum removal; with automatic adjustment, special provision will usually be made for doing this, as referred to in earlier chapters, but in one case at least it has been necessary to drill a hole in the face of the brake drum to gain access to the adjustment. Without slackening the adjustment, drum removal could be impossible if the drum had worn so as to leave a lip at its mouth; designers have sometimes avoided this possibility by ensuring that the braking path comes right to the edge of the drum or to a chamfer at the drum mouth.

With the drum removed, any steady springs can be removed and adjustable steady posts screwed back; the adjustment should then be slackened off completely, to release the tension in the pull-off springs, if this has not already been done.

The shoes, together with the various springs, handbrake mechanism and automatic adjuster parts should be removed in the recommended order; the job will often be made easier if a special tool, such as a Girling Shoe Horn (Fig. 12.2) is used and other useful tools are to be had. The claim is made for some large cam brakes that no special tools are necessary, nor is appreciable strength required, but in many cases the servicing of the largest drum brakes calls for a combination of strength and suitable equipment; in all cases the work will become easier as experience is gained.

Brake drums and other brake parts are likely to harbour the wear products of the brake linings and it is now recognised that, whether or not these are directly toxic, it is always foolish to inhale dust when this can be avoided. Compressed air should never be used to remove dust; the use of a vacuum apparatus or of liquids to suppress any dust being recommended instead. Special liquids for use when servicing brakes can be expensive and may, themselves, present problems; a cheap, effective and entirely harmless means of preventing dust from rising is to use water, to which a little liquid detergent has been added as a wetting agent. Water used in this way will wash away dust without harming brake linings, rubber components or anything else; it will have little effect on lubricating greases but will facilitate the removal of mud and most other kinds of dirt. Once the dust and general dirt have been removed, the brake can be cleaned further as necessary; hydraulic wheel cylinders must only be cleaned with ethyl alcohol, but more usual solvents can be used for non-hydraulic components.

When the brake is clean, components should be checked for wear or damage and account must be taken of the vehicle manufacturer's recommendation regarding any parts, such as hydraulic wheel cylinders, which may need servicing at a stipulated mileage; this is particularly to ensure that pressure seals are replaced before wear of their lips introduces the chance of leakage. In many cases, hydraulic components are replaced with exchange units, rather than change the seals in the often less than ideal conditions of the average vehicle workshop; to minimise the loss of brake fluid from the hydraulic system, another Girling service tool (Fig. 12.3) is recommended for use on flexible hoses, which it closes off without harm.

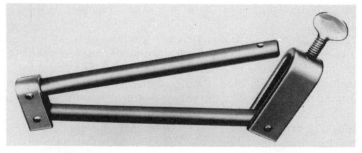

Fig. 12.3   Girling hose clamps can safely be applied to brake flexible hoses to isolate components when difficulty is experienced during bleeding (courtesy of Lucas Girling Ltd.)

Particular attention should be paid to such components as sliding wheel cylinders or other assemblies which are intended to equalise the force applied to the two shoes on a brake; as with handbrake mechanisms for disc brakes, sticking can easily cause one friction assembly to drag.

It may be necessary to transfer certain parts relating to automatic adjustment or to parking from the old shoes to the new ones, after which assembly should proceed in the reverse order to dismantling. Some brakes with pivoted shoes have adjustable anchor pins which must be reset to suit the new shoes; this is usually done by loosening the pin, forcing the shoes hard against the drum by means of the adjustment and relocking the pin. Adjustable steady posts are set in a similar way, ensuring that they lightly contact the shoe web whilst the linings are firmly in contact with the drum, then tightening the post lock nuts.

Finally, the brakes are adjusted using either the automatic or manual means provided; in the latter case, the brakes should be applied firmly after adjusting them, to ensure that the shoes are correctly settled in position, and then the adjustment should be checked, ensuring that the drum is just able to turn freely. After a short period of service, manual adjustment may need resetting; after this, further adjustment should only be needed at long intervals. Before considering the brake system to be ready for use, the level of the brake fluid in the reservoir should be checked and topped up if necessary.

Disc brake pads should be replaced when the friction material is reduced to 2.5–3 mm (0.1–0.12 in) thickness in the case of cars and light vehicles, or 5–6 mm (0.2–0.25 in) for larger brakes; in many cases wear indicators are provided which give an indication on the instrument panel, as described earlier, when replacement is needed. As has been detailed in the chapters dealing with disc brakes, there are many ways in which pads may be retained and special equipment is occasionally needed to make pad removal possible; usually, however, pad retaining devices are readily removable and the worn pads can then be withdrawn, some effort sometimes being needed if the pads are corroded on the edges. After pad removal, the calipers should be cleaned, much as for drum brakes, and pad retainers and other associated parts checked for fitness for further service, if new ones are not provided.

Hydraulic calipers will need to have the piston(s) retracted to make room for new pads and it is advisable, while this is being done, to run off the brake fluid which is displaced through the adjacent bleed screw and a bleed tube into a container for disposal; when pressing pistons back into their cylinders, only moderate pressure should be exerted with a suitable lever, taking care not to misalign them. Sliding calipers will need centralising (their sliding surfaces may need attention) while calipers which incorporate a parking mechanism are likely to require special procedures; the larger mechanical calipers will need to have their adjustment slackened off in an appropriate manner.

Before the new disc brake pads are fitted they should be lightly smeared with a suitable proprietary disc brake grease on those areas of the steel backplate which will come into contact with either the caliper body or the piston face; anti-squeal shims should be smeared with this grease on both sides. Sometimes the backs of pads are coated with a layer of special material which, yielding a little when under load, permits the pads to so align themselves between the piston and the disc that squeal is eliminated; grease should not normally be applied to these coatings.

Having ensured that handed pads or those with wear indicators are being put into the correct position, the new pads should be put into place with their shims, anti-rattle springs or other parts and retained in the appropriate manner. When all are in position, the brake pedal should be operated to take up clearances and restore the correct free play but, during this operation, care must be taken to maintain a sufficient brake fluid supply in the reservoir. Wear indicator leads must be connected to the wiring which operates the visual warning.

Sometimes in service, a stone thrown up by one of the wheels may become trapped between the brake disc and the dirt shield which is normally fitted, causing an unpleasant grating sound; if this does not work its way out within a short period of driving, it may be necessary to reverse in order to dislodge it.

The torque output of disc and drum brakes may not reach the full expected level, in terms of pedal effort, until bedding is largely complete; this is because the effective radius of disc brake pads may initially be displaced towards the disc centre, while brake shoe assemblies are usually designed to avoid initial toe and heel contact (which could cause leading shoes to grab) by bedding from the centre outwards, which initially reduces the shoe factor. Full torque will, however, be available at once should it be necessary at the cost of a slightly higher pedal effort than normal. During bedding, until the linings are in almost full contact with the mating surface, prolonged heavy braking should be avoided as far as possible otherwise local overheating may occur.

12.4 Brake linings

Assuming the disc or drum brake linings fitted to a vehicle (the second of the four areas to need attention) to be generally suitable for the purpose, there is virtually no direct action which should—or even can—be taken to maintain them in good working order; the indirect action—as considered in part above—is largely related to the functioning of the parts of the brake which present the friction material to the disc or drum, and to the maintenance of such items as oil seals to prevent contamination of the working surfaces. As designed, the area of the linings should be sufficient (once they are bedded) for their surface temperature to remain within acceptable limits under normal working conditions and the volume available for wear should be adequate to ensure a reasonable working life; where paired drum brake linings are used to match, for example, the differing loading of primary and secondary shoes they must, of course, be fitted on the correct shoes or both performance and life will be affected.

Drum brake linings are sometimes chamfered but, with moulded linings as are now normally used, this should not be necessary. When woven linings were usual it was often necessary to chamfer the ends, beyond the last rivet holes, to ensure that grab could not be caused by lining end lift; rigid moulded linings (and all bonded linings) should not be subject to end lift so chamfering should only be used, as an expedient when other remedies have failed, to attempt to eliminate any squeal which may occur, by reducing the shoe factor. A reverse chamfer, intended to scrape foreign matter from the drum has been used by Saab, who patented this feature, but it seems to have been of only marginal benefit. Disc brake pad linings have sometimes been chamfered to influence the position of the centre of area of the lining in its early service, so as to reduce audible vibration.

Grooving of disc brake pads has already been mentioned in Chapter 2, but a single longitudinal groove has also been used by Opel on drum brake linings, the groove being positioned centrally along the line of the shoe web, although it is not certain that any advantage was gained. Drum brakes are better protected from water than are disc brakes so there is little need to consider the use of transverse grooves on the linings for water dispersal.

Although linings do not need any attention in the form of maintenance, much can in fact be learned by an examination of them; in this respect, the trend to automatic adjustment reduces the chance of faults being identified by observation at regular intervals of the condition of brake linings. The change in the colour of friction material during bedding has already been remarked upon; if one lining from a set is noticeably darker than the others, this is a sure sign that it has been working harder and points to the need to identify the brake or actuation fault responsible. The effects of excessive surface temperatures are often visible on the edges of linings where, at high

Fig. 12.4   The effects of severe overheating of the working surfaces are often visible on the edges of disc brake pads

temperature, the film of accumulated dirt turns pale to a point corresponding to the depth of penetration of the heat into the friction material; this effect is visibly coupled with the progressive increase in temperature across the surface of disc brake pads in the pair shown (Fig. 12.4), which were removed from a saloon car driven to its limits on a test track. The breaking up of the friction material also seen is an indication that the temperature has been so excessive as to carbonise the resin binder and weaken the structure.

Whereas within the acceptable temperature range, the original colour of the linings is preserved, although much darkened, there is a universal blackening as carbon is formed at the surface; the effect is progressive over a temperature band, which is a measure of the reserves of safety formulated into the friction material, and experience is necessary for assessment of the degree of damage. At one stage, the polished black surface of a moderately overheated lining may be mistaken for glaze, but glaze is a condition brought about by prolonged light duty when, because of the negligible wear experienced, the normal friction surface becomes coated with a thin layer of partially degraded wear products and foreign matter which forms a glass-like covering having low friction. When glazing occurs and the duty cannot generally be changed, the lining surfaces should be regenerated from time to time by means of short spells of harder braking.

If conventional pads are used persistently in a style more appropriate to the race track, even the carbonised remains of the resin binder may be burned away, leaving only the fibre and traces of the fillers used; such degradation usually takes place first at the edges, because of the proximity to the atmospheric oxygen needed for carbon dioxide to be formed from the carbon present.

Another feature of used brake linings is that they necessarily bed in to the cross sectional profile of the disc or drum with which they have been in contact; they will, therefore, reveal whether scoring, grooving or uneven wear is present. New linings used with badly worn mating parts may yield indifferent results in their early service if they are used hard, when only a small part of their area is making contact; in the

Fig. 12.5   Longitudinal brake lining taper

case of disc brake pads, the mean radius will be reduced if the initial contact is largely towards the disc centre; there will, therefore, be a reduction in torque both because of this effect and because of any local fade which may occur.

Differences in the wear rate of corresponding linings in a set indicate a fault which should be identified and corrected before a shoe or a pad backplate can damage the mating surface; in particular, some types of sliding calipers are very prone to sticking, with expensive consequences if the fault is not put right. Taper wear of disc brake pads is uncommon but may indicate the use of unusually heavy pedal efforts, but taper wear of drum brake linings can readily occur if brake servicing is at fault; transverse lining taper is usually an indication that adjustable steady posts have not been set correctly, while longitudinal taper (Fig. 12.5) is usually caused by failure to lubricate the tips of sliding shoes adequately. It must, however, be remembered that while most car and van linings and many truck linings are initially parallel and should remain parallel in service, others are initially tapered and only become parallel when fully worn.

Modern moulded friction materials are not very porous and so are little affected by water; if, however, they become contaminated by oil their friction value will be affected and there is no worthwhile way of removing the oil. When a pair of pads or shoes has been affected in this way and is to be replaced, it is advisable to renew the parts on both brakes on the axle concerned so that no unbalance can occur across the axle.

By long tradition, linings suspected of contributing to unsatisfactory braking are often roughed up with a coarse file or abrasive cloth; this is, however, almost always dealing with the effect rather than the cause of the problem and is likely to be counter-productive. Even if the linings are glazed, abrasion of their surfaces necessitates rebedding and may cause overheating of high spots in the meantime;

it is unlikely that freehand working of lining surfaces can match the precision of the factory finish.

When linings are worn to the recommended limit, the need to change them is not because reduced thickness implies declining quality, but because of increasing heat flow or of the risk of damage to the drum or disc by rivet heads or backplate; on the other hand, some disc brake pads incorporate a layer of different material next to the backplate which may give benefits in terms of reducing heat flow or suppressing vibration, but which may not possess the frictional properties of the lining material.

12.5 Actuation

As designed and manufactured, the brake actuation causes input forces to be applied to the brakes in a predetermined relationship to the driver's brake pedal effort; these forces should be the same for the two brakes on any axle but will often differ between axles. Both air and brake fluid are, as has been described, used as working media—either singly or in combination—and a typical system consists of pipelines and moving elements of many kinds; in order that the complete system may continue to function correctly over an extended period of years, a certain amount of attention is required from time to time. However, unnecessarily frequent interference with actuation systems may do more harm than good, by increasing the likelihood of contamination in one way or another.

One maintenance requirement which applies to hydraulic but not to air systems is that the level of the fluid contained in the reservoir needs to be checked from time to time (a low level warning device is now usual) and, if necessary, topped up with fresh fluid of suitable quality; when doing this the fluid should preferably be poured directly from its can but, if this is not convenient, a clean glass vessel may be used to transfer it. In order to minimise the risk of contamination by dirt and of moisture absorption, both the can and the reservoir should be uncovered for as brief a period as possible; because of the difficulty of preventing moisture absorption, it is recommended that even unopened, sealed cans of brake fluid should not be kept for more than three years.

When drum brakes were common at both the front and the rear of a car, the expectation was that the level of the brake fluid in the reservoir would remain more or less constant, because in many cases the method of adjustment restored the wheel cylinder pistons to their original position; any noticeable drop in the fluid level was taken to be an indication of a loss from the system. With disc brakes now almost universal at least at the front of cars and vans, wear of the brake pads and the consequent piston displacement cause a slow but steady fall in fluid level which is entirely normal and which is specially provided for by the use of an enlarged reservoir.

Because of the hygroscopic nature of most brake fluids, it is common for the brake and vehicle manufacturers concerned to recommend replacement at intervals of eighteen months or 35000 km (24000 miles), whichever occurs first; this virtually guarantees freedom from any chance of fluid vaporisation, due to absorbed moisture, but some police forces replace at yearly intervals in view of the exceptional braking duty to which their vehicles are sometimes subjected. Brake fluid also needs to be replaced because its properties such as lubricity and corrosion inhibition gradually deteriorate with time; it is imperative that it is replaced immediately if it is known that it has become contaminated with any substance other than an equivalent brake fluid. The procedure for fluid replacement is dealt with below in connection with bleeding of hydraulic brake systems.

One other reason for having to service a hydraulic system is the presence of air in one of the pipelines, usually due to carelessness in letting the reservoir level fall excessively or to working on some part of the system; the presence of an air bubble leads to excessive pedal travel (spongy pedal) and, depending on the size of the bubble, may make it impossible to generate sufficient pressure in the system to stop the vehicle with any degree of safety. Whether the fluid is new or old, it is necessary to drive the bubble out by the procedure known as bleeding the system; this consists of using the master cylinder or some other means to pump fluid through the system and out of all bleed screws in turn until, the bleed tube used being immersed in liquid (Fig. 12.6), it can be seen that no further air bubbles are appearing (a special procedure is necessary with stored pressure systems to achieve the same result and the vehicle workshop manual should be consulted). It

Fig. 12.6 Bleeding air from a hydraulic braking system (courtesy of Automotive Products PLC)

is clearly important during bleeding to replenish the reservoir frequently with fresh fluid of the appropriate type.

Whether air is to be bled from the system or the fluid is to be replaced, it is desirable first to minimise the fluid capacity of components such as wheel cylinders and disc brake calipers. In the case of drum brakes with expanders operating on the shoe web, this is done by slackening the adjustment off completely, no attention being needed with adjusters which are situated at the shoe tips; the pistons of all disc brake calipers should be retracted fully and, as also with drum brakes, the fluid displaced should be expelled through the appropriate bleed screw. If a load sensitive valve is fitted and the vehicle is not supported by its wheels, it may be necessary to ensure that the valve is in the fully open position; if in any doubt, the workshop manual should be consulted. Special procedures may also be needed when other valves are fitted. After bleeding has been completed, brake adjustment should be carried out to restore pistons, shoes and pads to their former positions, the brake fluid level being maintained throughout this operation; load sensitive valves should be restored to their normal condition.

The actual method of bleeding will be one of two, but with a number of variations and will depend on the circumstances; the traditional method requires one person to pump the brake pedal while a second person attends to each brake in turn but apparatus is also available making it possible for one person to bleed brakes. Using the first method, no equipment other than a bleed screw and jar, as already illustrated, and a suitable spanner is needed; if a servo is fitted, the engine should not be running and the unit should be at atmospheric pressure throughout (achieved by operating the brake pedal hard at least a dozen times).

The number of bleed screws to be dealt with will depend very much on the actuation system layout used and the type of brakes fitted; an older, undivided hydraulic system with drum brakes front and rear may only have three in all, if the rear brakes are piped one from the other, but one four cylinder opposed piston caliper for dual circuit operation will have three bleed screws of its own, all of which must be bled in the order recommended, making a dozen or so in all for a vehicle so fitted at front and rear.

Usually, bleeding commences at the rear brakes and continues until no more bubbles are expelled from the bleed screw being attended to; when this is the case, the bleed screw should be closed while fluid is still flowing so that there is no chance of air finding its way back in, past the screw threads. If the fluid is being changed, flow is allowed to continue until the discoloured used fluid is followed by clear new fluid. If the master cylinder is pumped to displace the brake

Fig. 12.7   A pressure brake bleeder for garage use (courtesy of Alfred Teves GmbH)

fluid, the brake pedal should normally be pressed down at a moderate rate but allowed to fly back at its own speed; when, however, a Girling CV type master cylinder is used, some short, rapid strokes are necessary to agitate the fluid and so entrain any air which otherwise might remain in the central bore of the piston.

Pressure bleeding units (Fig. 12.7) are often used by the motor trade and allow one man to carry out the bleeding procedure; in the container a diaphragm separates a large quantity of brake fluid from air at a low pressure, the fluid being expelled through a valve by way of a tube to an adaptor screwed on to the master cylinder. Each bleed screw in turn may then be dealt with speedily without the need for frequent topping up. Simple one operator bleeding kits are also available for the do-it-yourself motorist.

An air braking system is free from the need for bleeding but there is, nevertheless, some maintenance required at intervals to ensure that the system does not become contaminated in one way or another; air filter elements may require to be changed, alcohol evaporators may need refilling and other items may require attention as specified by the vehicle builder. If excessive oil or carbon is being discharged by the compressor, to the extent that the air cleaning facilities provided are overloaded, then the compressor needs to be serviced or replaced.

12.6 Component checks

With both hydraulic and air systems, flexible hoses which connect wheel or axle mounted assemblies to the frame mounted pipelines need regular inspection to ensure that they are not rubbing on other parts or showing signs of damage; they should be renewed at the time of a major system overhaul. Brake pipelines should be inspected at similar intervals for any evidence of corrosion; they should be thoroughly cleaned of dirt on these occasions because moist salt laden mud is one of the most hostile environments for metallic components which are liable to corrosion. If renewal of pipework becomes necessary, the use of an alternative material with superior corrosion resistance—although possibly more expensive to purchase and install—may offer long term economy.

Assuming that they have not become scored by abrasive particles which have contaminated the fluid, hydraulic cylinders and similar components need servicing or replacement mainly because the lips of moving pressure seals become worn in service (especially if neglect of the fluid has permitted its lubricity to decline), so that their effectiveness becomes impaired; the corresponding components in air systems become worn and may be fouled because of imperfect filtration of the air and diaphragms eventually suffer fatigue. The recommendations which apply to the vehicle should be followed as regards the intervals at which renewal takes place and the units concerned should be serviced or renewed.

When choosing a source of replacement parts, it is well to make absolutely sure of the quality of items considered, particularly in the air braking component market. Manufacturers and reputable suppliers re-use only those components which lend themselves to this (and then only after a full inspection) but fit new springs, seals and other wearing parts; usually, also, the service replacement assemblies are then covered by a similar guarantee to new ones.

A special warning is needed with regard to spring brake units which, because of the very considerable energy stored in the spring, even when all air is discharged, can represent a real danger if they are put back on the market in an imperfect condition by an unqualified workshop; spring brake units should never be disposed of as waste for tipping without first being dismantled because of the danger of the casing or fasteners corroding and the unit then 'exploding'. Dismantling of these units should only be performed with the equipment recommended by the manufacturer.

Replacement of system components on an air braked vehicle is, of course, carried out with the vehicle safely parked and all air stored under pressure completely exhausted; in this connection, it is vital in any workshop that working procedures are established to ensure that nobody can, by mistake, start work on a system which is still partly or wholly charged. With a hydraulic system, complete overhaul requires that all fluid be drained off and fresh fluid eventually used to refill; when servicing or replacing a single wheel cylinder or caliper, however, fluid loss can be minimised by using a Girling clamp on the associated flexible hose as already mentioned and illustrated (Fig. 12.3). The hose clamp can also be used, singly or in numbers, to isolate parts of the system when a difficulty is experienced in locating a pocket of air which is responsible for a 'spongy pedal' condition.

A routine trial of the 'feel' of the brake pedal of a hydraulic system, perhaps on a daily basis, is recommended as a procedure which can identify the need for attention before any impending problem becomes serious; the amount of free pedal travel should hardly vary if all brakes are automatically adjusted and the pedal should always feel firm. A full effort application made on the brake pedal demonstrates that pipelines and seals may be expected to hold their pressure under normal conditions, at least for that day.

There are other items of equipment, particularly on air braked vehicles, which may need routine attention because their mechanical components not in contact with the working fluid may decline in performance over a period, or may need lubrication or adjustment; the workshop manual will identify these. Special maintenance procedures may also be required when braking systems for either cars or trucks include load sensing or anti-lock equipment; the workshop manual should be consulted in respect of this.

Because of the complexity of air braking systems and their extent on a large commercial vehicle, any aid to routine checking or fault diagnosis can save a great deal of time; one notable piece of equipment for this purpose is the Scrutineer (Fig. 12.8), manufactured by Hope Technical Developments Ltd. of Ascot. A Scrutineer with a cylinder of compressed air can be used to check a trailer air system for leaks, for the response of the emergency relay and quick release valves and for the free movement of the brake mechanism without the necessity of having a tractor available (it can also check the lighting circuits); it can also be used to check the storage pressure on a tractor, compare the pressures in a split system and check the effect of a load sensing valve.

Finally, in considering the maintenance of brake actuation systems, mechanical parking/emergency systems must not be overlooked. If neglected, these may become ineffective so that an inadequate force is applied to the shoe tips, they may fail to release fully so that the brakes affected are caused to drag or, in extremity, they may break and fail completely. These systems extend from the handbrake lever (some

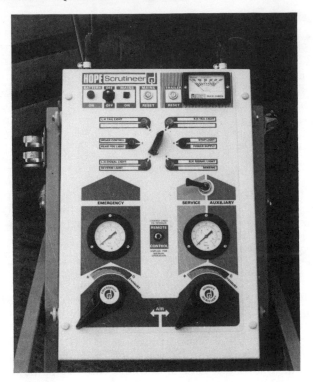

Fig. 12.8   The Hope Scrutineer for air brake system checking; trailer electrical circuits can also be checked and the latest model can deal similarly with anti-lock system warning light circuits (courtesy of Hope Technical Developments Ltd.)

pull type controls may still be found) to the brakes which they apply and the force is transmitted by way of either cables (open or guided in flexible conduits) or rods; trucks used to use multi-pull handbrake levers, requiring a measure of skill in operation, before servo assistance and power operation became acceptable legally.

Some flexible cables are sheathed in a plastics coating, so that they slide more easily in their conduits and are unlikely to corrode. Sometimes, provision is made for lubricating them; in many cases it has been found that the cable has worn a groove in its conduit which has caused excessive friction or has frayed, so cables may need regular attention. Open cables are sometimes turned through an angle by guides—which need greasing; both cables and rods may also be redirected by what are still popularly known as bell cranks, involving pivots and pin joints which will wear badly—or seize—if not adequately cleaned and lubricated. Handbrake cables may sometimes stretch in their early service, requiring adjustment if the hand control is to retain a sufficient margin of reserve travel.

Lastly, the pivot of the handbrake lever may require lubrication if, after a period of service, it becomes stiff; associated with this lever there will often be a switch which operates a warning on the instrument panel to show when the parking brake is on and this may occasionally require attention.

12.7 Drums and discs

Brake drums and discs in service, the last of the four areas to be considered, are subject to five particular effects; abrasion by the friction material, rapid heating during braking, contamination of the working surfaces by abrasive particles, corrosion (especially when roads are salted in winter) and distortion; there is little that the owner of the vehicle can do to prevent these effects from taking place but he must take note of them and, when the condition of the mating surfaces reaches a certain stage, take remedial action.

One of the requirements for friction materials is that they should not cause excessive wear of the mating surface with which they are in contact; at the same time, the cast iron used (this being the recommended material for discs and drums) should itself be of such a quality that it can well resist not only the abrasion experienced in service, but also the thermal and other effects. The fleet engineer who is responsible for many vehicles will, therefore, seek to optimise his choice of supplier of both brake linings and mating parts to obtain satisfactory results from the two in combination. Disc or drum wear should, therefore, be at a much lower rate than lining wear and the metal surface should remain substantially smooth, even when the wear is such as to leave a lip at the edge of the braking path (Fig. 12.9);

Fig. 12.9   Badly worn brake discs

Fig. 12.10   A badly scored brake disc

provided the mating part is not worn beyond the permissible limit, new linings can be used against it without their wear rate being increased. If drum brake linings are not quite flush with the edge of the braking path and much more drum wear occurs, a lip will be formed which can make drum removal difficult as noted earlier; it is, therefore, advisable to remove any such lip which forms, at each drum inspection.

It must be noted however, that whilst even wear of a disc does not affect brake output when new linings are fitted, even wear of a drum increases its radius; new drum brake linings made to match the nominal drum radius, which are used against an appreciably worn drum, will have pronounced crown contact until bedded in, lowering the shoe factor and creating the possibility of overheating the initial contact area. When drums are badly worn and have been remachined, suitable packing material is sometimes fitted between the lining and the shoe to compensate, or oversize linings may be available.

Sometimes, scoring of discs (Fig. 12.10) and drums may be caused, either by an unsuitable friction material or by the trapping of abrasive matter thrown up from the road surface; new pads could be used with such a disc as that shown and, after a rather longer than usual period of bedding, would develop normal braking, but the degree of scoring should first be considered or the lining wear rate may be excessive. Even the best of pad materials will generate circumferential marks on the disc surface, but these will only be shallow and may be discounted; a simple but useful test is to draw a finger nail over the braking path in a radial direction (Fig. 12.11) to distinguish between marks which cannot be felt and deep scoring. If scoring is not too severe, it may be

Fig. 12.11   A finger nail drawn across a brake disc as a simple check on the degree of scoring present

practicable to have the faces of the discs remachined, observing the recommended limits for metal removal; excessive machining would reduce both the heat capacity and the strength of the metal part.

Drums may become scored if successive sets of linings are worn until the rivet heads come into contact with the braking path; in extreme cases (Fig. 12.12) the lines of rivet heads eventually wear deep grooves in the drum, weakening it and making removal less easy. Brake output will be little affected by this type of neglect, because the metal of which the rivets are made will generate friction and will only form a small proportion of the total contact area, but lining wear rate may suffer and the soundness of the drum will be put in doubt.

Metals other than cast iron which are used for brake discs—either for the sake of appearance and the elimination of corrosion or in the attempt to improve heat dissipation—are more prone to scoring and some compromise becomes necessary; either a friction material is chosen which minimises scoring but which may be less than ideal in its performance characteristics, or one is selected on the basis of good performance regardless of the consequential effects on the disc surfaces.

Fig. 12.12   A brake drum which has been badly grooved by rivet heads when excessive lining wear was ignored

During a brake application, heat is generated at the surface of the disc or drum and instantly begins to dissipate itself; some will be radiated into the atmosphere (this effect is of limited significance at low temperatures), some will be removed by convection by way of the cooling air flow and the rest will flow into the metal of which the rotating member is made. With the disc or drum initially at a low temperature, different points in the metal will experience a rise in temperature at different times and to a varying degree as the flow of heat takes place—there will be what is called a temperature gradient; depending on the time which elapses before the next brake application, the mass of metal may reach an even temperature throughout or there may be an eventual temperature gradient as the starting point for the next braking cycle.

Because materials expand and contract as temperature rises and falls and because of the uneven distribution of temperature during a series of brake applications, stresses will be set up in the metal which will vary during each braking cycle; the ability of the metal to withstand many such cycles of stress without fatigue causing hairline cracks to occur is, therefore, an important measure of its quality. Grades of cast iron as specially developed for drums and discs have this ability, but others which may be found in the replacement market may not always be so satisfactory; crazing of either discs (Fig. 12.13) or drums (Fig. 12.14) may, therefore, occur and it is not likely that this condition is due to any shortcoming on the part of the brake linings. Remachining while crazing is barely detectable will prevent immediate extension of the fine cracks formed, but the condition is likely to recur; it is difficult—if not impossible—to define simply a limiting condition which renders the item unfit for further service. If ignored, crazing will increase in magnitude until the member breaks, possibly causing an accident; the fracture of the disc shown (Fig. 12.15) is bad enough, but the failure of the drum (Fig. 12.16) extends not only across the braking path, but also around much of the circumference at the corner adjacent to the stud holes.

Another feature of the drum just considered is the dark area through which the fracture passes; this is a severe case of what is known as blue spotting and in this example it may have contributed directly to the failure. Blue spotting, it seems clear, comes about as a consequence of a combination of circumstances relating particularly to four factors: the mating surface form, its metallurgy, the friction material and the braking duty. If there are high points on the mating surface such that the friction material cannot conform to it, if there are sudden and severe brake applications when the drums and discs are relatively cool and if the metallurgical structure of the cast iron used is of a certain type then rapid temperature rises will be experienced at

Fig. 12.13   Crazing of the braking path of a disc

Fig. 12.14   A badly crazed truck brake drum

the high points. With cold metal all around these heated areas, the dissipation of heat and the consequential temperature drop may be sufficiently rapid to equate to a quenching operation, such as is used to harden steel; with a certain structure of the iron there can, in fact, be such a hardening at the high points under these conditions, associated with an increase in volume of those parts affected.

Because of this transition to a different metallurgical structure, the high points initially existing and thus affected become higher and the effect—which at first is only on a small scale (Fig. 12.17)—becomes self perpetuating and increases in scale; the hard areas are also less

Fig. 12.15   A brake disc which has fractured after prolonged usage

Fig. 12.16   A truck brake drum with a serious fracture and associated blue spotting

ductile than the parent metal, increasing distortion occurs during drum rotation and, as has probably occurred in the case referred to above, fracture is likely to be the eventual result. Inspection of drums and discs from time to time is as important as the inspection of numerous other parts of a vehicle to establish continuing roadworthiness; replacement is the only cure when their condition is suspect.

Corrosion, an attack much accelerated by the use of salt on roads in winter, is another matter which has been mentioned and this applies particularly to discs; although exterior corrosion of drums may impair cooling a little, the undisturbed corroded surface does protect the parent metal beneath it to a certain extent. Corrosion of disc

Fig. 12.17   A car brake drum with blue spots

surfaces, however, seems to proceed at a pace which cannot be halted, the only variation relating to the manner in which the effect is manifested. In the case of cars covering an appreciable mileage, the braking paths usually remain bright, although their wear rate is likely to be enhanced; discs on low mileage cars, on the other hand, are likely to exhibit corrosion spreading across the braking paths (Fig. 12.18), which will shorten pad life. In either case, the outer edge of the disc will be likely to build up an undisturbed layer of corrosion products, which it is well to remove with a suitably hard hand tool, or pad removal will become difficult. Disc brake pads used on corroded discs usually reveal this fact by their profile, which will often feature the excessive wear at the edges which the very abrasive corrosion products cause.

The last of the factors to be considered in connection with discs and drums is distortion; this becomes apparent as run-out of discs (with which can be associated thickness variation) and ovality of drums (with which can be associated eccentricity). Although it is expected that the castings from which discs and drums are machined should first be treated to relieve them of residual stresses, it may be found in service that discs have an excessive run-out and drums are oval, these conditions sometimes giving rise, with hydraulic actuation, to a pulsating feedback at the pedal and they may be associated with noise of one form or another; components may be found already distorted when new, or may become so in use. An acceptable limit for disc run-out is 0.1 mm (0.004 in) but the limit for drums varies with diameter; it

Fig. 12.18   A pair of badly corroded brake discs

may be straightforward to remachine unsatisfactory discs but, as noted earlier, allowance needs to be made when drums have been skimmed.

Thickness variation of discs is likely to give rise to pedal feedback and judder and needs to be closely controlled when discs are machined; whereas at one time 0.025 mm (0.001 in) was thought to be an acceptable limit, it is now considered that a limit of 0.01 mm (0.0004 in) is necessary in order to be sure of freedom from ill effects. The desirable standards of surface finish for disc and drum braking path surfaces have already been considered in Chapter 2.

As distinct from ovality of brake drums, due to distortion of the castings, it should be noted that drums are sometimes found to have been machined so that their braking paths are eccentric to their mounting holes; such a condition can cause very severe wear of brake parts, as they move with drum rotation, accompanied by considerable noise. It is also known for hubs to be eccentric to their centres so, in difficult cases of drum brake judder, it is necessary to use a dial gauge to check drums for both ovality and eccentricity and also the hubs themselves; faulty hubs may also be responsible for discs failing to run true and, since they cannot be corrected, must be replaced.

12.8 Conclusion

It will now be appreciated that braking systems often comprise a great many parts of different kinds and can be of considerable complexity; over a period of some years, with routine replacement of some parts and renewal of others as may be found necessary, the system may become subject to a measure of uncertainty so that when the cause of a problem has to be found, everything should be checked and nothing should be taken for granted.

Between the case of a single privately owned vehicle, driven by its owner, and that of a number of similar vehicles driven by different drivers on shifts, it can become apparent that, in addition to all the other factors described in this book, there are those attributable to the driver. A driver may not abuse his vehicle but he may fail either to notice or to respond to warning symptoms; if these symptoms are reported, the statements made may be incomplete or inaccurate. When different drivers use the same vehicle it is likely that, overall, less care of it will be taken and it may be difficult to eliminate malpractices; brake usage over similar routes can vary greatly between different drivers and the brake linings are the components which will first show up those drivers who are hard on brakes.

When it comes to routine maintenance and repair, the human element must again be considered; for work to be done effectively, both the skill and an appropriate motivation are required and both need to be cultivated. The need for brake maintenance to be carried out should be as much accepted as the need to refill the fuel tank; the need for this work to be done properly should be recognised as readily as the need for the driver to have his eyes open. In describing the design and construction of the most commonly found components of braking systems, the work of many engineers throughout 25–30 years has been briefly summarised; their efforts to enhance road safety can easily be frustrated in practice by indifference and carelessness when braking systems are misused or neglected.

Index